Foucault

and the
Indefinite Work
of Freedom

Réal Fillion

Foucault
and the
Indefinite Work
of Freedom

University of Ottawa Press
2012

uOttawa

© University of Ottawa Press, 2012

The University of Ottawa Press acknowledges
with gratitude the support extended to its publishing list by Heritage Canada through the
Canada Book Fund, by the Canada Council for
the Arts, by the Federation for the Humanities
and Social Sciences through the Awards to
Scholarly Publications Program, by the Social
Sciences and Humanities Research Council,
and by the University of Ottawa.

www.press.uottawa.ca

Library and Archives Canada Cataloguing
in Publication

Fillion, Réal Robert, 1963-
Foucault and the indefinite work of
freedom / Réal Fillion.

(Philosophica, ISSN 1480-4670)
Includes bibliographical references and index.
Also issued in electronic format.
ISBN 978-0-7766-0781-8

1. Foucault, Michel. 2. Liberty–Philosophy.
3. History–Philosophy. I. Title.
II. Series: Collection Philosophica

B2430.F724F54
2012   194   C2012-905650-2

À mes parents.

TABLE OF CONTENTS

Acknowledgements

The following chapters incorporate material previously published.

Chapter One incorporates, with modifications, text published as: "'L'Idée de l'Histoire' chez Michel Foucault," *Science et Esprit* 55.1 (2003): 23–34.

Chapter Three incorporates, with modifications, text published as: "Foucault after Hyppolite: Towards an A-theistic Theodicy," *The Southern Journal of Philosophy* XLIII.1 (2005): 79–93.

Chapter Six incorporates, with modifications, text from both "Freedom, Responsibility and the 'American Foucault'," *Philosophy and Social Criticism* 30.1 (2004): 115–26 and, especially, "Foucault on History and the Self," *Laval Théologique et Philosophique* 54.1 (1998): 143–62.

I wish to thank the publishers of these journals for their permissions.

I would like to acknowledge the University of Sudbury for its support.

This book has been published with the help of a grant from the Canadian Federation for the Humanities and Social Sciences, through the Aid to Scholarly Publications Program, using funds provided by the Social Sciences and Humanities Research Council of Canada.

INTRODUCTION

Making Sense of History Making Sense of Us

Like our lives, does history unfold? To what extent is history relevant to our attempts to make sense of our unfolding lives? These are the underlying questions that animate the writing of this book. It is driven by the sense that we should not neglect history as a way of framing how we make sense of our lives, even as we should not abuse it either. It is a book born of the sentiment, like Nietzsche's, that history can be and is both "used" and "abused" and that history can be and is of significance "for life". But it is also a book that is born not only out of a sentiment but out of a commitment, like Hegel's, to the *intelligibility* of history, to the endeavour to draw out and to appreciate the *sense* that it contains. Note that both the sentiment and the commitment, taken together, suggest that history is both something we create (as we make use of it) and something larger than us, in which we participate. Karl Marx probably captured this double sense best when he wrote, "Men make their own history, but they do not make it just as they please; they do not make it under circumstances chosen by themselves, but under circumstances directly encountered, given and transmitted from the past."[1]

As the mention of the names of such thinkers as Nietzsche, Hegel and Marx suggests, this is an exploration in the philosophy of history; more specifically it is a work that appeals to what has come to be called *speculative* philosophy of history, so called as a contrast to *analytic* philosophy of history. This distinction between speculative and analytic philosophy of history is an interesting one but one that has outlived its usefulness. As a check against modes of philosophizing that would abusively pretend to give us the "meaning" of the historical process as a whole, and as a way of insisting that we examine more carefully and rigorously the kinds of claims put forward in the name of something called "history", a philosophy of history that calls itself "analytic" certainly makes sense and has produced important work. But as a

---

1. Karl Marx, *Selected Writings*, ed. Lawrence H. Simon (Indianapolis: Hackett, 1994) 188.

stricture against any effort to think about history as a process or as a whole (or both), and as a restriction to consider exclusively the production of the work of those who call themselves "historians", such an approach does not serve our sense of history well. Worse, it serves to block a fuller appreciation of the significance that history can have for making sense of our lives.

The principal reason I think the distinction between analytic and speculative philosophy of history has outlived its usefulness is the way it severs history from a consideration of the fact that our lives unfold, that it has a temporal structure that can be understood in terms of a present shaped by a past and moving into a future. In this, it is merely following upon the increasing disciplinarization of history and historiography. Hayden White has been writing for a long time about the kinds of limitations such a professionalization of historical investigation has had on our appreciation of history, and I will return to White's work a number of times in what follows. For the moment, I would like to mention two points he raises in a recent discussion on the public role of history.[2] The first he takes over from

---

2. Hayden White, "The Public Relevance of Historical Studies: A Reply to Dirk Moses," *History and Theory* 44 (2005): 333–38.

Michael Oakeshott, who asks us to consider how this professionalization increasingly drives a wedge between two senses of the past which he

> calls "the historical past," the preserve of professional historians interested in "disinterested" study of the past "as it really was" and "as an end in itself," on the one hand, and, on the other hand, "the practical past," the past considered as a storehouse of memory, ideals, examples, events worthy of remembrance and repetition, and so on, the kind of past ordinary people and politicians, ministers, ex-soldiers, and social reformers carry around with them as an imagined "reality" serving in lieu of both religion and metaphysics as a paradigm or bedrock of "the real."[3]

What this wedge does is increasingly alienate us from a fuller sense of our relation to history because it insists on treating a part of it as a distinct object understood independently as "the past", in explicit contradistinction to the correlative conceptions of "the present" and "the future". I do not mean to suggest that one cannot and should not bracket any of these correlative conceptions in order to focus one's attention on a single one, just as the historian

---

3. White, "Public Relevance" 334.

does when she focuses on "what has happened in the past", or as most of us do in our daily preoccupations with the demands of the present. But, of course, such present preoccupations are the preoccupations they are because they are framed not solely in terms of a self-contained present but also with reference to both the past and the future, through our various commitments, for example "I promised yesterday that I would be there tomorrow". To link these correlative conceptions explicitly is precisely what it means to say that our lives are *unfolding*. The historian, too, in her "disinterested interest" in what happened in the past, considers that past from a particular place in an unfolding present.

If a concern with this unfolding quality of the past, the present and the future is borne in mind, however, then the traditional concern of the speculative philosophy of history with the *whole* of history seems relevant, indeed, inasmuch as it enables us to frame questions concerning how we relate the past to the present and the present to the past. (For example, how did what happened in the past contribute to what is possible and impossible in the present, and correlatively, how do our present preoccupations determine our approach(es) to what came before us?) As well, we could raise questions concerning how the future figures in how we deal both with the past and with the present.

None of this is straightforward, despite the self-evidence of the correlativity of the notions themselves (as Augustine famously remarked in his discussion of time). But it is precisely this combination of self-evidence and convolution that invites a speculative philosophical approach. What is meant by a "speculative philosophical" approach is nothing more threatening than a combination of argument and imagination. The discussion takes the form of argument because it is committed to giving reasons for the views it puts forward, reasons that others would accept as reasons, ideally as their own but not necessarily so, given *other* reasons they might feel compelled to bring forward. Which is to say that, though the approach is committed to argument, it is not argumentative; it seeks neither to "win" nor even primarily to convince anyone else than the writer herself. In this I am following R. G. Collingwood who, in his *Essay on Philosophical Method*,[4] writes:

> Every piece of philosophical writing is primarily addressed by the author to himself. Its purpose is not to select from among his thoughts those of which he is certain and

4. R. G. Collingwood, *Essay on Philosophical Method* (Oxford: Clarendon, 1933) 209.

to express those, but the very opposite: to fasten upon the difficulties and obscurities in which he finds himself involved, and try, if not to solve or remove them, at least to understand them better.

On this view what is asked of the reader, then, is that she follow the writer's working out of her thoughts in order to see the extent to which they do work themselves out, that is, yield a better understanding in the reader's own mind. This is why the philosopher *writes*, instead of merely thinking: through this effort of communicating, there is an attempt to have the "difficulties and obscurities" (presumably shared with the reader insofar as she continues to read) work themselves out.

However, there is a speculative dimension as well in this approach, insofar as the attempt to work out the "difficulties and obscurities" encountered is not animated by a kind of frustration with the lack of clarity one is confronted with—as one finds in Descartes' approach, or Wittgenstein's, for example—but rather by a sense of *incompleteness* in what one is confronted with in one's thought. What such incompleteness signals is a sense of other *possibilities* to be discerned in the obscurities and difficulties encountered and this engages one's imagination as it considers such possibilities.

The "difficulties and obscurities" this book is attempting to work through, then, are those encountered when we try to work out how the unfolding of history as a whole connects to our efforts to make sense of our lives. Or put another way, it tries to make sense of history making sense of us. It does not, and will not, propose a "theory" of history as a whole. In fact part of its purpose is to encourage us to move away from the image of thought or thinking as the circumscribed consideration of particular or specific "objects" (for the historian, the past; for the speculative philosopher of history, history as a whole) and to move towards an engagement with thought as a shared *making sense* of our involvement in a world that confronts us with shared "difficulties and obscurities" which, even as they manifest themselves in thought and through thinking, are not primarily intellectual but which involve a broader sense of ourselves.

This brings me back to Hayden White and the second point I wanted to draw attention to. In his response to the critique of his work by A. Dirk Moses (who faults him for providing a vision of historiography that does nothing to guard against the "instrumentalization" of history to serve and foment ethnic and nationalistic exclusionary practices),[5] he quotes Michel de Certeau's reflection on the impossible scientificity of historiography (I will use the term "historiography" when the focus is explicitly on the "writing-up" and presentation of the results of historical investigations, the manner in which they are presented for appreciation and assessment):

> Envisaged as a "discipline" historiography *is a science that lacks the means of being one.* Its discourse undertakes to deal with what is most resistant to scientificity (the relation of the social to the event, to violence, to the past, to death), that is, those matters each scientific discipline must eliminate in order to be constituted as a science.[6]

White points out how this passage captures something about our ambiguous relation to history and to modern historiography's appropriation of history. The latter's project, as William Dray puts it (in a critique of White's own earlier critique of the politics of contemporary philosophy of history), must be conceived, *at a minimum,*

---

5. A. Dirk Moses, "Hayden White, Traumatic Nationalism, and the Public Role of History," *History and Theory* 44 (October 2005): 311–32.

6. White, "Public Relevance" 333.

as that of giving us "a true picture of the past: a picture of it seen steadily, whole and right side up—the way it 'really was'".[7] Dray is surely right in saying that this is what is expected of *historians*, those who engage in the study of the past. That, in itself, however, does not remove the ambiguousness of our relation to the past. However fascinated we are by historical attempts to provide a "true picture of our past", such attempts are never entirely satisfying, because of the continuingly problematic nature of the object whose true picture is sought by historians. Which is to say that, despite the work of historians, our relation to the past is not merely—indeed I would argue not even primarily—a *knowing* one (even if that is the privileged relation in modern culture in the sense that anyone wanting to make claims about the past will be assessed and appreciated in terms of whether or not he or she knows what he or she is talking about, based on criteria that will include those articulated by professional historians). It is, in fact, one that continues to present many "difficulties and obscurities". Following up on de Certeau's point, White comments:

---

7. W. H. Dray, "The Politics of Contemporary Philosophy of History: A Reply to Hayden White," *Clio* 3.1 (1973): 68.

History's subject-matter, that is, the past, is a problematic object of study—especially for a society that has lost its faith in religion and is disillusioned with metaphysics. The past is the realm of the dead, or, as Heidegger has said, the domain of the "once having lived." It is a place of fantasy that we confront with anxiety. It is not present to perception but is known only by the traces that its once living inhabitants have left behind. The past is an absent presence, the equivalent for a community of what one's ancestors or, indeed, one's own childhood, is for an individual person. The dead can be studied scientifically, but science cannot tell us what we desire to know about the dead. Or rather, those aspects of the past that can be studied scientifically do not yield the kinds of information or knowledge that drives us to the study of the past in the first place.[8]

What I will be suggesting and exploring in what follows is that what "drives us to the study of the past" are the "difficulties and obscurities" that recognizing a past to our unfolding lives generates as we attempt to work through them. That some of those "difficulties and obscurities" are epistemological (what can we *know* about the past) is undeniable; but the focus

---

8. White, "Public Relevance" 333.

here is much broader and has to do with the "absent presence" of the past in our attempt to make sense of our unfolding lives. For example, how does the fact that what was once considered to be "true" is no longer held to be true (fixed stars, a flat earth, a spirit world, the natural inferiority of certain kinds of human beings) impact on what is held to be true today? May not what we hold to be true today someday be seen to be untrue? Does recognizing this mean giving up on the truth we hold today as "truth"? What does this encounter with the differences that the past exhibits say about the grasp we have on our own present? In what sense is our present the future of the past and how does making sense of that past impact on our future? That is, how are we to appreciate that what was thought about the world and about what should be done in that world in the past did in fact yield unimagined futures currently lived as a particular present? Does the appreciation of such historicity loosen or tighten the grip we have on our present reality?

***

The attempt to think history not only in terms of the past but in terms of how the past relates to the present and the future is how we should understand the continuing relevance of speculative philosophy of history. It is "speculative" in the sense that it attempts to gather together in thought a whole that is not experienced as such; a whole that is not completed in our experience, as it were. We relate to both the past and the future in our unfolding lives, but the experience of living out those lives does not grasp, or encapsulate, the whole of those relations. There is much more to the past that we can remember or even know; the future is unknown to us even as we anticipate it in specific ways. Attempting to think those relations despite this experiential limitation is to engage in speculative thought. To characterize the relations of a whole in terms of the past, the present and the future as these engage our collective efforts to make lives for ourselves is to engage in speculative philosophy of history.

These comments are meant to give a little more precision to the more common distinction between the historian's preoccupation with history as the "past" and the philosopher's preoccupation with history "as a whole". It also allows us to see more clearly the relation between historians and philosophers of history. If historians are *explicitly* concerned with the past, indeed with knowing "what happened in the past", they are *implicitly* connecting the past to self-conceptions operative in the present and oriented in specific ways to the future. Philosophers of history are explicitly concerned with the connections and orientations themselves. (Historians, of course, can be more or less explicit about these connections and orientations as well. Indeed, you will often find them introducing these broader questions as background to the detailed and focused discussion of the specific object of their study, which is some feature of the past.)

How then to proceed? The question is worth asking because it is important to recognize that there are numerous ways in which one can do speculative philosophy of history, just as there are numerous ways in which one can do history. Let me appeal yet again to Hayden White, who argues in his *Metahistory* that "in any field of study not yet reduced (or elevated) to the status of a genuine science, thought remains the captive of the linguistic mode in which it seeks to grasp the outline of objects inhabiting its field of perception".[9] I think this is an interesting way to engage the relation between language and thought, between the modes we have for expressing our-

9. Hayden White, *Metahistory: The Historical Imagination in Nineteenth-Century Europe* (Baltimore: Johns Hopkins UP, 1973) xi.

selves and the thoughts we thereby find ourselves trying to express. And while I will not be following White's formalist analysis of particular modes (as fascinating as it is), nor will I be adopting his structuralist view of how the thinkers he examines are seen to be "captive" to those modes (as dazzling as that is), I will try to follow up on his view that the systematic approaches brought to the examination of history and the sense it can be said to have will in fact be kinds of "*formalizations* of poetic insights that analytically precede them".[10]

We will recall his earlier comment concerning the general appeal to history as giving us some kind of sense of the "real", now that both religion and metaphysics are afforded little public sanction. History counts as the real, presumably because it is about things that have really happened. The problem is, of course, that its "reality" is one that needs to be recovered through examination of the traces of a past in the present. Accessing this "reality" is therefore far from straightforward. White, in speaking of "poetic insight", is addressing the varied ways we appeal to and access this reality of history and the varied results that are produced (and this variety is, no doubt, what justified him in talking about

---

10. White, *Metahistory* xii.

something that is less—or more—than a "genuine science").

This is worth emphasizing. White's point is especially valuable in reminding us that, despite the careful work accomplished by historians in opening up the past as a field of study subject to developed canons of investigative rigor (one cannot say whatever one likes about the past and still claim to be speaking about the *historical* past), the past thereby opened up is *of interest to us* for reasons other than the objectivity of its (re)presentation. And those reasons need not be explicit to be effective in motivating an engagement with the past. But the point I would like to emphasize is that *we are already so engaged* insofar as we distinguish, within our unfolding lives, the past from our present in ways that connect them through the differences they exhibit. We are in fact drawn to exploring those differences *because* of the connection we maintain between the past and the present as a "field" of intriguing differences that we recognize as relevant to our own self-understanding, and this connection between the past and the present is not only intelligible but *significant.* If history, then, is more properly understood as a "field"—as opposed to an object—it is because its exploration contributes to our sense of orientation; indeed, making sense of it is a kind of self-orientation within a broader sense of our temporal existence.

Now, the point White is raising is that our engagement in such a field is already "prefigured" by our very *ability* to engage it as a field. To say, with White, that such a prefiguration is "poetic" captures the idea that we do *not* approach (because we already inhabit) this field as a particular object of investigation, but rather that we are already, in our approach (and in the ways that we inhabit it), *enveloped* in a language that already makes some sense of it, provides orientation and guidance, outlines expectations, gives words to our desires, but does so in a way open to be taken up in multiple ways, subject to different interpretations, eliciting ambiguous responses that are themselves open to interpretation.[11] In other words, the

---

11. I am using "poetic" here in the sense developed by John McCumber in *Poetic Interaction: Language, Freedom, Reason* (Chicago: U of Chicago P, 1989) 385, where he distinguishes modes of interaction in which the meanings of the utterances at play do not impose themselves by the constraints of the particular context of utterance: "for one reason or another, the utterances...leave it up to the hearer to decide how they are to be understood". Of course, this is not the case for most

poetry of the world as we live in it precedes any focused examination of it and the latter can replace the former only at the cost of its own expressive relevance. (For example, our welcoming and appreciation of the "rising" sun is enhanced but not ultimately replaced by our schooled and more accurate understanding of its relation to a rotating earth).

White, in *Metahistory*, proposes a fascinating tropological reading of the "poetic prefiguration of the historical field" (in terms of the literary tropes of metaphor, synecdoche, metonymy and irony) as articulated in the nineteenth-century "historical imagination". I will not follow him in his specifically tropological reading, but I do want to make brief use of his classification of the various *explanatory strategies* taken up by the figures he examines. He identifies three such strategies, which he then explores in terms of what he calls

---

of our utterances—hence the particular and relatively stable shapes our worlds have taken—but recognizing that some of them are is crucial if we are properly to *situate* our freedom to "interact" in the first place. For this latter point, cf. McCumber's *Reshaping Reason: Toward a New Philosophy* (Bloomington: Indiana UP, 2007). I will return to this point throughout and to this book in my conclusion.

their "modes of articulation" (all framed within the prefigured tropes enumerated above).

The first strategy is to explain by means of "emplotment" as this is evidenced in various narrative modes. While much interesting philosophy of history has turned its attention to the role that narrative can play in helping us make sense of history,[12] this approach will not be privileged here. Rather, my focus will be on the second form of explanatory strategy that White identifies, which he calls "formal argument". The third strategy—"ideological implication"—will be left for another time. I should say that I will not be making use of White's own manner of parsing this explanatory strategy through the particular modes he identifies, as they are focused on the historians and philosophers of history of the nineteenth century that interest him. Rather, I make use of his distinctions because they help us see how

---

12. Cf. Hayden White himself in *The Content of the Form: Narrative Discourse and Historical Representation* (Baltimore: Johns Hopkins UP, 1987) but also Paul Ricoeur, *Time and Narrative*, 3 vols., trans. Kathleen Blamey and David Pellauer (Chicago: U of Chicago P, 1984–1988) and David Carr, *Time, Narrative, and History* (Bloomington: Indiana UP, 1986) come to mind.

different strategies are indeed adopted
in various attempts to make sense of history. And I want in particular to contrast
an approach to making sense of history
whose explanatory strategy is focused on
"argument" rather than "emplotment",
which focuses on the narrative or story-like
features of making sense of history.

I have two basic reasons for doing this.
The first is that I think the attempt to
make sense of history through a strategy
that appeals to argument—that is, that
appeals to *principles* and *reason-giving*—is
a valuable way to engage our experience
of the correlativity of the past, present
and future in our unfolding lives. The
second reason is that I think it is important at this time to *disengage* philosophy
of history from that other "explanatory
strategy" that does focus on narrative and
"emplotment". That is, I do not think that
the particular demands being made on
our attempts to make sense of history, to
deal with our present "obscurities and difficulties" as we do so, are best responded
to by appealing to the structures of narrative and the expectations that are generated by those structures. Put simply, we
are aware and appreciative of too many
stories to accept the idea that *history as
a whole,* as we try to make sense of it as it
relates to our unfolding lives, can plausibly

be gathered up into the shape of a single, over-arching story, a "meta-narrative", to use Jean-François Lyotard's term.[13] The attraction of such a mode is still there, to be sure, to *look* at our lives, both individually and collectively, as story-like, as structured by beginnings, middles and ends, as being comic or tragic, etc. But, I would argue, however attracted to and appreciative of such a story-like approach to our lives we are, we do not *wholly buy into it* and do not accept it as *actually* or fully making sense of our unfolding lives or as being *ultimately* how we relate to the co-relativity of our experience of the past, present and future *when considered as a whole* (a kind of consideration I admit we pay less and less attention to but that nevertheless remains open to us).

Let me clarify what is being said here, because it is crucial to what I am trying to do in this book. I am not saying that a narrative explanatory strategy is not explanatory of what human beings do and have done (in the past). Indeed, I am rather sympathetic to those who even *insist*, when it comes to understanding what human

---

13. Jean-François Lyotard, *The Postmodern Condition: A Report on Knowledge*, trans. Geoff Bennington and Brian Massumi (Minneapolis: U of Minnesota P, 1984).

beings are doing and what they have done, on the explanatory potential of narrative, on its ability to *make sense* of human beings. Narratives (including fictional ones) *do* illuminate us in what they reveal about human beings as actors and agents. I am even prepared to grant that the most likely reason that narrative does illuminate our understanding (or, put more directly and bluntly, does *explain*) human actions and human agency generally, it is that human action and human agency *themselves* have a narrative structure, as someone like David Carr has argued. That is, we do not only make sense of our lives *through* narrative, or by imposing (or superimposing) upon them a narrative form, so this argument goes; our lives themselves, *as lived* and not merely recounted, have as their privileged form a narrative structure. As Carr has recently put it, "narrative goes all the way down".[14]

But this particular insistence on narrative concerns a conception of what we are as human beings in terms of how we *live* out our lives. Of course, if such an approach is so obviously relevant to his-

---

14. David Carr, "Narrative Explanation and Its Malcontents," *History and Theory* 47 (2008): 30.

tory, it is because history concerns itself with how human beings have indeed lived.

However, I want to mark a distinction between this conception of history as an account of how humans have lived and a conception of history-as-a-whole, history as the past-present-future complex to which we can *relate* our unfolding lives in the very fact that they unfold, the fact that they cannot be "wholly" grasped outside of this unfolding. It is this latter sense of history that, I am arguing, is not best captured by narrative modes of explanation. That is, history understood as a whole is not a narrative, does not tell a story, or at least we no longer believe that it does, not *really*. Of course, lack of such a belief has entailed the gradual abandonment of speculative philosophy of history. But this, in my view, is a mistake, and a very specific one that can now be formulated fairly clearly: it is to treat history-as-a-whole as a subject-term whose "story" it is the job of the philosophy of history to tell. And, of course, such a "story" is often said to be quintessentially told in Hegel's philosophy of history, the subject-term of history being Spirit and the story of Spirit to be its gradual (but by no means smooth!) self-realization as the Idea of Freedom, or as he puts it, "the development of the consciousness of Freedom on the part of Spirit, and of the consequent realization of that Freedom".[15] And in that story, the whole of the world is embraced, both temporally by reaching back to Antiquity and spatially or geographically, by including all of the regions of the world, famously summed up in the oft-quoted pronouncement, "The East knew and to the present day knows only that *One* is Free; the Greek and Roman world, that *some* are free; the German World knows that *All* are free."[16]

This "story"—the story of History as culminating in the modern European state-form—is the kind of master narrative that is rejected along with the speculative philosophies that sustain it.

However, a speculative appreciation of history-as-a-whole need not take a narrative form. History need not be treated as a subject-term. Even as we reject those master narratives that would sum up and give us the meaning of the self-development of history, it remains open to us to *think* our relation to the whole of history understood as a past-present-future complex. That complex does not disappear as we abandon master narratives of the self-realization of Reason and Freedom. And

---

15. G. W. F. Hegel, *The Philosophy of History*,
     trans. J. Sibree (New York: Dover, 1956) 63.
16. Hegel, *Philosophy of History* 104.

the attempt to think (i.e., to work out the difficulties and obscurities encountered in) our relation to such a whole itself remains *speculative.*

But even Hegel himself, in his *Philosophy of History,* does not always rely solely on a narrative treatment of Spirit's self-development. Even within the lectures themselves (and we would do well to remember that what we are reading when we are reading his *Philosophy of History* are lecture notes prepared by his son), we are meant to follow a mode of speculative thinking that, like all thinking, makes use of conceptualizations and principles, but now with the aim of *comprehending, of grasping* the whole of history. In fact, the sentence immediately preceding the famous one quoted above makes this point. Hegel says, "The History of the World is the discipline of the uncontrolled natural will, bringing it into obedience to a Universal principle and conferring subjective freedom". Thus, rather than see in history the "story" of something called "Spirit" (we might call this "the Providential view"), we can ask what it is, exactly, that enables us to distinguish something called "history" in the first place. How is an examination of "history", as a context within which human beings act and live out their lives, to be distinguished from an examination of, for example, "nature", which of course is also

a context within which human beings act
and live out their lives?[17] Further, just as we
seek in "nature" the *principles* that allow us
to make sense of it, so might we seek within
"history" (assuming we are successful in
establishing a clear enough distinction
between "nature" and "history") the principles that allow us to make sense of *it*. Thus,
rather than merely the subject of a narrative account, Spirit, within Hegel's thought,
is also a principle of intelligibility for making sense of history (as something distinct
from nature). Mark C. Lemon (in a book
on the philosophy of history that is meant
to serve as a guide to budding professional
historians) has us confront Hegel in the following, I believe, useful way:

> Thus, the challenge Hegel presents us
> is not whether we "believe" him, or in
> "Spirit," as in some religious act of faith,
> but whether we agree history *is* fundamen-

---

17. That "history" should become such a
    context for making sense of human lives is
    masterfully described by François Châtelet
    is his account of the "birth" of history
    in antiquity where we witness the deci-
    sion to account for human actions in a
    strictly "profane-sensible" way and thus to
    preserve them as distinctively "historical".
    Cf. *La naissance de l'histoire*, 2 vols. (Paris:
    Seuil, 1962), especially the introduction.

tally about what he calls "Spirit." To Hegel
a number of things seem obvious: that
there is a qualitative difference between
human beings and animals; that in being
self-conscious, humans introduce a revolu-
tionary, fundamental principle otherwise
absent from Existence—namely, that they
are beings imbued with a self-directing
energy to strive towards aims, however
petty or ambitious; that this is the very *condition* of there being any "history" at all;
and that the logical heart of this human
activity—will—seeks 'freedom,' whose
ultimate realm cannot but centre on individuals' relations to each other in terms of
"right"—in other words, the realm of the
political organization of 'the state' broadly
conceived. Equally obvious to him was
that different states and corresponding
national cultures have arisen in history;
and that, as much because of as despite
dreadful setbacks, Freedom's general characteristics have been progressively made
actual, as shown in certain parts of the
modern world. Viewed as a whole, then,
there would be no *intelligible* history without the phenomenon of Spirit, expressed
via the fact of human self-consciousness.
Therefore, without a prior understanding
of what Spirit means and involves (i.e. its
"principles"), we cannot hope to *understand* history but can only record its facts

and, wandering in the dark, make of them
(or not) whatever erroneous "framework"
or meaning might occur to us.[18]

Lemon's summary is useful because it
sets up a basic opposition that I would like
to make use of: because of the systematicity and coherence of Hegel's response, we
seem to be confronted with either accepting its basic thrust (which is to show that
only reason's free self-development in
and through history can provide what
John McCumber has called the "shakeable foundations"[19] needed to make sense
of ourselves and our world) or accepting
that when it comes to making sense of our
unfolding lives, any appeal to history will
in effect be a "wandering in the dark", the
facts of history bearing whatever "meaning
might occur to us".

***

The focus of the chapters that follow will
be on the work of Foucault, specifically
on his historical works, but not principally out of an interest in Foucault himself
as an intellectual figure with a particular

---

18. M. C. Lemon, *Philosophy of History: A Guide
    for Students* (London: Routledge, 2003)
    235–36.
19. John McCumber, "The Temporal Turn
    in German Idealism: Hegel and After,"
    Research in Phenomenology 32 (2002): 44–59.

stature around which a number of debates
and discussions circulate (when they do
not swirl). Foucault was something of a
formidable figure and, twenty-five years
after his death (which in terms of potential productivity was no doubt premature),
his figure continues to shape much of
the discussion his work invites. We can,
however, distinguish the work from the
figure and consider it—or features of it—
outside of the structures and insistences
that such a figure imposes, including the
self-understandings that both shape it and
are betrayed by it. As mentioned at the
beginning of this book, my primary concern is with the notion of history itself,
with the question of whether or not it can
provide us with a framework for—or put
more simply, help frame—our attempts to
make sense of our unfolding lives. History
becomes such a candidate notion because
considering our lives as "unfolding" confronts us with our relation to the past, the
present and the future. (History of course
is not the only candidate; there are other
ways to deal with the temporal dimension
of our lives: we could appeal to the cycli-
cal rhythms of nature or situate the time-
fulness of our existences within structures
deemed eternal or outside of time or within
certain genetic parameters of growth and
decay.) I have claimed that this requires a

speculative approach to history because its object is a whole that cannot be grasped as an object independent of the attempt to make sense of it. Such speculative attempts were undertaken by various thinkers in the past (Vico, Condorcet, Kant and Herder in the eighteenth century; Hegel, Marx and arguably Nietzsche in the nineteenth). No doubt the most systematic attempt at working out a *philosophy* of history in this speculative sense is Hegel's and therefore when I refer to "the philosophy of history *before*" Foucault I largely will mean Hegel's philosophy of history.

But why "before *Foucault*"? If my primary concern is with how the philosophy of history might help us make sense of our unfolding lives and if I claim that Hegel has provided us with what is probably the most systematic attempt to work this out, why do I not simply concentrate on Hegel's philosophy of history? Why do I place his philosophy of history (as an exemplar *of* philosophy of history) before *Foucault*? *Especially* Foucault, given the latter's apparent rejection of so many of Hegel's key conceptual moves and preferences, including the key concept of Spirit (and the self-consciousness it instantiates and promotes).

I do so for two basic reasons: One, Hegel's philosophy of history has become

incredible to us. While we might remain
impressed by its achievement in systematically gathering together so many features
that define our self-conception as "moderns",[20] the history of the world as it has
unfolded in the twentieth century leads
us ultimately to reject the overly synthetic
and "totalizing" dimension of his "world-
historical" claims. But it is precisely this
incredible synthesis, historically situated
in Hegel's work and time, that insists that
our philosophical efforts to make sense
of ourselves and the world are based on
an inescapably temporal (and therefore
"shakeable") foundation and that suggests that one place it *before* someone like
Foucault. That is, what interests me about
Foucault's work is precisely the ways it constitutes itself as a specific mode of "rejecting"
Hegel's conceptual moves and preferences
as these get systematized into a philosophy
of history (rather than merely affirming
the "figure" of Foucault as an anti-Hegelian
thinker). If we refer back to Lemon's summary statement quoted above where the
basic Hegelian point is that *without* such a
notion as Spirit expressed through human

---

20. See for example the concluding chapter
    in Terry Pinkard's *Hegel's Phenomenology:
    The Sociality of Reason* (Cambridge:
    Cambridge UP, 1996).

self-consciousness "there would be no *intelligible* history", then Foucault's work looks like an explicit counterpoint inasmuch as his engagement with the intelligibility of history precisely does *not* make use of the notions of Spirit or self-consciousness. However, what I would like to explore and to show is, one might say, *how* Foucault goes about *not* making use of such notions. As it turns out, this is a fairly significant dimension of his work that can be read as struggling with Hegel's systematic working out of a philosophy of history.[21] This struggle with Hegel's philosophy of history is interesting not only for the history of philosophy or for issues arising out of what is called "Continental Philosophy", but in terms of the stakes (or the substance of what is at stake) which involve, in my view, the intelligibility of history itself, as a mode of making sense of our lives. Recall Lemon's summary once again: with-

---

21. Do I need to insist that I am not claiming that this is the only thing going on in Foucault's work, nor even that it is the most significant? Foucault's work is very rich and multifaceted. I will claim, though, that close attention to it, and specifically the historical works, does reveal that this struggle is a *prominent* feature well worth investigating.

out an understanding of the *principles* that Spirit provides, or so the argument goes, "we cannot hope to *understand* history but can only record its facts, wandering in the dark, make of them (or not) whatever erroneous 'framework' or meaning might occur to us". Is that where we are, then? Is this what our various engagements with "history" amount to?

Perhaps this is too dramatic. Perhaps other principles can replace the structuring principle of Self-Conscious Spirit and allow us to produce intelligible history. Perhaps it is precisely the appeal to more pragmatic principles that will enable us to make better sense of our unfolding lives (the ostensible purpose of this investigation).

Interestingly, I think, a reading of Foucault's work suggests that things are not that simple. I want to show how his *histories* can be read as *making sense* of the claims of a philosophy of history like Hegel's *precisely* by challenging their credibility. That is, while most of us will merely affirm the incredibility of Hegel's synthetic view of history as the self-actualization of reason as the Idea of Freedom, Foucault actually measures the cost of such an affirmation by excavating its (in)credibility through the production of histories that challenge it (the self-realization of reason in *History of Madness* and its self-actualization as the Idea of Freedom in *Discipline and Punish* and the *History of Sexuality*). This, in any case, will be the crux of my reading of Foucault.

***

What makes Foucault's histories so interesting is the way they can be shown to challenge the very engagement of making sense of history by having it confront, through his own particular engagement, the "poetic prefiguration" of the historical field that White argues precedes that engagement. His particular mode of historical writing allows that "poetic prefiguration" to surface *through the very attempt to make sense of history* that his histories engage. This is what makes his histories so disconcerting to some. That is, appealing once again to White's classification of the different "explanatory strategies" that histories exhibit, Foucault's histories do not "explain" through a narrative form of emplotment, nor are they governed by an attempt to draw out the ideological implications of the way we relate the past to the present and the present to the past; they confront those strategies of making sense of history through argument with the poetic prefiguration that makes them the arguments that they are. And they do this because of the way they embody what

W. E. Connolly has called Foucault's particular *sensibility*.[22]

Rather than fret too much about whether or not to consider Foucault as a philosopher or as a historian (and there has been considerable discussion on this point in the literature), I will be concentrating less on *what* his historical investigations say about their ostensible objects—"madness" in the *History of Madness*, the "prison" in *Discipline and Punish*—than on the *way* they say what they say, the way they are suffused with a *sensibility* to what history reveals to us when we concern ourselves with our *relation* (in the present) to the past, to what the past can say about our present when we confront it with what the present insists upon in the past (and ultimately to how this positions us with reference to the future). If, as Hayden White suggests,

> the principal difference between history and philosophy of history is that the latter brings the conceptual apparatus by which facts are ordered in the discourse to the surface of the text, while history proper

22. William E. Connolly, "Beyond Good and Evil: The Ethical Sensibility of Michel Foucault," *Political Theory* 21.3 (1993): 365–89.

> (as it is called) buries it in the interior of the narrative, where it serves as a hidden or shaping device,[23]

then it makes sense to consider Foucault as a kind *philosopher of history* who philosophizes *through* history insofar as the conceptual apparatus he makes use of are precisely the histories he composes. Hence the claim he sometimes made that his histories should be understood as "fictions", not because what they dealt with was fictional or imaginary in the sense of "not real", but in the sense that the reality they reveal is *made* real only through the conceptual apparatus designed to grasp it.[24]

---

23. Hayden White, *Tropics of Discourse,* 126–27, qtd. in Keith Jenkins, *Re-Thinking History* (London: Routledge, 1991) xiv.
24. The following comment is often quoted when considering the particularities of Foucault's histories:

> I am fully aware that I have never written anything other than fictions. For all that, I would not want to say that they were outside the truth. It seems plausible to me to make fictions work within truth, to introduce truth-effects within a fictional discourse, and in some way to make discourse arouse, "fabricate" something which does yet exist, thus to fiction something. One "fictions" history starting from a political reality that renders it true, one "fictions" a politics that does not yet exist starting from a historical truth.

A "sensibility" in Connolly's sense here contrasts with those other things demanded or expected from thinkers, perhaps a "theory" or a "position", even a "doctrine", something to evaluate and to judge, to assess, ultimately to accept or to reject. A "sensibility" might be described as a preoccupation or concern with certain kinds of questions and issues that do not register explicitly and in explicitly accepted terms within the predominant modes of discourse, predominant modes of "making sense of things"; it describes an attentiveness to what these predominant modes are *doing* even as they "explain themselves" and "account for themselves" in what they are doing. Another way to put this, a way I will return to, is to say that "things said" are themselves "things done" and Foucault's sensibility is one that pays attention to what "things said and done" are themselves doing as they are said and done.

For my part, I will characterize Foucault's sensibility as a *modal* sensibility, one attuned to the play of possibility, necessity and contingency in the ways we relate to the

---

Foucault, qtd. in Hubert Dreyfus and Paul Rabinow, *Michel Foucault: Beyond Structuralism and Hermeneutics* (Chicago: U of Chicago P, 1983) 204.

past, the present and the future. Connolly quotes Foucault's own account of his general approach in such modal terms:

> We have to dig deeply to show how things have been historically contingent, for such and such a reason intelligible but not necessary. We must make the intelligible appear against a background of emptiness, and deny its necessity. We must think that what exists is far from filling all possible spaces.[25]

The imperatives formulated in this passage—which I will identify and discuss as the basic principles that inform Foucault's conception of history: the principle of *rarity* and the principle of *immanence*[26]—should be read as both reminders and invitations: reminders of our relation to both the past and the present and an invi-

---

25. Michel Foucault, "Friendship As A Way of Life," qtd. in Connolly, "Beyond Good and Evil" 367.

26. I have briefly discussed Foucault's work in terms of these two principles as providing something like "prolegomena to any future speculative philosophy of history" in my "Moving Beyond Biopower: Hardt and Negri's Post-Foucauldian Speculative Philosophy of History," *History and Theory* 44. 4 (2005): 47–72.

tation to explore its intelligibility without abstracting it from that relation. That this requires a particular "sensibility" is indicative of the ambiguity of that relation. It is not clear why we appeal to the past in order to make sense of things in the present; it is not clear why what appears *as* the past appears as it does. The past is not laid out before (or behind) us, complete and evident and consultable, the way we believe dictionaries are. It is rather a kind of beckoning at the limits of the self-understandings that structure our present. Think of your own personal archives, those things that you have accumulated in the course of your life that bear witness to the fact that you not only *are*, but have been: Perhaps a journal you kept in your late teens or an essay you had forgotten you had written, letters or cards you have kept from people you can barely remember, books you bought but never read, clothes you once wore, receipts from past purchases, pictures of yourself that you cannot look at without laughing, pictures of others who have died. The complex relation one has to all of these things informs one's sensibility to the past.

Perhaps one of the best places to appreciate the particular sensibility Foucault brings to thinking about the relation between the past and the present is a text

called *Lives of Infamous Men*,[27] which was to
serve as an introduction to a series of pre-
sentations of archival materials under the
title *Parallel Lives:* This included the memoir of Herculine Barbin, which Foucault
published by juxtaposing the memoir itself
with contemporary newspaper clippings
and the medical, including autopsy, reports
framing the life and death of a nineteenth-
century hermaphroditic individual.[28] The
point of the series was to present an
"anthology of existences" encountered
"by chance in books and documents". The
"principle of selection" used is explicitly
linked to Foucault's own sensibility:

> The selection found here was guided by
> nothing more substantial than my taste,
> my pleasure, an emotion, laughter, sur-
> prise, a certain dread, or some other feel-
> ing whose intensity I might have trouble
> justifying, now that the first moment of
> discovery has passed.[29]

27. Michel Foucault, "Lives of Infamous
     Men," *Power: Essential Works of Foucault,
     1954–1984. Vol. 3*, ed. James Faubion
     (New York: The New Press, 2000) 157–75.
28. Michel Foucault, *Herculine Barbin: Being the
     Recently Discovered Memoirs of a Nineteenth-
     Century French Hermaphrodite*, trans. Richard
     McDougall (Brighton: The Harvester Press,
     1980).
29. Foucault, "Lives of Infamous Men" 157.

The notion of being "guided by nothing more substantial" than his own sensibility here is what is significant. Rather than focus on the "nothing more", we should note how Foucault is indicating *what is guiding* his perusal of the archive. This is important. Historical archives are myriad and they are investigated always for specific reasons, some of them quite deliberate and purpose-driven, others more leisurely and fueled by something like curiosity. One can well imagine that Foucault's perusal of the specific documents in question was initially a function of his work on the history of madness and thus was not completely "by chance". However, apart from that project, his decision to peruse them "guided by nothing more substantial" than what I am calling his "sensibility" is interesting because, rather than lead him to produce a whimsical or idiosyncratic presentation of such "brief lives" in history (which may or may not be of interest to others), it shows how Foucault remains *open* to the "poetic prefiguration" that is in fact our access to something called the past as distinct from our present (such a "prefiguration" usually indicated by the historian's "interest" in a particular aspect of the past). What Foucault allows us to see more clearly here is how this prefiguration is indeed *poetic* because he shows how closely connected our access to the past is enabled through *language*, opening it up as a field eliciting a response that is not fixed in advance. Indeed, the "existences", the "brief lives" that Foucault wishes to present are actually encountered as *effects* of language, as it were:

> For the things said in these texts are so compressed that one isn't sure whether the intensity that sparks through them is due more to the vividness of the words or to the jostling violence of the facts they tell. Singular lives, transformed into strange poems through who knows what twists of fate—that is what I decided to gather in a kind of herbarium.[30]

However, this aesthetic appreciation, the impact that the brief texts have on Foucault's sensibility (and on ours), also *prefigure* that which we strive to understand

---

30. Foucault, "Lives of Infamous Men" 157. Of the two examples he gives, here is the second:

> Jean Antoine Touzard, placed in the castle of Bicêtre, 21 April 1701: "Seditious apostate friar, capable of the greatest crimes, sodomite, atheist if that were possible; this individual is a veritable monster of abomination whom it would be better to stifle than to leave at large." (Foucault, "Lives of Infamous Men" 158.)

or to make sense of. *These* "existences"—these "singular lives"—are noticed by us, again through language, only because, as Foucault puts it, "a beam of light had to illuminate them, for a moment at least". That "light" illuminates not only the past we are opening ourselves to, these singular lives themselves, but in the flash of our encounter with them, it illuminates how we relate, in the present, to that past and how that past relates to our present. As Foucault puts it, the light that illuminates these singular lives is:

A light coming from elsewhere. What snatched them from the darkness in which they could, perhaps should, have remained was the encounter with power; without that collision, it's very unlikely that any word would be there to recall their fleeting trajectory. The power that watched these lives, that pursued them, that lent its attention, if only for a moment, to their complaints and their little racket, and marked them with its claw was what gave rise to the few words about them that remain for us—either because someone decided to appeal to it in order to denounce, complain, solicit, entreat, or because he chose to intervene and in a few words to judge and decide. All those lives destined to pass beneath any discourse and disappear without ever having been told were able to leave traces—brief, incisive, often enigmatic—only at the point of their instantaneous contact with power.[31]

We see Foucault here working, through the poetic prefiguration of these (textual, archival) encounters, towards a mode of articulation of the historical field which is neither *narratively-driven* nor *ideologically-motivated* (to take up once again White's schema), but argumented in ways this book will attempt to make clear. Specifically, I will attempt to show how Foucault's essentially *modal* sensibility (to what is necessary, contingent, possible) can be articulated as an argument opening up a space that challenges *us* to question and to reconsider a notion of history that would or could provide sense to our unfolding lives; that is, lives open to relating to the past-present-future complex as a whole.

***

This last remark allows me to clarify how the philosophy of history has been changed *after* Foucault. My principal preoccupation is with the philosophy of history, with its continued possibility and relevance to thinking about our world and the "obscurities and difficulties" we encounter in that thinking. Foucault's work does not provide

---

31. Foucault, "Lives of Infamous Men" 161.

us with such a philosophy of history, but it
does not drive it into irrelevance either; it
is not the case that "after Foucault" it no
longer makes sense to claim *any* sense to
history understood as a whole. On the contrary, Foucault's work, through its dogged
commitment to the *intelligibility* of history,
actually compels us to *re*-pose the question
of the sense history can be said to yield as
we engage with it; that is, to pose this question in a way that does not cover over what
Hayden White calls the "historical sublime", by which he means consideration
of the possibility that, ultimately, history
understood as whole, that is, history as it
has been lived and is being lived, is in fact
without meaning, a kind of meaningless
spectacle, that inspires a kind of horror
(what Kant called "the idiotic course of
things human" and what Hegel referred
to as the "slaughter bench" of history.)
White's appeal to the ever-present possibility is neither cynical nor desperate (hence
his use of the notion of the sublime: the
sublime meaninglessness of the history of
human life); quite the contrary. According
to White, it is those "modern ideologies"
that pretend to give meaning to history
that prove to be the most desperate, in the
precise sense that they remove the essential role of human hopefulness in making
sense of our lives. He says this because, to

the extent that these "ideologies" are successful in imputing "a meaning to history
that renders its manifest confusion com-
prehensible to either reason, understanding or aesthetic sensibility", then

> these ideologies deprive history of the
> kind of meaninglessness that alone can
> goad living human beings to make their
> lives different for themselves and for
> their children, which is to say, to endow
> their lives with a meaning for which they
> alone are fully responsible. One can never
> move with any politically effective confi-
> dence from an apprehension of "the way
> things actually are or have been" to the
> kind of moral insistence that they "should
> be otherwise" without passing through a
> feeling of repugnance for and negative
> judgment of the condition that is to be
> superseded.[32]

The sublimity of contemplating the historical process as a whole does indeed
pose a formidable challenge to anyone
who would defend its intelligibility. And
yet careful attention to it *does* yield intel-

---

32. Hayden White, "The Politics of Historical
    Interpretation," *The Content of the
    Form: Narrative Discourse and Historical
    Representation* (Baltimore: Johns Hopkins
    UP, 1987) 72–73.

ligibility, as the works of both Foucault and Hegel demonstrate. Indeed, it is the goal of this book to show how Foucault's work, through its modal sensibility and read against the backdrop of the more explicitly speculative framework of Hegel's speculative philosophy of history—the latter understood less in terms of its *narrative* of the self-development of Spirit (what might be called the Protestant Storyline Hegel appeals to in his lectures) than in terms of the modal argument concerning the actualization of freedom—rises to this challenge of historical senselessness. In what follows, I draw a tighter connection between Foucault's work and Hegel's than is usually tolerated (largely because of Foucault's explicit opposition to certain key Hegelian conceptual moves). However, I think initiating such a *rapprochement* is worth it inasmuch as it illuminates a reading of Foucault's work that stays true to what I take to be its deepest and most lasting insights.

***

Foucault, in a discussion with historians concerning how best to approach his work *Discipline and Punish*, or even better, how best to approach his work generally, says the following: "My books aren't treatises in philosophy or studies of history; at most, they are philosophical fragments put to

work in a historical field of problems."[33]
I will have occasion to examine this statement more closely in what follows. For the
moment, I would simply like to point out
that, if we are to regard Foucault's books
as *philosophical fragments*, we are led to ask
or to consider the *whole* to which these
so-called fragments might be said—if not
to belong, which would be to say too much
too quickly—to *relate*. I think it is plausible
to suggest that these philosophical fragments should be read against precisely
the kind of reading that would approach
history both systematically and as a whole,
such as that proposed by Hegel.

My objective is not to recuperate
Foucault by reintegrating his thought
within Hegel's own particular problematic.
Such reference to proper names and the
doctrines said to be proper to them can
quickly get in the way of the effort to work
through the "difficulties and obscurities"
that thinking about history and our relation to it generates. But the work denoted
by these names remains a rich source and
guide to such an effort. It is my hope that
the particular juxtaposition that governs

---

33. Michel Foucault, *Power: Essential Works of
Foucault, 1954–1984. Vol. 3*, ed. James D.
Faubion (New York: The New Press, 2000)
224.

the reading proposed in this book might
be useful to others who share this interest
and concern with relating our unfolding
lives to a history that can help make sense
of them.

PART A

Philosophical Underpinnings

I
Foucault and the Idea of History

My concern in the general introduction was with the speculative philosophy of history and with raising the question of its relevance in helping us make sense of our unfolding lives. It led to a consideration of the work of Michel Foucault, which will be the primary focus of this book, specifically because Foucault's engagement with history, through its particular sensibility, argumentative strategies and basic principles, poses an interesting challenge to the notion that something like the philosophy of history can help us make sense of our unfolding lives.

This chapter will serve as an overview of Foucault's work through a general reading of the way it can be said to relate to the questions raised by the philosophy of history. After this general reading of Foucault's work, the next chapter will examine what might be called Foucault's

own specific conception of the general
nature of history and the challenges that
such a conception sets up.

While there are many important works
dealing with Foucault's engagement with,
and challenge to, traditional historiography,[1] my approach here will be slightly
different. It will mirror my own initial
engagement with Foucault's work which
interested me because of its potential to
illuminate and to help bring about what,
following R. G. Collingwood, I took to be an
urgent task of contemporary philosophical
thought: that of bringing about a *rapprochement* between philosophy and history. My
understanding of what Collingwood meant
by this was that philosophical thought
needed to take the historical conditions

1. I will signal two of the most significant in
   my view: Thomas R. Flynn, *Sartre, Foucault,
   and Historical Reason: A Poststructuralist
   Mapping of History* (Chicago: U of Chicago
   P, 2005) and Mitchell Dean, *Critical and
   Effective Histories: Foucault's Methods and
   Historical Sociology* (London: Routledge,
   1994). I should also mention Paul Veyne's
   piece "Foucault révolutionne l'histoire,"
   which appeared in his *Comment on écrit
   l'histoire* (Paris: Seuil, 1978). In English:
   Paul Veyne, "Foucault Revolutionizes
   History," trans. Catherine Porter, *Foucault
   and his Interlocutors*, ed. Arnold I. Davidson
   (Chicago: U of Chicago P, 1997) 146–82.

of its articulation more seriously and historical investigations needed to become more aware of the principled character of their commitments and that the juxtaposition of these two imperatives set the agenda for reflective thought. Accepting this agenda, I turned to Foucault's work because I thought that his philosophical engagement *through* historical investigations would surely yield important insights. I was not disappointed (even as I was challenged and surprised by his work).

In addition to setting this particular agenda, Collingwood will be useful to set up a framework for mapping relevant considerations of Foucault's work, specifically with regard to what can simply be called Foucault's "idea of history" as it joins (and contests) a long line of related ideas which Collingwood so ably surveyed in his lectures and papers and which were posthumously collected and published by T. M. Knox in 1946 in a volume called *The Idea of History.*[2] What Collingwood traces in this work is the working out of a progressively more adequate conception of what is involved in thinking historically

---

2. (Oxford: Clarendon Press). A revised edition including an introduction and additional material edited by Jan van der Dussen was published in 1993 by the Clarendon Press.

as this is reflected in historiographical practices. Collingwood shares, then, in this sense, the epistemic concerns characteristic of what we have come to know as analytic philosophy of history, that is, concerns that have to do with historical knowledge. Collingwood's specific concern is with affirming the *autonomy* of historical knowledge, by which he means that any affirmation of the criteria by which it can be said that something is *known* historically arises out of the *practice* of historical thinking itself and is not dependent on some other form of thoughtful activity, like natural science. It should be said that, in insisting on this, Collingwood is not merely defending a disciplinary division of what it means to know the things we claim to know. If historical knowledge is not dependent on the forms and practices of the knowledge typical of the natural sciences, it is because historical knowledge is not about "nature" (understood as the controlled observation of regularities) but about human activity (understood in terms of actual realizations in relation to intentions and consequences). However, the point here is not merely to affirm the distinction between *Naturwissenschaften* and *Geisteswissenschaften*; Collingwood wants to go further and claim that the point of affirming the autonomy of historical knowledge is to allow us to see how the problems raised by our efforts to think historically are the *essential* problems faced by our contemporary engagement with the world. For example, in *The New Leviathan*, Collingwood's last published work (in 1942; Collingwood died in 1943), at the end of a section called "Theoretical Reason", he states the following:

> The object of scientific study, for a man who has taken part in the progress of human thought down to the present time, is history. The world of Nature, first the law-abiding Nature of modern science and secondly the end-seeking Nature of Greco-Medieval science, is as real as you will; but it is not history, it is the background of history... It is in the world of history, not in the world of Nature, that man finds the central problems he has to solve. For twentieth-century thought the problems of history are the central problems: those of Nature, however interesting they may be, are only peripheral.[3]

---

3. R. G. Collingwood, *The New Leviathan* (Oxford: Clarendon Press, 1942) 129. For those who would dismiss such a claim now, in the twenty-first century, by pointing out our urgent need to reconsider the problems of Nature, citing climate change as an example, I would suggest that the *urgency*

The bulk of *The Idea of History*, then, sets out to discuss how history has been conceptualized from Herodotus to what Collingwood calls the "scientific history" of the present (and by "scientific" here Collingwood does not mean appeal to a methodology developed in the natural sciences—the natural sciences are themselves specific, not exclusive, examples of "scientific" thinking—but more broadly a kind of thinking that conceptualizes and poses questions that it sets itself to answer in a systematically intelligible way). Retracing this history, for Collingwood, forms part and parcel of our own current conception of what we are doing when we are doing history (unlike the natural sciences whose history, while interesting, is not an ingredient of the current self-conception of the project of investigating nature; or, at least, has not been so until recently, but that is a subject for another time).

Foucault's historiographical practices do not leave anyone indifferent. The eminent historian Paul Veyne, in fact, sees in his work "the culmination of history" and claims that this "philosopher ... might also be the author of the scientific

referred to in this return to the problems of Nature indicates that something like climate change is in fact a problem for *historical* thinking.

revolution around which all historians have been gravitating".[4] But even without Veyne's hyperbole, and despite Foucault's own likely reaction to being included in such a continuist conception of historical self-consciousness, I think considering Foucault's work within the terms articulated by Collingwood is important for two reasons. First, Foucault's various ways of interrogating our appeals to the past can themselves be seen as a contribution to our historical self-understanding. Second, I think Foucault's work can be fruitfully read as engaged in the *rapprochement* that Collingwood promoted. Therefore, I would like to describe in general terms Foucault's contribution to our historical self-understanding in the context of such a *rapprochement*. I also think that this Collingwoodian framework helps us grasp Foucault's overall approach to history in a way that respects its various manifestations.

As mentioned in the Introduction, the question is often asked: should one consider Foucault a historian or a philosopher?[5] It gets asked because Foucault wrote *histories*,

4. Veyne, "Foucault Revolutionizes History" 147.

5. For example, Clare O'Farrell, *Foucault: Historian or Philosopher?* (New York: St. Martin's, 1989). Or, more recently, Béatrice Han-Pile, "Is Early Foucault a

which would imply that he should be treated as a historian. However, *what* he treats in those histories seem to belong more properly to philosophical discussion and reflection, namely the relation of reason to madness, of power to knowledge, of relations to self. We will recall Foucault's own characterization cited in the Introduction: "My books aren't treatises in philosophy or studies of history; at most, they are philosophical fragments put to work in a historical field of problems." I have already indicated the importance I am according this particular formulation, especially as it juxtaposes the notion of "fragments" and that of a "field". Right now, however, I will simply point out how this situates his work at the nexus of philosophical questioning and historiographical practice, thereby engaging and effecting a form of the *rapprochement* Collingwood called for. In other words, Foucault's work situates itself precisely within the double task formulated by Collingwood: first, to show how history is possible; and, second, to show how history affects or impacts our conception of philosophical inquiry.[6]

Historian? History, History and the Analytic of Finitude," *Philosophy and Social Criticism* 31.5–6 (2005): 585–608.

6. For Collingwood, philosophy, because it is the ultimate expression of our thinking,

In order to outline the space of this confrontation and encounter between philosophy and history, I will make use of the four questions identified by Collingwood as the basic framework to understand philosophically our relation to history. These four questions concern: 1. the nature of history; 2. its object; 3. its method and 4. its value, or what it is for.[7] Collingwood stipulates the following conditions or qualifications that anyone answering these questions must have: first, they must themselves have engaged in active historical work; and, second, they must have reflected on their practice. Foucault surely

---

must deal with the specific problems—those obscurities and difficulties—that confront it. For the ancient Greeks, philosophy needed to confront the problems posed by mathematical thinking; for the Middle Ages, philosophy needed to confront the problems posed by theological thinking; for Moderns, philosophy confronted the problems generated by the natural sciences; and since the nineteenth-century, philosophy needs to come to terms with the work of historians and the problems generated by a developing historical consciousness.

7. Collingwood, *The Idea of History* 7. *The Idea of History* will hereafter be referred to as "*IH*".

possesses both qualifications; my own task here is merely to tease out the answers to these questions implicit in his work.

***

1. First question: what is history? The general answer Collingwood gives is that history consists in a form of research or inquiry, which is to say that it is a form of thought that purports to be "scientific" in a very broad sense, that is, included in those "forms of thought whereby we ask questions and try to answer them",[8] or more specifically, we ask questions about something we do not know in order to correct our ignorance.[9] This is a sufficiently general answer to accommodate a variety of different investigators who are free to develop or elaborate their specific approach (which will gain recognition, be contested or rejected, perhaps ignored by others). Let us examine Foucault's.

---

8. *IH* 9.

9. As Collingwood puts it:

> That is why all science begins from the knowledge of our own ignorance: not our ignorance of everything, but our ignorance of some definite thing—the origin of parliament, the cause of cancer, the chemical composition of the sun, the way to make a pump work without muscular exertion on the part of a man or a horse or some other docile animal. Science is finding things out: and in that sense history is a science. (*IH* 9)

Foucault, who sometimes confesses to
a nominalistic approach, has left a number of names characterizing the nature
of his historical investigations: "archaeology", "genealogy", "problematization".
Not surprisingly, many have taken up the
discussion of the continuities and discon-
tinuities evident in these diverse conceptions.[10] Rather than take up this discussion
in those terms, I would like to connect
his archaeological and genealogical
approaches more simply to his sensibility.
His archaeological investigations are animated, in my view, by an *archival* sensibility,
as it were: an openness to the particularities of the enunciative struggles that strike
him as he sets himself up to work within
a particular field of questions (concerning
madness, the clinic, the human sciences)
that the *archive* opens up. Foucault the
archivist, as Deleuze calls him,[11] situates

10. Probably the most systematic of these
    would be Flynn's; another recent dis-
    cussion can be found in Amy Allen's
    *The Politics of Our Selves: Power, Autonomy,
    and Gender in Contemporary Critical Theory*
    (New York: Columbia UP, 2008). Cf. also
    her review of Flynn's book in *Notre Dame
    Philosophical Reviews* (2006), 31 Mar. 2012
    <ndpr.nd.edu/review.cfm?id=5721>.
11. Gilles Deleuze, *Foucault*, trans. Sean Hand
    (Minneapolis: U of Minnesota P, 1988).

himself at the level of *énoncés* (things said, statements). The conceptual, archaeo-logical task he sets himself is not first and foremost to interpret or to understand these "things said", but to lay them out, to spread them out as things said within their discursive formations. According to Deleuze, Foucault the archaeologist is in fact a kind of *cartographer*, whose task is not to attempt to discern some kind of secret or hidden meaning but to make *evident* the constellations of sense that crystallize beneath a gaze that sustains itself through an engaged sensibility. As Deleuze puts it, Foucault places himself within the archive like someone attentive to murmurings oth-ers ignore: "It is within this murmur with-out beginning or end that Foucault would like to be situated, in the place assigned to him by statements."[12] But, of course, this is not a merely passive disposition. By engaging the archive in this way, Foucault is joining others also at work in the archive as they work and re-work historical mater-ials in ways that challenge more traditional views of historiography, those "new histor-ians" that follow in the footsteps of the school of *Annales* founded by Marc Bloch and Lucien Febvre. That is, as Foucault himself notes, "where once one sought

12. Deleuze, *Foucault* 17.

to decipher traces left by men, where once one tried to excavate what they had been, history deploys a mass of elements that must be sifted, grouped, rendered pertinent, put into relation, constituted as wholes".[13] Concretely, what this meant for Foucault's own investigations into our relation to madness, for example, was that "instead of perusing, which we nevertheless did, only the library of scientific books, we had to visit a whole ensemble of archives which included warrants [*décrets*], regulations, hospital and prison registries, and jurisprudential acts".[14]

This kind of activity engaged Foucault for many years and inspired a number of books published in the fifties and sixties.[15]

---

13. "là où on déchiffrait des traces laissées par les homes, là où on essayait de reconnaître en creux ce qu'ils avaient été, [ces historiens] déploie[nt] une masse d'éléments qu'il s'agit d'isoler, de grouper, de rendre pertinents, de mettre en relations, de constituer en ensembles." *L'archéologie du savoir* (Paris: Gallimard, 1969) 15.

14. Michel Foucault, *Dits et écrits*, vol. I (Paris: Gallimard, 1994) 842, my translation. Foucault's *Dits et écrits* will hereafter be referred to as "*DE*", with the volume number following the acronym.

15. *History of Madness*, ed. Jean Khalfa, trans. Jonathan Murphy and Jean Khalfa.

However, this archival work eventually became "genealogical", which, in the terms being suggested here, engaged Foucault differently such that he became more explicitly preoccupied with his relation to the present (a "present" marked by the events and aftermath of May, 1968). His archival investigations no longer restrict themselves to paying attention to the "murmuring" of things said in the past; rather, they seek to show the effective past that is obscured by the justificatory discourses that structure the present. Foucault recognizes much more explicitly in his genealogical works the fact that the historian's work gets formulated and articulated within a particular context that makes it possible (and traces its limit). While genealogical investigations obviously continue to exploit the archive, Foucault no longer positions himself primarily as a "listener" (or as an open sensibility to what it reveals); the point now is to have the archive speak and expose its

(London: Routledge, 2006); *The Birth of the Clinic: An Archaeology of Medical Perception.* (London: Routledge, 1973); *The Order of Things: An Archaeology of the Human Sciences.* (London: Routledge, 1989); *The Archaeology of Knowledge*, trans. Alan Sheridan. (New York: Pantheon, 1972).

relation to a knowledge that shows itself to be directly invested in relations of power as these inscribe themselves upon bodies. Formerly, archaeologically, he had placed himself at the level of discourses structuring what is and is not said. But now we find ourselves at a "microphysical" level that more properly speaks to what is and is not done. Things said are also things done.[16]

Foucault here shows his own particular epistemic commitment, one where historical inquiry does not pretend to an "objectivity" that would split off the past from explicit concerns manifest in the present, but rather seeks to *problematize* that very relation to the past (especially as "objectified" in traditional historiographical discourse). In his courses at the Collège de France, Foucault insisted that his genealogical investigations sought

> a way of playing local, discontinuous, disqualified, or nonlegitimized knowledges off against the unitary theoretical instance that claims to be able to filter them, organize them into a hierarchy, organize them in the name of a true body of knowledge,

---

16. Michel Foucault, *Discipline and Punish; The History of Sexuality: An Introduction*, trans. Alan Sheridan (New York: Vintage Books, 1977).

in the name of the rights of a science that
is in the hands of a few.[17]

Foucault engages the concrete and immediate knowledges of nurses, of those suffering, of delinquents and of inmates
themselves; those knowledges that both
oppose and confront the expert knowledges of criminology and psychiatry,
which Foucault calls "grotesque" in the
sense that these latter knowledges have
"the curious property of being foreign to
all, even the most elementary, rules for the
formation of scientific discourse", but even
so are given a status that enables them to
have "effects of power that their intrinsic
qualities should disqualify them from having".[18] In appealing to such knowledges as
contrasts to the organized expert knowledges, Foucault remains attuned to the
broader context of historical unfolding
as it actually occurs and not merely those
forms that have obvious sanction in dominant forms of discourse. He is pointing to
other areas of relevance within the overall

---

17. Michel Foucault, *"Society Must Be Defended":*
    Lectures at the Collège de France, 1975–1976,
    trans. David Macey (New York: Picador,
    2003) 9.
18. Michel Foucault, *Abnormal: Lectures at the*
    Collège de France, 1974–1975, trans. Graham
    Burchell (New York: Picador, 2003) 11.

movement of history. Here, too, Foucault shows his affinity with other historians working to broaden our appreciation of what is of "historical significance".

Arlette Farge, who collaborated with Foucault during this period—publishing together a presentation of select *Lettres de Cachet* of the eighteenth century, those solicitations made by subjects to their king to incarcerate unruly members of their families[19]—gives a good description of this dimension of movement at the heart of any historical context which is always only partially grasped by official discourses and pronouncements. In connection with the notion of *public opinion* in the eighteenth century—a public opinion contrasted with the more formalized notion of public opinion thematized by Habermas[20]—she writes:

---

19. Michel Foucault and Arlette Farge, *Le Désordre des Familles. Lettres de Cachet des Archives de la Bastille* (Paris: Gallimard Julliard, 1982).

20. J. Habermas, *The Structural Transformation of the Public Sphere: An Inquiry into a Category of Bourgeois Society*, trans. Thomas Burger (Cambridge: MIT Press, 1991); cf. Arlette Farge, "Le parcours d'une historienne: entretien avec Laurent Vidal," *Genèses* 48 (2002): 115–35.

Proferred speeches, pamphlets written
out on walls, ordinary social practices do
not exhaust the opinions and the sentiments within a population's grasp in order
to reflect and to act: the refusal to speak,
implicit language, dreams and illusions,
fear, expectation, silent denials are some
of the major areas that require our attention. Fantasies and dreams create culture
and history.[21]

One must be careful here: The point
is not to refuse or to seek to delegitimize
those knowledges that connect their
claim to "truth" to their particular forms
of expertise and modes of justification
(institutional knowledges such as criminology and psychiatry). Rather, by insisting on these *other* knowledges as they
are covered over, Foucault seeks to show
how they nevertheless do have a historical existence and take shape within the
interstices of dominant forms of thought.
Further, he effectively seeks to "play" (*faire
jouer*) these other knowledges against the
emergence of those specific forms called
"expert" and given institutional sanction.
What we might call Foucault's "counter-
investigation", as it were, of these other
forms of knowledge (*savoirs*) at play, as

---

21. Arlette Farge, *Des lieux pour l'histoire* (Paris:
    Seuil, 1997) 102. My translation.

we shall see, raises questions about how dominant forms of knowledge consolidate themselves through this process of their disqualification of other knowledges. Thus, the questions raised and the answers provided by Foucault's investigations serve to open the field of history as a site, not only of the emergence of those forms of thought that work themselves out and are transformed (according to a broadly Hegelian kind of description), but of what we can call a *struggle for intelligibility.*[22]

***

2. Let us turn now to Collingwood's second question: What is the object of history? What is the focus of its attention? We have already noted in this chapter a number of focal points (even as we have raised in the Introduction a number of questions about the practice of abstracting the past from its correlativity with the present and the future in order to privilege it as an "object" capable of "objective" knowledge). The

---

22. One can find a number of interesting discussions concerning the activist and engaged character of Foucault's historigraphical investigations in a work edited by Didier Eribon, entitled *L'infréquentable Michel Foucault: Renouveau de la pensée critique* (Paris: EPEL, 2001). I recommend in particular the article by Philippe Mangeot, "Foucault sans le savoir," 89–100.

general answer Collingwood provides is
the following: history concerns itself with
res gestae, "actions of human beings that
have been done in the past".[23] One needs
to understand action here in a very broad
sense, that is, as referring to purposive
activity that is structured such that we
can reconstruct it as recognizable activity
from what is given to us in the present.
It is important to note that the activity
is intentional in structure, because for
Collingwood it is the goals and intentions
that structure actions taken that enable
a reconstruction and a reconstitution by
the historian. In other words, what makes
human activity *human* is this reference to
its intentional structure (thought).[24] Of
course, the extent to which these goals

---

23. *IH* 9.

24. Which is another way of saying that human
    activity is "free" activity. Here we can see
    why Collingwood connects our actual
    realization as free beings to our increas-
    ing ability to give a historical account of
    ourselves, to recognize the "autonomy" of
    historical knowledge. That is, as he writes
    in *The Principles of History,* "the activity
    by which man builds himself his own
    constantly-changing historical world is a
    free activity. There are no forces other than
    this activity which control it or modify it or
    compel it to behave in this way or in that,
    to build one kind of world rather than

and intentions are actually *realized* through
the efforts of human beings as they engage
in these activities is something that always
needs to be determined. And, in fact, one
can say that the origin and development
of this mode of thought called "historical" can be found precisely in this interest
and attention paid to the gap between the
goals and plans expressed and proposed
by human beings as they attempt to live

---

another." (Oxford: Clarendon Press, 1999)
98. And then a little further:

> The discovery that the men whose actions
> he studies are in this sense free is a discovery
> which every historian makes as soon as he
> arrives at a scientific mastery of his own subject.
> When that happens, the historian discovers
> his own freedom: that is, he discovers the
> autonomous character of historical thought, its
> power to solve its own problems for itself by its
> own methods. He discovers how unnecessary it
> is and how impossible it is for him, as historian,
> to hand these problems over for solution to
> natural science; he discovers that in his capac-
> ity as historian he both can and must solve
> them for himself. It is simultaneously with this
> discovery of his own freedom as historian, that
> he discovers the freedom of man as an histor-
> ical agent. Historical thought, thought about
> rational activity, is free from the domination
> of natural science, and rational activity is free
> from the domination of nature. (Collingwood,
> *Principles of History* 101)

out and make sense of their unfolding
lives and the actual results and consequences of those efforts (which results
and consequences they find themselves
having to reintegrate into their structured
intentional actions). In a word, historical
thought preoccupies itself with the real
and concrete effects (as opposed to hypothetical or regulative or normative ideals)
of human action.[25]

I think it is important to see that
Foucault, too, is concerned with *res gestae,*

I will return to this explication of the
notion of freedom as it relates to Foucault's
work in the conclusion of this book.

25. Arlette Farge nicely describes those kinds
of "historical interrogations" that remain
sensitive to a sense of history that is filled
with gaps allowing

for the imperceptible movements, the multiplicity of social experiences, the plurality of
singular destinies, strategies that permit brief
dislocations, or again those different modes of
subjectivation of individuals that result in shifts
of their identities. The world of the historian
recounts the norms, the constraints and the
fixity of rules while at the same time unearthing
the multiplicity of possibilities, the incomplete
routes nevertheless undertaken, the ruses of
men and women, their dead-ends and their
failures. (*Des lieux pour l'histoire,* 124–25, my
translation)

that this is, for him as well, the object of history. Indeed, if Foucault is the focus of this book, it is because of his singular appreciation and sensitivity to *res gestae* as one actually encounters it, both through the glimpses of unique struggles—as evidenced in the "lives of infamous men"— and through his efforts to track the more insidious forms of its effects (by examining more closely how things said are also things done). Emphasizing this dimension of Foucault's appreciation of history does entail downplaying another feature of his thought that has been a matter of concern for some[26] who see in Foucault's "anti-humanism" an attempt to undermine the foundations of a certain conception of rational agency. And it entails downplaying Foucault's own provocations that would announce something so thrilling— intellectually speaking—as the "death of man". These are distractions, in my view, for those who commit themselves to taking history seriously.

In fact, the kinds of things Foucault himself says and the way he sets himself up to

---

26. I am thinking in particular of Luc Ferry and Alain Renaut, *French Philosophy of the Sixties: An Essay on Antihumanism*, trans. Mary H. Cattani (Amherst: U of Massachusetts P, 1990).

say them in *The Order of Things* does not, I submit, give us the best sense of what for him, and for us, is the actual object of history, namely *res gestae*.[27] Foucault, in *The Order of Things*, exhibits a certain impatience with such an "object", largely because of the manner in which it is unselfconsciously treated as more or less transparent to itself. There, the "object" of history in *The Order of Things* would seem to be language itself as it formal-izes itself in successive constellations of sense (which Foucault calls *epistemes*). An interesting project, executed with consid-erable brio, despite the questions such a project raises for those who would take history seriously, which no doubt includes Foucault himself. Because, of course, it is not language "itself" that is Foucault's con-

---

27. What follows gives some indication of why, given the particular angle Foucault takes on "history" in *The Order of Things* ("his-tory" understood as epistemically bounded and constellated), that discussion will not be privileged here. For a reading that does privilege that discussion, cf. the work of Béatrice Han-Pile, both the already cited "Is Early Foucault a Historian? History, History and the Analytic of Finitude," but also *Foucault's Critical Project: Between the Transcendental and the Historical*, trans. Edward Pile (Stanford: Stanford UP, 2002).

cern, but language in its particular, that is, *historically-specific* constellations as these are successively (re)constituted. As he will explain in his *Archaeology of Knowledge*, his concern is not the linguist's concern with the structural features and possibilities of language itself as a system of signs, but with the archival evidence of *things said* (*énoncés*). And inasmuch as they are things *said*, and not abstract features of language itself, then they call up the historical circumstances of their being said. This need not lead us to look for particular individuals saying these things said: the archive is evidence of itself, no further appeal is required. However, the circumstances themselves of their enunciation are not so easily dismissed, not, that is, if one wants to insist on their *particular* character as things said. In *The Order of Things* Foucault wants to *generalize* that particularity by drawing our attention to the constellated character of such things said, especially as these concern the shapes that constitute knowledge. But he also wants to show the remaining particularities of those generalized constellations.

It is this focus on such constellations of sense-making that invites a *rapprochement* between Foucault and structuralism. However, like the distinction between Foucault's specifically *historical* concerns and those of the linguist's, the *rapproche-ment* in fact points to a basic difference. What distinguishes Foucault from the structuralist approach is his particular application of what I have been calling his principle of *rarity*, an emphasis on the particularity of the constellated structures he investigates. A comment by Paul Veyne seems to me to be useful in this regard:

> Through his theory of discourse, Foucault might have seemed to belong to what is called structuralism, a word that is as inviting as it is vague. He believes in the historicity of truth-saying (*dire-vrai*), in singularity and in "rarity." Through these three features, he shares with structural-ism the admission that thought does not generate itself and must be explained by something other than itself: by the histor-ical *dispositif* for Foucault, by structures for structuralists. In fact, the two doctrines actually only shared their negations: both affirmed that between things and con-sciousness there was a *tertium quid* beyond the grasp of the sovereign subject.[28]

---

28. Paul Veyne, "Un archéologue sceptique," *L'infréquentable Michel Foucault: Renouveau de la pensée critique*, ed. Didier Eribon (Paris: EPEL, 2001) 38. My translation. I do not agree with Veyne that Foucault, in focusing on the historical *dispositif*, is saying that

What is most interesting to note, however, is how the *tertium quid* between things and consciousness identified by Foucault as a language differentially constellated in *The Order of Things* would soon enough be abandoned under the pressure of his more fundamental appreciation of the proper object of history, namely *res gestae* (things done).

On this point, it is worth considering Arpad Szakolczai's interesting reading of what he calls Foucault's "life-work".[29] Although I am, in this book, attempting to distance myself from those readings that insist on treating Foucault's work in terms of his own attempt to describe its overall coherence (which is fascinating in itself) in order to have it speak *to* rather than *against* the philosophy of history, Szakolczai's conceptualization of a "life-work" allows us to understand why *The Order of Things* actually skews the appreciation of history that, I am arguing, animates Foucault's repeated return to it.

---

thought does not "generate" itself, suggesting it is generated by something other than itself, but only showing that it is not self-transparent.

29. Arpad Szakolczai, *Max Weber and Michel Foucault: Parallel Life-Works.* (London: Routledge, 1998).

Szakolczai's approach is to contextual-
ize and to thematize the "life-work" of a
thinker (in this case Weber and Foucault,
where the point is less to compare them
than to present them in "parallel", which
has the interesting effect of reinvigorating
one's reading of the texts) in terms of a
triple relation concerning self, work and
world, which he plots out on a three-by-
three schema reproduced in Table 1:

Thus, if we take the terms as they relate
to the professional work of academics (the
middle column 2, 5, 8), one's sense of self
is invested in one's professional identity.
For most of us, such an identity tracks
both our discipline's priorities and our
institutional affiliation(s). As professionals
and academics, this sense of self connects
to and relates to the work we are engaged
in, which can be defined as the particular
problem or set of problems we are working
on. And this work that engages us relates
to the wider world in the specific ways in
which it is received. This, then, is how the
relation between self, work and world can
be seen under the general rubric of work
itself. If one wants to examine the relation
of self, work and world under the general
rubric of the self (the first column 1, 4, 7),
as opposed to that of work, then it is more
a question of one's *personal* identity as
distinct from one's professional identity.

Table 1: Szakolczai's conception of the "life-work" of a thinker

	Self		Work		World	
Self	personal identity	(1)	professional identity	(2)	national identity	(3)
Work	status	(4)	problem	(5)	relevance	(6)
World	recognition	(7)	reception	(8)	modernity/West	(9)

Reprinted from Arpad Szakolczai, *Max Weber and Michel Foucault: Parallel Life-Works* (London: Routledge, 1998) 85, formatting changed.

Work itself relates to this personal sense of identity more abstractly, as simply the *status* one has within the wider world which is, again abstractly considered, a sphere of recognition. Under the final rubric, the world itself (third column 3, 6, 9), one's self-identity is, for example, national, while one's work is considered more or less relevant within a specific characterization of the "wider world". For Weber and Foucault, according to Szakolczai, this "wider world" is best characterized both temporally and spatially as "modernity" and the "West".

What is interesting about this approach is the way it reminds us how academic work fits into a broader schema even when features of this broader schema are bracketed. For example, most of us focus on these relations strictly in terms of work (insofar as we identify with our work), where our professional identities are invested in the particular problems as identified and circulated in our disciplines. However, the broader context of the work we do involves our *own* sense of ourselves in relation to that work and the wider world that values that kind of work (the diagonal line cutting across the schema 1, 5, 9). This can be more or less explicitly recognized. Those who do explicitly recognize and take up these relations between self, work and world can be said to be engaged in a "life-work". That is, their own personal identity is invested in working out problems that are relevant not only within the disciplinary parameters of the work undertaken, but to the unfolding of the world itself.

Foucault was someone so engaged in a "life-work". At the core of his work, the working out of a number of "philosophical fragments within a historical field of problems" was a personal investment and engagement rooted in his personal experiences (evidenced in my terms in his particular modal sensibility to the contingent possibilities within what is claimed as necessary) that was nevertheless directed towards illuminating the broader significance of our shared experience of the present. Szakolczai makes the case that, in 1963, because of his disappointment in the reception of his work *History of Madness* (the work we will focus on in Chapter Four below), Foucault takes up projects—namely, a book on the writer Raymond Roussel and eventually *The Order of Things*—that, in fact, are *deviations* from "the diagonal axis" of the schema (1, 5, 9) which is descriptive of the way self, work and world are combined in a "life-work". That is, these works, unlike the earlier and later works, are less grounded in his attempt to write and to think from his own experience—or what I am calling

his own particular sensibility grounded in
his experience of the world—than written and "conceived under the impact of
a negative experience, a disappointment
due to the reception of his first major
books".[30] Thus, as dazzling as they might
be in their execution (I am thinking in
particular of Foucault's brilliant discussion of Velasquez's *Las Meninas*), they do
not capture the sense of *history* that animates his other works, indeed his "life-
work", and therefore, I will be arguing,
are not the primary site of the challenge
and contribution his work makes to the
questions raised in this book concerning our ongoing attempt to make sense
of history.[31] This is not to say, of course,
that *The Order of Things* is completely unre-
lated to the themes and concerns that animate his "life-work" (how could it be?). As
Szakolczai himself remarks, "if conceived
as a Husserlian bracketing of change in
order to render the analysis of different
systems of truth and meaning possible so

---

30. Szakolczai 216.

31. It is in this sense, then, that my work
    demarcates itself from those who see in
    The Order of Things the centre of Foucault's
    critique of historical consciousness, which
    in effect ties the importance accorded to
    something called "history" to an *episteme*
    that Foucault sees as ending.

that it would be possible to return to a conceptualization of change beyond evolution and dialectics, the work fitted well into Foucault's project". But, as he immediately goes on to say, "This was not, however, the way in which Foucault conceived and saw it in the 1960s."[32]

The focus here in this book, then, is on Foucault's engagement in his "life-work" because it is there that the questions he raises resonate most with its preoccupations with our unfolding lives.

If the "object" of history thus remains *res gestae* both for Foucault and for historians themselves, his particular mode of engaging that "object" in terms of *practices* is what renders that work so rich and interesting. Indeed, his appeal to a principle of immanence (along with his appeal to a principle of rarity), as mentioned in the Introduction to this book, is largely an appeal to the practices that give shape to the historical field he sets out to explore. Todd May, who has written extensively on Foucault and contemporary French philosophy, also wrote a useful book entitled *Our Practices, Our Selves: Or, What It Means to Be Human*[33] which argues that, in response

---

32. Szakolczai 216.

33. (State Park: U of Pennsylvania P, 2001). In defending his argument concerning the centrality of the notion of practice,

to the philosophical question of "who we are", we should examine the practices we are engaged in (rather than appeal to some metaphysical notion or other or, for that matter, some "scientific" notion or other). That is, he claims that "by understanding the role that practices play in our lives, we can learn much about what we do, how we think about ourselves and the world", and that "a picture of who we are will begin to emerge that is a picture worth having".[34] He defines the notion of a practice as "a regularity (or regularities) of behavior, usually goal-directed, that is socially norm-atively governed".[35] Without going into detail, his conception is that to understand ourselves, we need to look at the different things we are engaged in doing in terms of the regularities they display, the goals they

---

May appeals to Wittgenstein and specific-ally the work of Theodore R. Schatzki, *Social Practices: A Wittgensteinian Approach to Human Activity and the Social* (Cambridge: Cambridge UP, 1996), where the basic claim is that "practices are the site where human coexistence is established and ordered: All dimensions of human coexist-ence ultimately refer to practices." (May, *Our Practices, Our Selves* 172).

34. May, *Our Practices, Our Selves* 3.
35. May, *Our Practices, Our Selves* 8.

seek to accomplish and the norms—which spell out the right and wrong ways of proceeding—that govern them and that are socially sanctioned. For example, reading this book is engaging a practice: its regularities involve having it before you, deciphering its print, having sufficient light (for some of us, a pair of glasses), turning the pages; its norms involve reading from left to right down the left page and then the right page, holding it upright, attempting to understand what it is trying to say, assessing its significance; its goal is either instruction, entertainment, completing an assignment, pleasing someone (me!) and so forth. The practice of driving a car involves controlling its acceleration, turning the wheel (regularities) in order to get from point A to point B (goal) by following the path laid by streets and their accompanying signs and stoplights (norms).

This reference to practices goes beyond Collingwood's emphasis on intentional structure to include considerations not only of the purposes and goals of various human activities, but the way those activities, as practices, are structured by regularities and norms.

Paul Veyne also insists on Foucault's focus on practices. Foucault's contribution to our comprehension of what is involved

in historical work is to show how the particular objects that fuel our research "are
only correlatives of practices".[36] This,
according to Veyne, would be Foucault's
central and most original thesis: "*What is
made*, the object, is explained by what went
into its *making* at each moment of history;
we are wrong to imagine that the *making*,
the practice, is explained on the basis of
what is made."[37] This is to say that what
we call the "objects" of history are in fact
crystallizations or materializations of what
human beings *do*; human beings do not
conform themselves to pre-established
"objects". This is illustrated in the way
Foucault takes up those "objects" (within
a historical field of problems) called "madness" and "sexuality".

But Veyne also points to the other
interesting, indeed, crucial feature of
Foucault's approach to the historical
field (which will be taken up in the next
chapter): what Foucault, through his
work, through his histories, enables us to
appreciate, that which might be said to
constitute his "object", is not only human
actions, Collingwood's *res gestae*, but these

---

36. Veyne, "Foucault Revolutionizes History"
    160.

37. Veyne, "Foucault Revolutionizes History"
    160–61.

actions undertaken within the *rarity* of their actual occurrence, and this

> in the Latin sense of the word. Human phenomena are exceptional: they are not ensconced in the plenitude of reason; there is empty space around them for other phenomena that we in our wisdom do not grasp; what is could be otherwise. Human phenomena are arbitrary in Mauss's sense. They cannot be taken for granted, although for contemporaries and even for historians they seem to be so self-evident that neither the former nor the latter notice them at all.[38]

Given this rarity—I won't say that structures the historical field for that would be to totalize it precisely in the way that is being challenged; within which structuring occurs, rather—Foucault's work as a whole (his "life-work") can be appreciated as an effort to have us see, understand and notice that what we take to be unquestionably the case is in fact only questionably (and contingently) so, leading us to reconsider the *grasp* we nevertheless insist we have on such "objects" as madness and sexuality.

***

---

38. Veyne, "Foucault Revolutionizes History" 147.

3. How does he do this? We raise here the third question, that of method. Collingwood is quite happy to say simply that the method used by historians is the interpretation of evidence. The only "method" historians need adopt is one that will allow them to interpret that which is in the present in order to reconstitute that which was, but is no longer. Foucault would presumably agree; as an avid reader of Nietzsche, he would no doubt insist that interpretations are all there is. However, the point to recall here is the one emphasized by Veyne, that all these interpretations are produced by practices and these are in fact *rare*.

We can illustrate this notion of rarity by thinking of a library as an assemblage of practices—including the reception and classification of documents, but also as a hub of their circulation and presentation—that both constitutes and is constitutive of a certain "knowledge". If one examines this library a little more closely in terms of its *practices*, one might want to pose such questions as the following: What criteria are used for the reception and classification of documents? To what extent do these developments represent the "knowledge" they claim to exhibit? How are such documents renewed and updated? What is gotten rid of when the allocation of space is restricted? Of course, any answers to these questions (as well as others one can easily imagine: what are the relations between those documents that actually get published and the thoughts that inspired and motivated their creation?) are particular interpretations.

In order to respect the rarity within which we find them, Foucault sets himself the task of tracking the interpretive practices that "circulate" (to continue to use the metaphor of the library) at a given time by making use of a conception of *power*, or power-relations; or rather, he uses this notion of power as a way to describe the links between these practices which otherwise might appear to the inattentive as too dispersed or simply uninteresting. (The notion of power will be taken up in more detail in Chapter Five.)

Of course, Foucault is indebted to others for his particular methodology: indebted, for example, to Georges Dumézil, because, as Foucault puts it himself,

> it was he who taught me to analyze the internal economy of discourse quite differently from the traditional methods of exegesis or those of linguistic formalism. It is he who taught me to refer the system of functional correlations from one discourse to another by means of comparison. It was

he, again, who taught me to describe the transformations of a discourse, and its relation to the institution.[39]

Foucault is indebted as well to Georges Canguilhem, because, he continues:

I owe it to him that I understand that the history of science did not necessarily involve, either an account of discoveries, or descriptions of the ideas and opinions bordering science either from the side of its doubtful beginnings, or from the side of its fall-out; but that one could—that one should—treat the history of science as an ensemble, at once coherent, and transformable into theoretical models and conceptual instruments.[40]

---

39. Michel Foucault, "The Discourse on Language," *The Archaeology of Knowledge*, trans. Alan Sheridan (New York: Pantheon, 1972) 235.

40. Foucault, "The Discourse on Language" 235. Foucault then goes on to discuss his indebtedness to Jean Hyppolite; this is less a methodological indebtedness than one that informs the basic parameters of his "life-work" as I will attempt to show in Chapter Three below. The focus here is merely on his basic interpretive strategies. For a good discussion of Foucault's claimed intellectual debt to Canguilhem, cf. Gary Gutting, *Michel Foucault's Archaeology of Scientific Reason* (Cambridge: Cambridge

But what marks Foucault's distinctive approach is his development of this particular "conceptual instrument" that is the notion of power which presents itself as a kind of *grid of intelligibility* that makes sense of the relational dynamics of our practices as they striate the historical field, dynamics that, *through* the very expression of our intentions and our explicit projects (and the norms and regularities of the practices through which they happen), configure a present that is something other than what is grasped as such.[41]

UP, 1989); and for his debt to Georges Dumézil, cf. Didier Eribon, *Michel Foucault et ses contemporains* (Paris: Fayard, 1994).

41. Much has been said and written about Foucault's conception of power and yet, as Veyne remarks:

> He did not have a diabolical sense of it. Power is the capacity to conduct conducts non-physically, to make people walk without having to place their feet and legs in the appropriate positions. It is the most quotidian of things and that which is most widely shared; there is power within families, between lovers, at work, in the workshop and on one-way streets; millions of little powers thus form the woof of society while individuals make up the warf. Political philosophy is in the habit of conceiving power exclusively as a central Power, the State, the Leviathan, the beast of the Apocalypse. But the Leviathan, who

Let us stop and consider for a moment this reference to the present. It is at the juncture of this present that Foucault the philosopher interrogates Foucault the historian, an interrogation that leads him to deny that he is one or the other while being both: someone who, in working through the difficulties and obscurities encountered in his thinking, explores the past in order better to grasp our present, or rather, to loosen the grip that such a grasping exerts. Foucault explores the open field of history through his philosophical fragments, that is, forms of questioning that do not seek out the certainty of definitive answers allowing him to "think differently".[42] This expression,

---

no doubt exists, would be powerless without the myriad of little Lilliputian powers; the railway mechanic at Auschwitz obeyed the Monster because his wife and children had the power to demand that he bring home a salary. What moves or blocks a society are these innumerable little powers as much as the action of a central Power. (Eribon, *L'infréquentable Michel Foucault* 35, my translation)

42. Michel Foucault, *The Use of Pleasure*, trans. Robert Hurley (New York: Vintage, 1990) 9. Michel Foucault, *Histoire de la sexualité*, t. 2, *L'usage des plaisirs* (Paris, Gallimard, 1984).

often quoted and commented on, comes from the introduction to the second volume of the *History of Sexuality* where Foucault gives an account of his relation to history and to philosophy:

> The studies that follow, like the others I have done previously, are studies of "history" by reason of the domain they deal with and the references they appeal to; but they are not the work of an "historian." Which does not mean that they summarize or synthesize work done by others. Considered from the standpoint of their "pragmatics," they are the record of a long and tentative exercise that needed to be revised and corrected again and again. It was a philosophical exercise. The object was to learn to what extent the effort to think one's history can free thought from what it silently thinks, and so enable it to think differently.[43]

Foucault's distinction here between his "studies in history" and the works of historians is important for the overall theme of this book. Although he does not explicitly thematize the distinction this way, works of historians are specific kinds of historical studies insofar as they are constituted by bracketing one's implication in a present,

---

43. Foucault, *The Use of Pleasure* 9.

which includes anticipations of the future, in order to focus exclusively on the "past" as the object of one's attention. Foucault's historical studies are not "histories" in that sense, given that they are meant precisely to *question* rather than bracket one's relation to the present. Foucault, then, is to be distinguished from the historians because of his explicit preoccupation with the present and how it relates to the past specifically as an open field permitting a questioning of the present. Thus, he sometimes says he is involved in producing a "history of the present". Of course, historians are far from oblivious to these relations and the open field in question; however, their own preoccupation is with the "past" itself, with its transformation into an "object" of study (as distinct from its status as a relation).

But what of this preoccupation with the "present" and his effort to engage in a "history of the present"? It is not simply an appeal to history in order to "illuminate" the present (though, in the end, this kind of notion often ends up being the justification for "doing" history when study-for-its-own-sake is deemed to be insufficient; even when such justifications generate accusations of "presentism" understood as reading back into the past the significance of our present

values).[44] Though there does seem to
Foucault to be a question of "enlightenment". In an important text for this study,
Foucault takes up the "enlightenment
question", acknowledging explicitly Kant's
contribution and response to the question *Was ist Aufklärung?* Kant is interesting for Foucault because he considers the
enlightenment as a new way to interrogate
our actuality, our present. Traditional
responses see in the present either (a) a
"belonging to a certain era of the world,
distinct from the others through some
inherent characteristics" or (b) a dark or
obscure moment which however "may be
interrogated in an attempt to decipher
in it the heralding signs of a forthcom-
ing event"[45] or, yet again, (c) "a point of
transition toward the dawning of a new
world".[46] Kant's approach is different. He

---

44. For a sophisticated discussion of the
    different forms that presentism takes in
    contemporary considerations of historio-
    graphy, cf. W. H. Dray, "Some Varieties
    of Presentism" in his *On History and
    Philosophers of History* (Leiden: Brill, 1989).

45. Michel Foucault, "What Is Enlightenment?"
    in *Ethics: Subjectivity and Truth (Essential
    Works of Foucault, 1954–1984, Vol. 1)*
    (New York: New Press, 1997) 304, hereafter
    referred to as "*EW*".

46. Foucault, "What Is Enlightenment?" 305.

focuses on the present in itself, as it were, as a fully contemporary reality, an *actuality*, and he asks of it, specifically, "What difference does today introduce with respect to yesterday?" Note how the question posed in this way speaks to the relation of the past to the present, and of the relation of the present to the past, but not in order to trace some kind of continuity or connection, *but to mark a difference.* One might say: of course the present is linked to the past, or the past has led to the present; but that does not capture an important feature of what it could be said to mean to say that we live in a specific *present*, one that, as present, as the focus of our attention, distinguishes itself from the past. How does it do so? What marks that difference? How are we to think are being-in-the-*present*? Why and how is it different from what we take to be our being-in-the-past?

This leads to an interesting question of how to understand our relation to the question itself, which requires that we not submit completely to such being-in-the-present, all the while remaining attentive to its difference and specificity. How is this to be done? Especially if one considers the extent to which we are implicated in that present, are in fact constituted by it and sustained within it.

The trick here, again, is to appeal to a principle of rarity, to remind ourselves that we are so constituted within a field or configuration that itself is *rare*; it is not a plenitude but a particular configuration that stands as it does at this particular time (the present) and marks a difference (within the broader unfolding of time).[47] But to say this is also to say that such a present *contrasts* with what is different from it, which includes its past-as-different (it also contrasts with its possible futures, but that is a concern for another time and around a figure other than Foucault).

Now, the idea of a present-as-marking-itself as distinct from the past-as-different is also to be found in the way we use the notion of "modernity". To be "modern" is to take up, in the present, a view of things that marks itself as distinct and demarcates itself from the past-as-(essentially)-

---

47. John McCumber appeals to such a principle in his development of a notion of "demarcation" which insists on the temporal character of our attempts to think the world, where to "demarcate something means to open up a defining gap at its core, as a way of bringing about its future" in his *Reshaping Reason: Toward a New Philosophy* (Bloomington: Indiana UP, 2007) 99. I will return to McCumber's work a number of times in what follows.

different. Foucault thus takes up this
notion of "modernity" but precisely as
an "attitude" and as defining a particular
kind of "philosophical ethos that could be
described as a permanent critique of our
historical being".[48] In doing so, Foucault
is marking a distinct approach to history
understood as a whole, that is, history as
the past-present-future complex that outlines a particular way of relating past and
present. This outline is to be discovered or
traced (I will attempt to show) in a mode of
analysis that presents itself as "a series of historical inquiries that are as precise as possible...oriented toward the 'contemporary
limits of the necessary,' that is, toward what
is not or is no longer indispensable for the

---

48. Foucault, "What is Enlightenment?" 312,
    translation modified. Foucault writes "cri-
    tique permanente de notre être historique"
    which is translated as historical *era* which
    makes sense given that the discussion is
    connecting the Enlightenment to modern-
    ity; however, I think a stricter translation
    is required in order to capture the full
    significance of what is at stake here. As we
    shall see, Foucault speaks in terms of a his-
    torical *ontology* of ourselves, which explicitly
    refers to our "being", and the critical work
    he is engaged in is meant to exploit the
    gap opened up by treating our present-as-
    distinct-from-the-past-as-different.

constitution of ourselves as autonomous subjects".[49]

Thus, we have Foucault's version of a rapprochement between the critical work of philosophy and historiographical investigations. And such a rapprochement requires an approach that gives up on any transcendental or metaphysical aims; that is, it adopts an approach that is:

> genealogical in its design and archaeological in its method. Archaeological—and not transcendental—in the sense that it will not seek to identify the universal structures of all knowledge [*connaissance*] or of all possible moral action, but will seek to treat the instances of discourse that articulate what we think, say, and do as so many historical events. And this critique will be genealogical in the sense that it will not deduce from the form of what we are what it is impossible for us to do and to know; but it will separate out, from the contingency that has made us what we are, the possibility of no longer being, doing, and thinking what we are, do, or think. It is not seeking to make possible a metaphysics that has finally become a science; it is seeking to give new impetus, as far and wide as possible, to *the indefinite work of freedom.*[50]

49. Foucault, "What is Enlightenment?" 313.
50. Foucault, "What is Enlightenment?" 315–16, my emphasis, and translation modified:

Throughout Foucault's work, we will find this concern with *situating* our efforts within the discursive practices that structure what we are thinking, saying and doing, not only to render them intelligible per se (given that they themselves are the vehicles of intelligibility), but to contribute within those efforts to the actualization of the possibilities of a present-as-distinct-from-the-past, while recognizing how it is nevertheless constituted and constraining in specific ways.

***

"le travail indéfini de la liberté" *DE* IV 574. While it makes sense to translate "*indéfini*" as "undefined", especially if one wants to respect the sense in this passage, and in Foucault's work in general, of open possibility and the challenge to modes of thought structured, when relating to truth, around appeals to necessity, I think a better appreciation of what is modally at stake in this passage, and in particular in this expression, is the way critical work on ourselves needs to be taken up ever anew, *indefinitely,* and that this better captures the overall *movement* of history within which Foucault sees himself as working out the "difficulties and obscurities" he has encountered. I will return to this crucial and central point—hence the choice of this expression as the title of this book—in the chapters that follow.

4. This brings us to the fourth question posed by Collingwood: What is the value of history? What is it for? Collingwood's answer is that history is "for" human self-knowledge, though he seems to hesitate, saying it is, in fact, a harder question to answer than the others, because it involves thought about more than just history in the sense that "to say that something is 'for' something implies a distinction between A and B, where A is good for something and B is that for which something is good".[51] If he puts the "for" in scare-quotes in his ultimate decision to say that history is "for" human self-knowledge, it is because, on his account, there isn't really a distinction between A=history and B=human self-knowledge. They are, in an important sense, the same thing. Nevertheless, he does settle on this claim and glosses on it as follows:

> Knowing yourself means knowing, first, what it is to be a man; secondly, knowing what it is to be the kind of man you are; and thirdly, knowing what it is to be the man *you* are and nobody else is. Knowing yourself means knowing what you can do; and since nobody knows what he can do until he tries, the only clue to what man

---

51. *IH* 10.

can do is what he has done. The value of
history, then, is that it teaches us what man
has done and thus what man is.[52]

I think this is quite interesting and worth
looking at a little more closely both for
what it is saying about the value of history
directly, and what it says indirectly about
an approach such as Foucault's.

If self-knowledge is a function of what
we can do, and if we cannot know what
we can do until we try, then it would seem
that self-knowledge is not something that
we could ever possess. It is, rather, an
engagement. Saying history is "for" self-
knowledge points to our relation to history
in terms of that engagement and therefore
points beyond a conception of history as
exclusively the study of the past. It is an
engagement, in the present, with the past.
What does this engagement tell us about
ourselves? Through its accounting of
what we have done, it gives us a "clue", as
Collingwood puts it, as to what is open to
us in what we can do. I think it is important to emphasize this notion of history
as providing a "clue" to what we are (and
pointing us to what we can do). History
informs our engagement with our world
as a present structured by the past and
faced with the future. It does not, however,

---

52. *IH* 10.

tell us what to do. It can only tell us what we have done. And insofar as this tells us something about what we are, it does so by reminding us of our free engagement with a world structured by the past and faced with the future. But the particular way we are "reminded" is by engaging in understanding or making sense of what we have done such that we continue to pose the question of what we are. One might even go further and argue, as Collingwood does, that it is only by engaging in this attempt to make sense of what we have done that we *realize* our freedom, or as he puts it in a short section included in the *Idea of History* given the title "History and Freedom", we need to realize that "our knowledge that human activity is free has been attained only through our discovery of history".[53] Again, what he means by this is that

> the activity by which man builds his own constantly changing historical world is a free activity. There are no forces other than this activity which control it or modify it or compel it to behave in this way or in that, to build one kind of world rather than another.[54]

---

53. *IH* 315.
54. *IH* 315.

I take Collingwood here to be re-articulating what might be called the basic claim of the philosophy of history (as it appeals to a principle of immanence) which insists on the specificity of the human realm within which we make sense of our unfolding lives, one that is distinct from what we take to be nature, the latter understood as a realm whose intelligibility is approached differently, according to rhythms and regularities that effect us as human *animals* but not as human beings (where human beings understand themselves as free beings, that is, as activated and animated by intelligent engagement with each other and with the world).

Now, where does Foucault's work stand with regard to this question? We will recall that I am not suggesting in this study that Foucault's work provides us with a philosophy of history, but rather that it presents the philosophy of history with interesting challenges and insights through its particular engagement with history. With regard to the value of historical investigations (as a response to the question of what history is "for"), Foucault tells us in his last works that the importance of history, as we engage it, lies in the way it enables us to "free ourselves from ourselves" (*se déprendre de nous-mêmes*). Or at least this is what engaged *him* in his discussion of what motivated his particular historical investigations (and we touch on here, once again, the importance of considering the *particular* sensibility that Foucault brings *because* of the insights they yield) which he says was quite simply:

> It was curiosity—the only kind of curiosity, in my case, that is worth acting upon with a degree of obstinacy: not the curiosity that seeks to assimilate what it is proper for one *to know*, but that which enables one to get free of oneself. After all, what would be the value for the passion for knowledge if it resulted only in a certain amount of knowledgeableness and not, in one way or another and to the extent possible, in the knower's straying afield from himself? There are times in life when the question of knowing if one can think differently than one thinks, and perceive differently than one sees, is absolutely necessary if one is to go on looking and reflecting at all.[55]

We will see in more detail in the final chapter the significance of these particular formulations. For the moment, I want to stress once again what I have called

---

55. Foucault, *The Use of Pleasure* 8, emphasis added.

Foucault's *modal sensibility* to what presents itself as imposing its necessity by appealing to historical investigations as a way to re-engage our free appropriation of the world. Note again that, if history is "for" self-knowledge, as Collingwood puts it, it is not for "knowledge's sake", as it were, but for the self that seeks knowledge *of* itself. Foucault's particular sensibility engaged him in investigating the ways in which the formation and pursuit of *knowledge* itself could take on such constraining forms that only a historical appreciation of its actual *formation* could loosen. Even more than Collingwood, then, Foucault shows us how history *captures* us and *shapes* us in our activities, but he does so from the imperative to "free ourselves" (*se déprendre*) from such captivity. Thus, Foucault's self-awareness is a kind of attempt to break free (*une déprise*) of the grip and grasp of certain historically specific discursive formations, an attempt that is wary of the type of historical consciousness that would see in history either a complacent unfolding of itself or a developing realm of increasingly evident mastery. Foucault, as we shall see, installs himself more firmly *within* history, within its contingent, changing, *rare* present, not in order to disappear into its flow, but to contribute, in his own way, through his work, to what I call—in contradistinction to the theme of an increasing historical self-awareness—a kind of *self-wariness*. It is through this wariness that animates his critical project of interrogating the forms of intelligibility that structure our relation to the past and the present that he will engage the transformation of the necessary into the possible, the natural into the normalized and the inevitable into the contingent in order better to be able to face our world with courage and lucidity.

II

History Considered Generally: Thinking Freedom through Domination

In the last chapter, my aim was to place Foucault's work within the general field of history as a preoccupation for philosophers of history. We can now see how Foucault's work is responding to basic questions it raises concerning history's nature, object, method and value.

In this chapter I would like to consider what overall or general conception or sense of history (understood as a whole, as an overall process) might be said to inform his specific historical investigations. It is interesting to note that, although consideration of Foucault's work makes us think hard about history, his own conception of history is hard to pin down. However, if asked to pick a single passage that might capture the general sense of history contained in his work, I am guessing many would pick a passage from his "Nietzsche, Genealogy, History" where he writes,

"Humanity does not gradually progress from combat to combat until it arrives at universal reciprocity, where the rule of law finally replaces warfare; humanity installs each of its violences in a system of rules and thus proceeds from domination to domination."[1]

This is a bleak view indeed, and yet it does square with a widespread sense of Foucault's so-called "postmodern" challenge to traditional conceptions about the unfolding of history, including contemporary "cosmopolitan" arguments that in many ways resemble these views.[2] However, the passage might be considered an odd choice, at least for describing Foucault's view, given that using "humanity" as a subject-term does not really fit Foucault's style of writing or his mode of conceptualizing the basic features of historical unfolding (again, I use this expression simply to point to the

---

1. Michel Foucault, "Nietzsche, Genealogy, History," *Aesthetics, Method, and Epistemology: Essential Works of Foucault, 1954–1984, Vol. 2*, ed. James D. Faubion (New York: The New Press, 1998) 378. Hereafter referred to as "*NGH*".

2. See my *Multicultural Dynamics and the Ends of History: Exploring Kant, Hegel, and Marx* (Ottawa: U Ottawa P, 2008).

notion of history as a past-present-future complex).

Put in its context, however, it makes sense because here he is not—at least explicitly—commenting on his own approach to history, but rather on Nietzsche's conception of genealogy, specifically its object, in this case *Entstehung* or "emergence", which, together with *Herkunft* (understood as "descent"), Foucault tells us "are more exact than *Ursprung* in recording the true object of genealogy; and, though they are ordinarily translated as 'origin,'" he would like to "attempt to reestablish their proper use".[3]

But what of this particular context? Foucault is commenting on Nietzsche's conception of "genealogy", specifically with reference to its "true object" which, rather than "origin", should be thought in terms of "emergence" and "descent". And this in the broader presentation of genealogy as "gray, meticulous, and patiently documentary",[4] which, of course, likens it to historiography (as opposed to philosophy) inasmuch as genealogy "does not oppose itself to history as the lofty and profound gaze of the philosopher might compare to

---

3. Foucault, *NGH* 373.
4. Foucault, *NGH* 373.

the mole-like perspective of the scholar; on the contrary, it rejects the metahistorical deployment of ideal significations and indefinite teleologies".[5] There is, then, a *rapprochement* of genealogy or a genealogical mode of investigation to history *against* a certain conception of philosophy as "lofty" and "profound" in its "deployment of ideal significations and indefinite teleologies". The conception of philosophy that is targeted here would seem to be Hegel's, or more precisely Hegel's philosophy of history, at least as it finds itself supporting conceptually the work of the traditional history of ideas. As Foucault puts it later on in the article, when he inquires about the relationship between genealogy and history in the traditional sense, Nietzsche himself,

> beginning with the second of the *Untimely Meditations*, always questioned the form of history that reintroduces (and always assumes) a suprahistorical perspective; a history whose function is to compose the finally reduced diversity of time into a totality fully closed upon itself; a history that always encourages subjective recognitions and attributes a form of reconciliation to all the displacements of the past;

---

5. Foucault, *NGH* 370.

a history whose perspective on all that precedes it implies the end of time, a completed development.[6]

I think it is important to stress here that Foucault is explicitly referencing a *kind of history* that, although obviously reliant upon a certain conception of Hegel's philosophy of history, is not named as such. As I have indicated already and will increasingly seek to demonstrate throughout this book, Foucault's relation to Hegel, specifically when it is a question of relating philosophy to history, is actually quite complex, and by no means a simple opposition or rejection. This is evidenced in the very text we are considering here. Often taken as a key text for understanding Foucault's own conception of genealogical "method", despite its explicit discussion of Nietzsche and the relationship between genealogy and history, it is not often noted that the text appears in a volume introduced by Foucault himself, entitled *Hommage à Jean Hyppolite*[7] and one cannot help but think that the choice of its title, "Nietzsche, Genealogy, History", is a wink to what Gilles Deleuze, another of Hyppolite's students, describes as the way their teacher

---

6. Foucault, *NGH* 379.

7. S. Bachelard et al., eds. (Paris: Presses universitaires de France, 1971).

"rhythmically beat out Hegelian triads with his fist, hanging his words on the beat..."[8] I will take up this text, with a more detailed discussion of the relation of Foucault's thought to Hyppolite's appreciation of Hegel, in Chapter Three. For now, I merely want to point out that this is not *obviously* or straightforwardly a commentary either on Foucault's own appropriation of something called "genealogy" or indicative of the conception or general sense of history that animates his work and which many take to be an indictment of the philosophy of history.

And yet the passage quoted at the beginning of this chapter does seem to capture *something* about Foucault's overall conception of history, which does *contrast* his ultimate concerns with those of someone like Hegel, whom we recognize in the idea being rejected, namely that of a humanity that is gradually progressing "from combat to combat until it arrives at universal reciprocity", the kind of narrative treatment of history that we ques-

---

8. G. Deleuze and Claire Parnet, *Dialogues*, trans. Hugh Tomlinson and Barbara Habberjam (New York: Columbia UP, 1987) 12; qtd. in Bruce Baugh, *French Hegel: From Surrealism to Postmodernism* (London: Routledge, 2003) 188n45.

tioned in the Introduction to our study above. Therefore, what I want to do in this chapter is examine why the contrasting view, namely that "humanity installs each of its violences in a system of rules and thus proceeds from domination to domination" does indeed seem to capture something about Foucault's overall conception of history and why he could be said to think of history in this way. More importantly, however, I want at the same time to suggest that, in fact, the passage, taken at its face value, despite appearances, actually *only indirectly reveals* the general conception that animates Foucault's work. It seems to me that there is much more going on, and many more interesting things going on, in Foucault's conception of history, even in this passage, and it might be worth our while to examine it a little more closely.

***

The passage undoubtedly does capture something about Foucault's overall sense of the movement of history, if one considers it with reference to his two classic histories: *History of Madness*[9] and *Discipline and*

---

9. We now have in English a full translation by Jonathan Murphy and Jean Khalfa (London: Routledge, 2006) of *Histoire de la Folie* which replaces the abridged version of that text known as *Madness and*

Punish: The Birth of the Prison.[10] These two
works are the core works for the purposes
of this book insofar as they both can be
and are read as profound challenges to the
key notions at the heart of the philosophy
of history's account and defence of "reason" (which Foucault challenges through
an examination of "unreason" and madness) and "freedom" (which Foucault
challenges by examining the "birth" of the
prison). They are also core works in terms
of Foucault's "life-work" as discussed in the
last chapter.

Both works give meticulous descriptions
of what can be called the installations of
"systems of rules" that at the same time
reveal themselves to be kinds of "violences"
and we come away from reading those histories with a definite sense, not of a movement of progress or development, but of
having moved from one system of domination to another system of domination. This
is especially true of the effect of *Discipline*

---

*Civilization: A History of Insanity in the Age of
Reason*, translated by R. Howard (London:
Tavistock, 1967). For a review of this full
translation, cf. Alain Beaulieu and Réal
Fillion, "Review Essay of Michel Foucault,
History of Madness," *Foucault Studies* 5
(2008): 74–89.

10. Translated by Alan Sheridan (New York:
Vintage, 1979).

and Punish, where the spectacular violence depicted in the description of the punishment of Damiens is followed by the unsettling account of the pervasive installation of a different kind of "violence" in the construction and control of those docile bodies we seem all to have become. And, not surprisingly, this is precisely what many people dislike about Foucault's histories: not so much because they deny progress in history—such denial is fairly widespread by now—but because, as Charles Taylor has put it, "they seem to offer an insight into what has happened, and into what we have become, which at the same time offers a critique, and hence some notion of a good unrealized or repressed in history, which we therefore understand better how to rescue" and yet Foucault immediately "dashes the hope, if we had one, that there is some good we can *affirm*, as a result of the understanding these analyses give us".[11] Taylor, along with other critics, find this unacceptable and, as Taylor puts it, "rather paradoxical, because Foucault's analyses seem to bring *evils* to light; and yet he wants to distance himself from the

---

11. Charles Taylor, "Foucault on Freedom and Truth," *Philosophy and the Human Sciences: Philosophical Papers 2* (Cambridge: Cambridge UP, 1985) 152.

suggestion which would seem inescapably
to follow, that the negation or overcoming
of those evils promotes a good".[12]

What are we to make of this? We might
follow Paul Veyne, who after all knew
Foucault quite well, and merely point
out that Foucault, like Montaigne, is best
understood as a skeptical philosopher,
showing through his historical studies
the empirical singularities that undermine any claim to general and definitive
truths.[13] Such a view can be amply sup-

---

12. Taylor 152.

13. Cf. Paul Veyne, *Foucault. Sa Pensée,
    sa Personne* (Paris, Albin Michel, 2008),
    especially chapter III, "Le Scepticisme
    de Foucault", where he writes:

    we can no longer decree what is the true path
    of humanity, the meaning of its history, and we
    need to get used to the idea that today's cher-
    ished convictions will not be those of tomorrow.
    We have to renounce all definitive and general
    truths: metaphysics, philosophical anthropo-
    logy or moral and political philosophy are
    all but vain speculations. [. . . *nous ne pouvons
    plus décréter quelle est la vraie voie de l'humanité,
    le sens de son histoire, et il faut nous habituer à
    l'idée que nos chères convictions d'aujourd'hui ne
    seront pas celles de demain. Il nous faut renoncer
    aux vérités générales et définitives : la métaphysique,
    l'anthropologie philosophique ou la philosophie
    morale et politique sont autant de vaines spécula-
    tions*]. (Veyne, *Sa Pensée* 64)

ported by Foucault's texts. But, for my part, I do not find it satisfying. It fails to capture something about Foucault's histories that Todd May pointed out: Many of us find ourselves not only reading them, but returning to them as well. May suggests we do so because Foucault's histories serve "as reminders, reminders of who we are and how we got to be that way, and, even more important, of the contingency of both".[14] To be sure, many readers return to the works of skeptical philosophers like Montaigne as reminders of our fallibility and folly. And perhaps that is something that can be taken away from Foucault's histories. But it seems to me that there is something more going on in Foucault's histories. If we return to them, it is perhaps because they reveal something, not only about us, about "who we are and how we

---

14. Todd May, "Philosophy as a Spiritual Exercise in Foucault and Deleuze," *Angelaki: Journal of the Theoretical Humanities* 5.2 (2000): 227. May is here, like most defenders of Foucault, emphasizing the contingent character of what we are said to know. This is fine so far as it goes, so long as the notion of contingency is not treated as some kind of end in itself. It is, after all, a contrastive modal category and its affirmation carries with it implicit relations to the correlative notions of necessity

got to be that way", as Todd May affirms,[15]
but about the *world* and about how we situate ourselves within its unfolding. In fact,
contra Veyne's suggestion, my sense is that,
if we return to Foucault's histories, it is not
because of the skeptical story they might
be said to tell, but rather because they
perhaps give an indication of how we are
situated with regard to what is *true* about
the world. This is the question I want to
explore.

***

A central feature of Foucault's understanding of history—where we call history, as he

---

and possibility. Part of the impetus behind
this study is to work out that correlativity
more fully.

15. I do not intend this to be a criticism
of Todd May's approach to Foucault.
I find his book *The Philosophy of Foucault*
(Montreal: McGill–Queen's UP, 2006)
very valuable largely because of his focus
on this question as a way into Foucault's
work that can appeal to many different
kinds of readers, cf. his first chapter, titled
"Introduction: Who Are We?" My focus,
however, is not a (re)-introductory one, not
even to the notion of philosophy—which
I think is May's purpose in this work—but
on what Foucault's *histories* actually contribute to our reflective attempt to make sense
of history as a context for appreciating our
unfolding lives.

does, the "archive", that is, those "things said" somehow made available within a culture (but not necessarily "easily" made available), which of course includes such "things said" as contained within countless dusty cardboard boxes in the back rooms of government offices and other administrative buildings or record-keeping rooms (and, now, of course, various databases)— is his refusal to treat its composition as forming a whole or totality. Indeed, it is because of this refusal and commitment on his part that he is *not* to be considered as a philosopher of history as that expression is intended in this book (given that that is precisely the task of the philosopher of history: to consider what sense can be made of considering history-as-a-whole, as a past-present-future complex). On the contrary, as we saw in the last chapter, he brings to his examination of these various "things said" (*énoncés*, or "statements") an appreciation of their *rarity*. These boxes, as it were, and the "things said" that they contain do not form a seamless whole that would somehow contain the past in some kind of totality: the whole past, there to be discovered and revived. This is an illusion we are meant to guard against: for example, as one rummages through these boxes and begins to organize their contents, one might be tempted to see in, say, the gap between one set of baptismal certificates and another set dated a few years later, a space somehow *necessarily* filled with a set of certificates that just happen to be missing (possibly provoking one into an arduous but nevertheless unsuccessful hunt for the missing set). Foucault would have us resist the assumption being made here and accept the principle of rarity that governs the appearance of "things said" as well as have us acknowledge that in the chronological gap we notice between the two sets of certificates there is a space that remains *unfilled*. Or better, that the space opened up by our effort to organize the contents of the box in the form of sets of certificates is a *rarified* one, not a dense thicket of signification to be hacked through but a *dispersion* one pieces together in the particular ways that one does.

It should be noted that what is being said here does not *preclude* the intelligibility of *postulating* a missing set of certificates leading one to engage in a search for it if, for example, one has reasons to believe that it will contain information or facts one would need to make a particular kind of claim. Indeed, one can even make certain kinds of claims about the postulated series, inferentially speaking. That is, indeed, the way historians proceed with their evidence. The point being raised by Foucault is more properly an "ontological" one: the spaces between the different "things said" we consider are "empty" (they "are not" as it were); relatively speaking, of course, because "postulates" can come to occupy them. But such postulates themselves then become "things said" alongside of others.

What we have here is a way of seeing how and why Foucault does not consider himself to be a "historian" despite the fact that he writes histories. If he sometimes calls his histories "fictions", it is not because they make no claims to truth, but rather, it is their mode of composition that likens them to "fictional" works; their composition is guided by Foucault's sensibility rather than the presumed "plenitude" of a historical record imaginatively considered as somehow complete. Foucault's perusal of the archive is not governed by any other dictate—like that of the Rankean imperative to give an account of "what really happened"—than his own interest, delight, dismay, concern, in a word, "curiosity", a curiosity we do not begrudge the writer of fiction. The historian conceives of his relation to the "truth" quite differently than does Foucault.

To get a better sense of the relation to truth that consideration of the principle of rarity implies and the kind of space it assumes (in order to get a better sense of Foucault's overall sense of history), I will be considering Heidegger's "On the Essence of Truth"[16] which, along with the *Nietzsche* volumes, according to Paul Veyne, would have been the extent of Foucault's engagement with Heidegger; an engagement that nevertheless was sufficiently significant for Foucault to say as late as 1984 that "Heidegger has always been for me the essential philosopher. . . . My entire philosophical development was determined by my reading of Heidegger."[17]

This remark has generated considerable comment and speculation about how to draw out this relation between Heidegger's thought and Foucault's,[18] and I think it would be useful to consider the remark a little more closely. Paul Veyne seeks to

---

16. This text can be found in Martin Heidegger, *Basic Writings*, ed. David Farrell Krell (New York: HarperCollins, 1993) 115–38, hereafter referred to as "*BW*".

17. Michel Foucault, *Politics, Philosophy, Culture: Interviews and Other Writings, 1977–1984*, ed. Lawrence D. Kritzman (London: Routledge, 1990) 250.

18. I recommend Stuart Eldon's *Mapping the Present: Heidegger, Foucault and the Project of a Spatial History* (London: Continuum, 2001).

downplay its implications, pointing out that
the importance that Heidegger had was in
connection with his reading of Nietzsche.
And this is indeed what Foucault says in
his remark. He is responding to a question posed in the context of a discussion
about his turn to the "Greek experience of
morality" in his last works which, of course,
represented a significant shift of focus or,
in the terms I have been using, a shift in
the "the historical field (of problems)"
that concerned him, which for most of his
career had spanned the sixteenth century to the present. I will discuss this shift
more fully in Chapter Six below. What is
relevant to our discussion here is that the
question that prompts Foucault's response
names Heidegger specifically in terms of
the relations of history, freedom and truth,
as these are explored in his "turn to the
Greeks". Foucault is asked:

> In what you describe [in the Greek experi-
> ence of morality], you have found a point
> of convergence between an experience
> of freedom and of truth. There is at least
> one philosopher for whom the relation
> between freedom and truth was the begin-
> ning of occidental thought. This philo-
> sopher is Heidegger who, on this basis,
> established the possibility of an ahistor-
> ical discourse. Whereas previously you had

Hegel and Marx in your line of sight, did you not have Heidegger in mind here?[19]

What I would like to do now is give Foucault's full response with commentary in brackets:

Certainly. For me Heidegger has always been the essential philosopher. I began by reading Hegel, then Marx [*presumably under the guidance first of Hyppolite and then of Althusser*], and I set out to read Heidegger in 1951 or 1952 [*in Daniel Defert's chronology of Foucault's life published in the first volume of the collected* Dits et écrits *published by Gallimard in 1994, this reading is identified as taking place in October, 1951, in the year where Foucault is considering leaving both France and the Communist Party which he had joined the year before; he is considering Denmark and is reading Kafka and Kierkegaard, authors being taught at the Sorbonne by Jean Wahl,[20] also an important figure at the time, through his reading of the works of Heidegger, Husserl, and Nietzsche*]; then in 1952 or 1953—I don't remember any more—I read Nietzsche [*in August 1953 on the beach in Italy, according to his friend Pinguet, who suggests that this encounter*

---

19. Foucault, *Politics, Philosophy, Culture* 249–50.
20. The importance of the figure of Jean Wahl is emphasized by Baugh in *French Hegel*.

with Nietzsche was against the backdrop of his
"references" at the time, namely: Hegel, Marx,
Heidegger and Freud. Interestingly, Defert com-
ments that Foucault "often said" that he came
to read Nietzsche via Bataille and Bataille via
Blanchot, even as he recognizes Foucault's
later reference to Heidegger].[21] I still have
here notes that I took when I was reading
Heidegger. I've got tons of them! And they
are much more important than the ones
I took on Hegel or Marx. [*Defert mentions*
these in his chronology—October 1951—which
he says are worked out as lecture plans, on both
Heidegger and Husserl. The latter has recently
been the focus of yet further explorations of the
influences that feed into Foucault's work![22]]
My entire philosophical development was
determined by my reading of Heidegger.
[*Presumably, he is speaking of this early read-*
ing, when he was considering leaving both
France and the Communist Party; there is
also a later reading to be mentioned below.] I
nevertheless recognize that Nietzsche out-
weighed him. [*This is the point emphasized*
by Veyne and the point emphasized by most com-
mentators when discussing this famous remark,

---

21. Foucault, *DE* I 19.
22. Cf. R. Visker, *Truth and Singularity: Taking*
    Foucault into Phenomenology (Dordrecht:
    Kluwer, 1999); Johanna Oksala, *Foucault on*
    Freedom (New York: Cambridge UP, 2005).

cf. Stuart Eldon's discussion of this point.]
I do not know Heidegger well enough:
I hardly know *Being and Time* nor what has
been published recently. My knowledge
of Nietzsche certainly is better than my
knowledge of Heidegger. Nevertheless,
*these are the two fundamental experiences I have
had.* [*My emphasis. Foucault, then, is talking
of reading experiences, rather than influences;
something that marked him and in some way
confirmed or affected the direction of his thinking, its shape, one might say.*] It is possible
that if I had not read Heidegger, I would
not have read Nietzsche. I had tried to read
Nietzsche in the fifties but Nietzsche alone
did not appeal to me—whereas Nietzsche
and Heidegger: that was a philosophical shock! [*This is an interesting remark. It
would be interesting to know when this "shock"
occurred. My guess would be sometime in 1962
or 1963. Defert tells us that Foucault met
Deleuze in February 1962, the latter having just
published his* Nietzsche et la Philosophie.[23]
*Defert also notes in his chronology that Foucault
re-reads Heidegger in December 1963. Heidegger
published his* Nietzsche *in 1961; translated
into French only in 1971. In noting Foucault's
re-reading of Heidegger, Defert also notes that
Foucault stopped working on the outline of*

23.   (Paris: Presses universitaires de France,
       1962).

The Order of Things. *Evidence of the shock he is alluding to here? It is certainly true that Nietzsche's presence in* The Order of Things *is much more marked and singular than it is in* History of Madness, *where Nietzsche is usually evoked in conjunction with his alternative Pantheon of writers and artists, which includes Artaud and Van Gogh.*] But I have never written anything on Heidegger, and I wrote only a very small article on Nietzsche; they are nevertheless the two authors I have read the most. I think it is important to have a small number of authors with whom one thinks, with whom one works, but about whom one does not write. Perhaps I will write about them one day, but at such a time they will no longer be instruments of thought for me. In the end, for me there are three categories of philosophers: the philosophers that I don't know; the philosophers I know and of whom I have spoken; and the philosophers I know and about whom I don't speak.[24]

While I know I should resist falling into the trap of this last sentence—where Foucault is, I would say mischievously, both provoking and defusing the kind of interpretive mayhem among young scholars interested in his work his response to

---

24. Foucault, *Politics, Philosophy, Culture* 250.

the question will have generated—I cannot help but add the figure of Hegel as
one of those philosophers both "with" and
"against" what Foucault thinks, and that
recognizing this throws considerable light
on what he is doing. And this, even as he
affirms immediately after this response
that

> I am simply Nietzschean, and I try to
> see, on a number of points, and to the
> extent that it is possible, with the aid
> of Nietzsche's texts—but also with anti-
> Nietzschean theses (which are neverthe-
> less Nietzschean!)—what can be done in
> this or that domain. I am not looking for
> anything else but I'm really looking for
> that.[25]

But enough of these proper names. For
now, I would like to follow up on Foucault's
claim to be thinking "with" Heidegger and
consider the relevance of what would have
been an important text for him: "On the
Essence of Truth". Jean Hyppolite, who,
upon Foucault's arrival in Paris as a young
man, introduced him to philosophy[26] and
would play key roles in the development of
his career and whom Foucault eventually

---

25. Foucault, *Politics, Philosophy, Culture* 251.
26. Cf. D. Eribon, *Michel Foucault* (Paris: Flammarion, 1989) 34.

replaced at the Collège de France, makes the interesting remark that this text might more accurately be called "On the Essence of Error".[27] And it is indeed this ultimate concern with showing the intimate relation between truth and the "untruth" of concealment that might enable us to get a better sense of this notion of history both as the "installation of systems of rules" and as a series of "violences".

For Foucault, to take up the terms elaborated in the *Archaeology of Knowledge*, which seem most appropriate here, "systems of rules" are to be understood in terms of their *discursive formation*, quite literally in terms of their formation through "discourse". Discourses themselves are composed of *things said* (and in that sense are *res gestae*) or *énoncés* (translated somewhat awkwardly as "statements"; one should think of statement as in "policy statement" rather than as "proposition", which is too easily and traditionally analyzed in isolation from its conditions of utterance, something less easy to do when one thinks of "policy statements"), which are themselves events within a certain historically

---

27. J. Hyppolite, "Ontologie et phénoménologie," *Figures de la pensée philosophique* (Paris: Presses universitaires de France, 1971) 616.

specifiable field that, we have seen, is in fact
a rarefied one (that is, a field that is not a
plethoric totality, but the space of a dispersion). It is important to note that Foucault
develops this notion of discourse in explicit
contradistinction to the idea of language,
in the sense that discourse does not designate some kind of independent sphere of
meaning that its users (speakers, writers)
dip into in order to express themselves and
that somehow underlies everything they
may say. This would be to deny the historicity of the formation of that which is effectively said. As *things said*, discourse "is made
up of the totality of all effective statements
(*énoncés*) (whether spoken or written), in
their dispersion as events and in the occurrence that is proper to them".[28] The point
here, of course, is that, while the study of
language includes consideration of particular instances of it, the point is to produce
"a finite body of rules that authorizes an
infinite number of performances"[29] which
Foucault wants to contrast with the definite
occurrences of events. He writes:

> The field of discursive events, on the other
> hand, is a grouping that is always finite

---

28. Michel Foucault, *Archaeology of Knowledge*,
     trans. Alan Sheridan (New York: Pantheon,
     1972) 27. My emphasis.

29. Foucault, *Archaeology of Knowledge* 39.

and limited at any moment to the linguistic sequences that have been formulated; they may be innumerable, they may, in sheer size, exceed the capacities of recording, memory, or reading: nevertheless they form a finite grouping. The question posed by language analysis of some discursive fact or other is always: according to what rules has a particular statement been made, and consequently according to what rules could other similar statements be made? The description of the events of discourse poses a quite different question: how is it that one particular statement *appeared* rather than another?[30]

Let's focus on this latter question then: how is it that one particular statement (as some "thing said") appeared rather than another? It is in light of this particular question that Heidegger's text may prove illuminating. Heidegger allows us to consider the manner in which statements are in effect things that appear and in their appearance effectively disclose the particularities of a world. But he also allows us to see how this "disclosedness" or "unconcealment" is not the simple revelation of a world that is already there waiting to be illuminated, the lifting of a curtain and the shining of a spotlight—an object before an

---

30. Foucault, *Archaeology of Knowledge* 27.

investigating and ultimately knowing subject—but that this "unconcealing" of the
world through our actively engaging it is at
the same time a "concealing" of its truth,
and this not only despite but *because* of our
commitment to experiencing it truthfully
(that is, as we shall see, freely).

Let us look at this more closely, again
with reference to Foucault's question: how
is it that *one* particular statement appeared
rather than another? I am going to answer
by saying: because what is said is meant
(in the sense that it takes its place within
a prefigured field that receives it). "Things
said" are said truthfully. (Indeed, that
is what discloses the world.) In "On the
Essence of Truth" Heidegger develops an
example making use of two five-mark coins
on a table. He means to show how our
being-in-the-world is fundamentally one
of *accordances*. What can we say about the
accordances that hold between two such
coins? For one, two coins accord with one
another as two objects, namely, two distinct
five-mark coins. However, more interestingly for our purposes (and Heidegger's)
the *statement* "this coin is round" accords
with the coin as well. Heidegger notes:

> Here the statement is in accord with
> the thing. Now the relation obtains, not
> between thing and thing, but rather

between a statement and a thing. But wherein are the thing and the statement supposed to be in accordance, considering that the relata are manifestly different in their outward appearance? The coin is made of metal. The statement is not material at all. The coin is round. The statement has nothing at all spatial about it. With the coin something can be purchased. The statement about it is never a means of payment. But in spite of all their dissimilarity the above statement, as true, is in accordance with the coin. And according to the usual concept of truth this accord is supposed to be a correspondence. How can what is completely dissimilar, the statement, correspond to the coin? It would have to become the coin and in this way relinquish itself entirely. The statement never succeeds in doing that. The moment it did, it would no longer be able as a statement to be in accordance with the thing. In the correspondence the statement must remain—indeed even first become—what it is. In what does its essence, so thoroughly different from every thing, consist? How is the statement able to correspond to something else, the thing, precisely by persisting in its own essence?[31]

---

31. *BW* 120–21.

Thus the important question becomes not merely how two dissimilar things can "correspond" to one another, but how they can do so and remain the things that they are in their dissimilarity and, more specifically, how the statement can be what it is, given its dissimilarity from every *thing* else. To come to grips with this, one needs to look at how they relate to each other, which Heidegger describes in the following way: "the statement regarding the coin relates 'itself' to this thing in that it presents [*vor-stellt*] it and says of the presented how, according to the particular perspective that guides it, it is disposed".[32] Thus, the relation between the statement and the thing is a kind of mutual presentation within an open field which, and this is the important point, is "not first created by the presenting but rather is only entered into and taken over as a domain of relatedness".[33] Thus statements, like other things, are what they are through their relatedness within the open field of their very possibility of being presented as what they are. The openness of this field is, for Heidegger, a function of what he here calls "comportment" in the sense that "every open relatedness is a comport-

---

32. *BW* 121.
33. *BW* 121.

ment. Man's open stance varies depending on the kind of beings, with regard to what they are and how they are, can properly take their stand and become capable of being said."[34] For a statement and a thing mutually to be presented in accordance with each other as correct (true) they must be placed or, rather, "take their stand" within a field opened up through comportment in such a way that, as beings, they "present themselves along with the presentative statement so that the latter subordinates itself to the directive that it speak of beings *such-as* they are".[35] Now, the point Heidegger wants to emphasize is that this *self-subordination*, as it were, of the presentative statement presupposes a prior freedom within the field opened up by comportment, that is, "to free oneself for a binding directedness is possible only by *being free* for what is opened up in an open region" or, stated more succinctly, the "openness of comportment as the inner condition of the possibility of correctness is grounded in freedom".[36] Or to put it another way, which will be taken up in more detail in Chapter Five: it is not the truth that sets us free, it is freedom that

---

34. *BW* 122.

35. *BW* 122.

36. *BW* 123.

sets up truth. Here's how: the freedom "for what is opened up in an open region lets beings be the beings they are. Freedom now reveals itself as letting beings be."[37] Such a letting be is not to be understood in a passive sense; on the contrary, it "means to engage oneself with the open region and its openness into which every being comes to stand, bringing that openness, as it were, along with itself".[38]

We now have a clearer, more specific context for understanding what it means for statements to *appear* at a given time and place, which we will recall is Foucault's question concerning the eventfulness of "things said". Statements—now understood as claims to truth or truthfulness—present themselves within an open field that is the condition of their appearance. Within this open field, particular statements present themselves as standing in particular relations with other things (or in the case of statements as they present themselves in the archive, establishing a relation between the present and the past, the relations are with other statements), which is also descriptive of a particular relatedness and "letting be". These statements and the disclosedness of beings they

37. *BW* 125.
38. *BW* 125.

manifest is what we need to understand as the historical world (which opposes itself to the natural world or "nature", which, in Heidegger's terms, "here does not yet mean a particular sphere of beings but rather beings as such as a whole"[39]) insofar as "history begins only when beings themselves are expressly drawn up into their unconcealment and conserved in it, only when this conservation is conceived on the basis of questioning regarding beings as such".[40]

I think these considerations give a better sense of what Foucault is doing when he appeals to a principle of *rarity* in his overall appreciation of our relation to the historical world through an archival examination of things said. These various "things said" that make up the archive are the things they are insofar as they have "taken their stand" with reference to other things and thereby disclose the particularity and determinateness of a world. That this world can be described as a "system of rules" is a function of this "taking of stands" between statements, which is how the relations between them get established or are "installed".

And Heidegger's text continues to be useful as we consider this "installation".

---

39. *BW* 126.

40. *BW* 126–27.

"Systems of rules" are not arbitrary and haphazard constructions, but nor are they necessitated by anything other than themselves; they are the free attempt to "let be" the meaningfulness of the world disclosed in our comportment (what we say, think and do, or, in Foucault's terms: our discursive practices). We are speaking here of *rules* because our comportment is an "attunement" to what is, and not arbitrary and capricious (which would seem to characterize a conceptualization of what we think, say and do as in some way independent of our engaging in a world through comportment). And, again, such an attunement needs to be understood through our freedom to "let beings be". As Heidegger puts it:

> Letting beings be, which is an attuning, a bringing into accord, prevails throughout and anticipates all the open comportment that flourishes in it. Man's comportment is brought into definite accord throughout by the openedness of being as a whole.[41]

However, as he immediately goes on to note, this "openedness of being as a whole" is *immediately forgotten,* or lost from view, in our active rule-governed engagement *in* the world. The world, *as* a world disclosed

---

41. *BW* 129.

through our free engagement, gets lost *as* a world, through our (systematic) engagement *in* (what becomes) the world (as a system of rules).

Let me use a personal example to illustrate. Language use is governed by a system of rules. I happen to be bilingual. I say "happen" because, although French is my "mother tongue" I do not remember learning English and thus both languages are for me, to speak like Heidegger, equiprimordial as disclosive of the world. But such equiprimordiality is singularly revealing. Whenever I open my mouth to speak or set words down, two systems of rules make themselves available to me, and I make use of one or the other (sometimes—too often according to some—I mix them). I am writing this book in English despite the accent in my name and the language I have taught my children to speak. At some point, I might have abandoned the accent and taken to writing my name as "Ray" to better accord with what most of my friends called me when I was growing up in Manitoba. I might not have married a woman from France, might not have had children, might not have taught them my mother tongue. I might have become "assimilated" into the majority of English speakers around me. I might also have undertaken to write this book in French.

When I consider these various possibilities, just as when I am confronted with certain kinds of occasions (and in a country that officially declares itself to be "bilingual", thus reflecting a number of demographic and historico-legal tensions, such occasions are not infrequent), I sometimes become acutely aware of the very act I am engaged in, that is, speaking one language rather than the other, and that in doing so I am letting one language frame my speech rather than the other. This awareness affords me a glimpse of the "free letting-be" of "taking a stand" that is my being the speaker that I am, ontologically speaking. But, as I say, this is a glimpse, normally immediately forgotten, as the words themselves are indeed uttered, in French, in English, in a mix of both, and are systematically worked over according to the various sets of rules that govern their use in the situation. As Heidegger puts it, "Precisely because letting be always lets beings be in a particular comportment that relates to them and thus discloses them, it conceals beings as a whole. Letting-be is intrinsically at the same time a concealing."[42]

Thus, "systems of rules" form out of the letting-beings-be at the heart of our comportment which at the same time conceals

---

42. *BW* 120–30.

disclosedness as such, the open region or field of beings as a whole. My suggestion, then, is that we consider this concealment the "installation" of those "systems of rules" that govern our comportment.

In what sense should these "installations" be understood as "violences"? Precisely in the sense that the free letting-be that is at the heart of our being-in-a-world, in its concealing of the world-as-a-whole, *forces* that free possibility that we are into specific *modes* of being that shape the world as the world one comes to know. Saying things in this way does seem to suggest an implicit distinction between a "forced" mode of being and one that would be "unforced" and *therefore* free. But the point of putting things this way is to insist on the logical priority of the free letting-be upon which force is exerted, as it were. Or put another way, to speak of a *forced* mode of being is to speak pleonastically. To be a specific mode of being is already to be forced within a system of rules that qualifies it as the mode that it is.

That such force is exercised and "installed" is everywhere present whenever one considers the *historicity* of our ways of being in the world. As a simple illustration, think of the process by which as newborns we are taken up and, in many cases, placed in our exhausted mothers' arms and our cheeks and lips are poked and prodded with a nipple or her breast. The elation everyone exclaims when we "take" to that breast actually underscores the sense in which this event is historical rather than natural, an "installation" of a regulated relation between mother and child (more or less) systematically developed. It sounds, of course, unnecessarily harsh to qualify such an event as a "violent" one. I certainly won't here. But it is a forceful one insofar as we need to be picked up and presented with nipples, whether fleshy ones or synthetic ones, and the nourishment and succor we are given generally is structurally and (more or less) systematically enforced.

Or think of the games we play. The systems of rules that structure them and make them the games they are and that provide us not only with satisfaction and enjoyment but allow us to realize ourselves, are historically-specific sets of events installed on the free letting-be within the parameters of the playground, the basketball court, the swimming pool. To speak of the notion of violence as it relates to our bodies surely is no exaggeration when we consider the systems of rules they submit to as they are trained to leap, collide, twist and sail through the air.

Or again think of our musical instruments, the drums we beat, the keys we
strike, the strings we pluck, the air we blow
and suck and force through bored wood
or twisted copper and brass. Music, dance,
sport: it is important to remind ourselves
of the historicity of these things that we
do, that their development describes a distinct process from those we call "natural"
(whatever the role dispositions or predis-
positions can be said to play in that development; the distinction between history
and nature is not descriptive of two separate realms, but points to how the former
arises or emerges out of the latter, shapes
itself into its myriad forms). And it is in fact
this focus on the eventfulness of the way
human beings carve out for themselves the
particularities of their existences and shape
them forcefully through systems of rules
that suggests one is ignoring the detail and
thrust of such events when one insists on
seeing in them the singularity of purpose
of something called "humanity" as it is said
to progress gradually "from combat to combat until it arrives at universal reciprocity".
But does this mean that Foucault, for his
part, is insisting that attention to the eventfulness that shapes our lives shows rather a
humanity that "installs each of its violences
in a system of rules and *thus proceeds from
domination to domination*"?

Only if one wants to insist on the notion of "humanity" as the "subject" of history, of the eventfulness evidenced in the archive. If I am not prepared to ascribe this statement to Foucault's overall conception of history, it is because of the way Foucault's explorations of history help us *decouple* history-as-eventfulness from humanity-as-subject. As I will attempt to show in the following chapters as we examine some of those histories, Foucault is not proposing an alternative picture of history that, in denying the *telos* of universal reciprocity, seeks to recognize its movement as one that "proceeds from domination to domination". To accept such a picture is to occlude the central role that "freedom" plays in his thought (and leads to the kinds of misguided critiques like the one proposed by Taylor). More specifically, and this is the focus of my study, it does not allow us to account adequately for what Foucault calls the "indefinite work of freedom"[43] that he sees his work as promoting. I have modified the translation of this key phrase where Foucault speaks of the critical ethos he would have his work contribute to—a phrase that follows the description of the archaeological and genealogical approaches cited in the last chapter—and

---

43. Foucault, "What Is Enlightenment?" 316.

which seeks "*à relancer aussi loin et aussi largement que possible le travail indéfini de la liberté*".[44] "*Indéfini*" is translated as "undefined" but, as I will seek to show in more detail in the chapters that follow, I believe "indefinite" better captures what is at stake here. While one can appreciate that when speaking of the work of freedom, if one wants to insist on its character *as free*, one might want, like Foucault, to insist on qualifying that character as undefined. The target in mind here would be those who would insist on the *telos* of freedom in a specific form like the development of all our natural faculties, as in Kant, the self-realization of Reason, as in Hegel or the free development of each and therefore all, as in Marx.[45] Truly to respect our freedom would be to leave it undefined. This conception, however, seems to me to appreciate insufficiently the fact that it is the notion of *work* that is being qualified and that it is not a work that is "undefined" but "indefinitely" taken up as freedom, that it is this indefinite "taking up" of working freely that drives Foucault's own work and allows us to engage our own.

And turning yet again to Heidegger's text can help us get a better sense of what

---

44. Foucault, *DE* IV 574.
45. Cf. my *Multicultural Dynamics*.

might be claimed here. If it is claimed that *humanity* "proceeds from domination to domination" as it "installs each of its violences in a system of rules", it is because *humanity*, as Heidegger suggests, *errs* in its ever-renewed forgetfulness.

> Man errs. Man does not merely stray into errancy. He is always astray in errancy, because as ek-sistent he in-sists and so already is caught in errancy. The errancy through which man strays is not something which, as it were, extends alongside man like a ditch into which he occasionally stumbles; rather, errancy belongs to the inner constitution of the Da-sein into which historical man is admitted. Errancy is the free space for that turning in which insistent ek-sistence adroitly forgets and mistakes itself constantly anew. The concealing of the concealed being as a whole holds sway in that disclosure of specific beings, which, as forgottenness of concealment, becomes errancy.[46]

I want to suggest that we have here a better expression of what can be called Foucault's general sense of history, one that better captures the movement of his thought with and concerning history; much better, in any case, despite its obvi-

---

46. *BW* 133.

ous attractiveness, than the notion that
humanity "proceeds from domination to
domination". Rather, we should see at the
heart of history an "insistent ek-sistence
adroitly forget[ing] and mistak[ing] itself
constantly anew". Within that general historical perspective, and according to what
he calls "a philosophical ethos that could
be described as a permanent critique of
our historical era",[47] Foucault proposes
histories that track that insistence, the discursive forms that it takes, in such a way
that we are made to glimpse its contingent
character *as* an unconcealed/concealed
world and, in so doing, ask for ourselves
how, through our systems of rules, it is that
we insist on it as the world that it is.

---

47. *EW* 312.

III

Foucault after Hyppolite: Toward an A-Theistic Theodicy

My primary concern in this book is to explore the way Michel Foucault's work challenges the notion that a sense of history (like the sense of history developed in classical philosophies of history like Hegel's) can help us better make sense of our unfolding lives. This is a concern for me because, while there would seem to be an obvious link between our unfolding lives and the larger context of an unfolding history (because of the shared temporal character of both our lives and history), the sense that history does provide a larger context for understanding our lives is regarded with suspicion by most philosophers. Or rather, there is a suspicion about any *claims* that might be made concerning the overall significance of some general process called "history" (or indeed History). Philosophers, generally, seem either tacitly or explicitly to

accept Jean-François Lyotard's suggestion
that a basic characteristic of our present
"condition" (whether or not one wants to
call it "postmodern") is incredulity with
regard to the integrative and legitimating
function of "metanarratives".[1]

But a general sense of history need not
take the form of a meta-*narrative*. A general sense of history can also be explored
through conceptual considerations of its
particular temporal characteristics, the
ways in which it involves consideration of
the past, the present and the future both
in themselves and in the ways these notions
are related. This is the general sense that
is being privileged in this study. Making
sense of history, it is here being argued, is
making sense of this conceptual nexus.

If the figure of Hegel repeatedly returns
in this study, it is because of the way his
philosophy provides a sustained conceptual elaboration of the sense that history
can be said to have. And the basic claim
of this study is that it is this sustained conceptual elaboration that Foucault is both
challenging and grappling with in his historical work.

---

1. Cf. the introduction to Jean-François
   Lyotard, *The Postmodern Condition: A Report
   on Knowledge*, trans. Geoff Bennington
   and Brian Massumi (Minneapolis:
   U of Minnesota P, 1984).

Hegel's basic claim is that there is "Reason in History", or rather—because Hegel's whole philosophy aims at showing how any claim anyone might put forward will, upon examination, reveal itself to be caught up within a developmental movement of thought that is working itself out—that "Reason" in actuality *is* history and history is the self-realization of "Reason". What I will be offering in the next part of this book are readings of Foucault's histories as, in effect, what might be called concrete challenges to this broad philosophical conception. That is, it is not a challenge in the sense of a simple *rejection* of Hegel's view, but it is rather a *test* of its cogency and applicability and, perhaps more importantly (to play on the subtitle of one commentary on the works on Hegel), a test of reason's *self-satisfaction.*[2] For example, if Reason is history and history Reason, what of Unreason, what of that which is not taken up in history's progressive self-realization? As we will see in the next chapter, Foucault, in his *History of Madness*, has the reader confront the "torn presence" that is *not* taken up, or *grasped,* by Reason's accounting of itself.

---

2. Robert B. Pippin, *Hegel's Idealism: The Satisfactions of Self-Consciousness* (Cambridge: Cambridge UP, 1989).

This, ultimately, is the disconcerting effect of the book. It bears witness, as it were, to that which reason *silences* as it assures its own development, but it does so *through* an account of that development which, as an account, is a kind of grasping, a kind of conceptualizing that itself cannot *but* be caught up in "reason".

My readings of Foucault's histories will stress Foucault's own awareness and *grappling* with this question of being "caught up" in reason's self-developmental unfolding. I will not, however, be stressing the various ways he might be said to have succeeded in "freeing" himself from the *grasp* of reason. On the contrary, I will continue to insist (indeed to "in-sist", in Heidegger's sense, and thereby continue, in a sense, to "err" within Foucault's texts) on Foucault's constant preoccupation with the grasping character of reason's hold on our attempts to make sense of our unfolding lives, the way we are "caught up" in our own conceptualizing (as a form of grasping), because to do so is in fact to insist on our freedom, or our free engagement with the unfolding character of our lives and historical world.

The best way to show this, it seems to me, is to insist on the close proximity of Hegel's thought to Foucault's histories. But before turning to them, I would like

to situate further my particular reading
of Foucault by drawing out this connection to Hegel through a discussion of
Foucault's relation to one of his teachers:
Jean Hyppolite.

***

If one of Foucault's most significant contri-
butions is the way in which he has thought
confront its historically-constituted discursive conditions, then, in this, he can—and
should—be seen as participating in a long-
standing tradition of thinking that goes
back to Hegel. The importance of Hegel
for twentieth-century French philosophy
is well known. Although emphasis is usually placed on the influence of Alexandre
Kojève's lectures, a recent work by Bruce
Baugh[3] has both widened and sharp-
ened the focus on Hegel's reception in
France by privileging the impact of Jean
Wahl's *Le Malheur de la Conscience dans la
Philosophie de Hegel.*[4] If Kojève's reading of
Hegel remains focused on the dialectic
of the master and slave, Wahl's reading
stresses the unhappy consciousness and
the divided self. Baugh successfully shows
how "Hegel's description of how a reality

---

3. Bruce Baugh, *French Hegel: From Surrealism
   to Postmodernism* (New York: Routledge,
   2003).

4. (Paris: Reider, 1929).

divided against itself continually passes
from one opposed term to the other,
without finding repose or reconciliation,
constitutes a dominant theme in French
philosophy from the 1920s up to the
present."[5] This emphasis on the unhappy
consciousness is in effect a refusal of the
dialectical synthesis that otherwise characterizes Hegel's thought. What unites much
of twentieth-century French philosophy,
according to Baugh—from existentialism
and surrealism to postmodernism—is "an
anti-finalism, a denial of any ultimate telos
that would allow one to overcome divisions
and to understand them as interrelated
moments of a fully realized 'totality'".[6]
Let me call this the "standard" reading
of Foucault's relation to Hegel's thought.
While it is true that, like Hegel, Foucault
is concerned with exploring philosophy's
relation to history (describing his own
work, we will recall, as "philosophical
fragments within an historical field of
problems"), it is not in order to describe
Spirit's ultimate reconciliation with itself,
but rather to trace the dispersals and
deployments of systems of thought.[7] One

---

5. Baugh 2.

6. Baugh 6.

7. We will recall that the Chair that Foucault
   held at the Collège de France was given the
   title Chair of the History of Systems of

might even be tempted to see in Wahl's development a distant image of Foucault's own struggle. Wahl's initial claim was that "the truth of Hegel is to be found not in the Encyclopedia's 'desiccated' results of the dialectic, but in the striving and pathos of the dialectical movement itself, which corresponds to consciousness' search for reconciliation with itself"; however, as Baugh notes, "Wahl himself later rejected as illusory the Hegelian attempt to reconcile existence through speculative thought, and so turned away from the mediation of the Begriff and the dialectic based on it."[8] One might read the development of Foucault's "archaeological" and then "genealogical" approaches in a similar light. However, as Baugh also notes, Wahl's influence on Foucault was indirect, passing through Jean Hyppolite.[9]

I would like to explore further this "passage" via the work of Hyppolite in order to flesh out what I take to be persisting Hegelian motifs in his historical works,

---

Thought, and replaced Hyppolite's Chair of History of Philosophical Thought.

8. Baugh 24.

9. Though Defert mentions in his chronology of Foucault's life that, in 1951, Foucault was reading Kafka and Kierkegaard, both authors Wahl was commenting on at the Sorbonne. Foucault, *DE* I 17.

even as I readily grant the standard reading's view that Foucault rejected, and saw
his work as promoting the rejection of,
the kind of "finalism" and "totalism" often
attributed to Hegel's philosophy. In a word,
focusing on the relation between Foucault
and Hyppolite requires that we abandon
the view that Foucault is an essentially
anti-Hegelian philosopher (in the way that
Deleuze can be said to be). Foucault's concern with history runs too deep. Focusing
on this relation, though, leads me to
question Baugh's claim at the end of his
work that Foucault (albeit after a long
struggle that Baugh ably describes) has,
with his genealogical innovations, moved
us "beyond" Hegel and, together with
Deleuze, "inaugurate[d] a new conception of historical reason, concerned with
establishing the singularity of events, and
the limitations and possibilities for historically determined perspectives".[10] Baugh
of course is quite right that Foucault strug-

---

10. Baugh 172; which, of course, sounds a lot
    like Hegel! Cf. the work of commenta-
    tors such as John Russon, "Temporality
    and the Future of Philosophy in Hegel,"
    International Philosophical Quarterly,
    48 (2008): 59–68, and more gener-
    ally his *Reading Hegel's Phenomenology*
    (Bloomington: Indiana UP, 2004).

gled with Hegel's conceptions of teleological development, necessity and dialectical
synthesis as well as with the ideal of reconciliation. But this struggle, and the stakes
of the struggle, he learned from Hyppolite.
And Foucault learned from Hyppolite that
this struggle was ongoing, just as history
is ongoing. Thus, I will suggest in what
follows that we tarry a while longer with
this struggle that attempts to understand
the place of history within philosophy
and philosophy's place within history
and rather than follow Baugh and place
Foucault "beyond Hegel", we will consider
the place he created for himself "after
Hyppolite".

***

Foucault expressed his indebtedness to
Hyppolite on a number of occasions, the
most notable of which was surely his inaugural lecture at the Collège de France
on December 2, 1970. Foucault begins
that lecture in what is the premier intellectual institution of France by suggesting
that rather than begin a new discourse he
would have preferred to slip into a discourse already under way, pronounced
by a nameless voice, allowing Foucault
simply "to enmesh myself in it, taking up
its cadence, and to lodge myself, when
no one was looking, in its interstices as if
it had paused an instant, in suspense, to

beckon me".[11] At the end of his elocution, he returns to this idea, this voice, at the beginning nameless, that he now acknowledges as being the voice of Hyppolite.

Foucault is not merely evoking both his relation to discourse and Hyppolite in this manner to open and close the speech inaugurating his new position out of a kind of institutional deference. The nameless discourse in which he might "enmesh" himself, before explicitly identifying Hyppolite, might indeed be a reference to the discourse of Hegel's *Logic* itself, which, according to Hyppolite's reading in *Logic and Existence*, "is the authentic unity of that of which one speaks and of the one who speaks, of being and of the self, the sense which appears only in the medium of intelligible language".[12] Hyppolite was the teacher responsible for bringing Foucault to philosophy, and this encounter with philosophy was in effect an encounter with the philosophy of history.[13] And we could

---

11. Foucault, "The Discourse on Language" 215.

12. Jean Hyppolite, *Logic and Existence*, trans. L. Lawlor and A. Sen (New York: State U of New York P, 1997) 37.

13. According to his biographer, D. Eribon, a young eighteen-year-old Foucault freshly arrived in Paris would have fallen under the spell of Hyppolite and philosophy

take the notion of "philosophy of history"
here in its original Voltairian sense as a
contrast to all "theological" understand-
ings of history. That is, if a theological
interpretation of history is concerned with
how our actions in this world relate to
God's ultimate plan for us, a philosophical interpretation of history is concerned
with whether or not there is any discern-
ible plan or meaning in what we accomplish in this world (which is another way of
saying that philosophies of history appeal
to a principle of immanence). Indeed,
the development of a concern for a philosophy of history from the eighteenth century onwards was precisely a concern with
the importance and significance, with the
intelligibility, of our experience of the lived
world. It expressed a concern with what
was perceived to be the *movement* of this
lived world (its unfolding), with its development. (We will need later on to distinguish more clearly the difference between
the concepts of unfolding and development. For the moment, we will simply note
how the former does not have as much
telic emphasis as the latter.) The philosophy of history wanted to understand that
movement, and it was motivated to do so

---

because of their ability to make sense
of history. Cf. D. Eribon, *Michel Foucault*
(Paris: Flammarion, 1989) 34.

out of its commitment to rationality, to seeing in the actions of human beings more
than what Kant called "the idiotic course
of things human", that is, the past seen as
"everything in the large woven together
from folly, childish vanity, even from childish malice and destructiveness".[14]

In other words, it is my suggestion that
we should read Foucault as engaged in an
ongoing struggle with the figure of Hegel
(initiated and sustained by his reading of
Nietzsche and Heidegger), wrestling with
his vision of Reason and History and, I
will further suggest, attempting to continue the transformation already under-
way in Hyppolite's readings of Hegel's
works (specifically his *Logic and Existence*
more so than his *Genesis and Structure*,
which, however, did figure in Foucault's
early studies).[15] I will characterize this
transformation as one that can perhaps

---

14. Immanuel Kant, *On History*, ed. Lewis
    White Beck (Indianapolis: Bobbs-Merrill,
    1963) 12.
15. Cf. for example his complementary thesis
    entitled "*Genèse et structure de l'Anthropologie
    de Kant*", in Foucault, *DE* I 23. For a good
    discussion of the importance of *Logic and
    Existence*, not only for Foucault but for
    much of subsequent French philosophy in
    the sixties, see Len Lawlor's introduction
    to the English translation.

best be understood as the attempted articulation of an *a-theistic theodicy*: a theodicy
because, as will be discussed further below,
this is how Hegel ultimately describes the
project of the philosophy of history, which
traces "the recognition of the process of
development which the Idea has passed
through in realizing itself—i.e. the Idea of
Freedom, whose reality is the consciousness of Freedom and nothing short of it".[16]
However, much more explicitly (or much
less ambiguously) than in Hegel, such a
theodicy must be understood a-theistically
(not atheistically; we are not concerned
with denying the existence of God, not
even with affirming his nonexistence,
but only recognizing the affirmation that
God is dead), that is, it is a theodicy that
does not make reference to the plenitude
afforded by the notion of God and is intent
on avoiding all eschatological temptations
when contemplating (or attempting to
comprehend) this "best" of all possible
worlds (i.e., the actual world).

***

Hyppolite's primary concern, Foucault
tells us, and in this he is surely right, is our

---

16. Hegel, *Philosophy of History* 457. And in
     the last paragraph Hegel says: "this is the
     true Theodicea, the justification of God in
     History".

relation to Hegel's philosophy. What is
meant here by "our" relation is contemporary philosophy or the possibility of philosophy today. What is meant by "philosophy"
here is, I will suggest, not a particular discipline but the attempt to comprehend
the world, to *grasp* it in thought. It is in
this sense that for Hyppolite, according to
Foucault,

> the relationship with Hegel was the scene
> of an experiment, of a confrontation in
> which it was never certain that philosophy
> would come out on top. He never saw the
> Hegelian system as a reassuring universe;
> he saw in it the field in which philosophy
> took the ultimate risk.[17]

We have an echo here of what we have
encountered already as one of the ways he
characterizes his own work: as philosophical fragments in a historical *field* of problems. It would seem that the risk assumed by
Hyppolitian/Hegelian philosophy would
have resulted in its fragmentation and
dispersal into a field—a historical field—
that philosophy no longer contains. More
of this in a moment.

But why should the attempt to comprehend the world philosophically be considered an "ultimate risk"? A risk for what?

---

17. Foucault, "Discourse on Language" 236.

For philosophy? Or for reason? If Hegel's attempt fails, does that signal the end of philosophy as a relevant and fruitful enterprise? Or, more radically, does it announce the fading of any hope of having reason rule the world?

Hyppolite's work brings out the fundamental pathos at the heart of Hegel's philosophical achievement by tracking its ambiguities, and he does this, according to Foucault, by "shifting" the senses or directions that Hegel himself seems to have given his work, resulting in what Foucault calls the *inversion* of five "themes" running through Hegel's work.

First theme: rather than a total comprehension, philosophy becomes for Hyppolite's Hegel an *unending task* against the background of an infinite horizon. Philosophy's work is never complete and always begins anew "given over to the forms of paradoxes and repetitions".[18]

Second theme: given this background, the theme of an achieved, completed or accomplished self-consciousness becomes that of a *repeated interrogation* that constantly draws philosophy away from itself and its abstractions and generalities in order to "reestablish contact with the nonphilosophical; it was to draw as close as

18. Foucault, "Discourse on Language" 236.

possible, not to its final fulfillment, but to that which precedes it, that which has not yet stirred its uncertainty".[19]

Third theme: thus, the *sense* that philosophy is meant to give to existence in its comprehension of the world is accomplished by "a philosophy that was *present, uncertain, mobile* all along its line of contact with non-philosophy, existing on its own, however, and revealing the meaning this non-philosophy has for us".[20]

Fourth theme: if philosophy's ultimate task is to provide the meaning or sense of that which is manifested non-philosophically, then this raises the question of philosophy's status itself. Is it already within that which it is not, "secretly present"? If so, it is perhaps superfluous already. If it is not, what precisely is its role? What kind of justification can it give of the task it has set itself? If its only justification is itself, then it may legitimately be considered absolute. However, given its relation to non-philosophy, does not its absoluteness appear merely arbitrary?

Fifth and final theme: "if philosophy really must begin as absolute discourse, *then what of history*, and what is this begin-

___

19. Foucault, "Discourse on Language" 236.
20. Foucault, "Discourse on Language" 236; my emphasis.

ning which starts out with a singular individual, within a society and a social class,
and in the midst of struggle?"[21]

I will not ask here the extent to which
this interpretation of the "shifts" and "dis-
placements" accurately reflect Hyppolite's
appropriation of Hegel. My interest rather
lies in showing how these shifts and dis-
placements are reflected in Foucault's own
conception of the task of philosophy as
he himself "shifts" it through his historiographical practice.

Here it would perhaps be best to take
these themes in reverse order because
the fifth theme is no doubt the one
that underscores Foucault's work most
emphatically. Philosophy must confront
history in Foucault's work (as it does in
Hegel's), not as a chronicle of events that
needs to be given order and sense but as
problematized and problematizing *practices* of making sense of the world as these
emerge historically. Hyppolite, in *Logic
and Existence*, emphasized this sense of the
Hegelian *logos*, how it is the movement of
thought as it comprehends, in an unfolding world, the manifestations of objects
that, in their particular determinateness,

21. Foucault, "Discourse on Language" 236;
    my emphasis.

are inadequate in themselves, and must be taken up in thought:

> Philosophy thinks as genesis what presents itself in experience as object. All the universal determinations of existence present themselves as figures of consciousness in the *Phenomenology* or the *Philosophy of History*. The Logos conceives them as the being which thinks itself in its universality, and by thinking itself, thinks also its own alienation in nature and in finite spirit.[22]

Rather than speak of the *universalizing* movement of the Logos as it "reflects itself and expounds itself as intelligible speech",[23] through its appropriation of historical "objects", that is, the particularities that define and demarcate the actual individual things that make up the world, Foucault instead considers it as an *ordering* of discourse (the title of his inaugural speech, translated as "The Discourse on Language" is *L'ordre du Discours* or the "order of discourse"). If philosophy is said to begin as "absolute discourse", it is because philosophy, for Hegel, is that which *grasps* the movement of discourse, of the *Logos*. For Foucault, this grasping is an ordering and "history" or the "singular

---

22. Hyppolite, *Logic and Existence* 91.

23. Hyppolite, *Logic and Existence* 36.

individual" caught up, as it were, "in the midst of struggle" is the problematizing of that ordering. Thus Foucault, as he—in his singularity, his singular sensibility—runs through the archive, that "mass of documentation with which [a society] is inextricably bound", interrogates it via his own singular *sensibility*, his own reaction to its ordering principles and structures and the *sense* they are supposed to provide.

The interrogative approach, this questioning of the archive that Foucault operates, echoes Hyppolite's reworking of Hegel, where the emphasis is less on the narrativity that an appreciation of history might provide than on the multifariousness of the world it reveals. The third and fourth themes, according to Foucault, have to do with the precariousness and uncertainty of philosophy's contribution as a sense-giving project to processes that are initially seen as unphilosophical (i.e., whose principles are uncomprehended in Hegel's sense). If Hegel has extended the reach of philosophy immeasurably by having it reach right into the irrational itself, then Hyppolite, and Foucault after Hyppolite, shows a concern with the impact such an extension has on philosophy itself.

Hegel's grasp of Absolute Knowing becomes in Hyppolite noticeably more

tentative if still attentive or, as Foucault
puts it, revealed by a philosophy that is
"present, uncertain, mobile" and whose
primary concern, according to Hyppolite,
is to apprehend in the manifestations of
the world the meaning that it contains,
"as we find life in the midst of everything
living".[24] The idea of life, of linking philosophy to life, to life's multifarious manifestations, is important for Hyppolite,
echoing Hegel's attempt at Jena of linking
life and infinity:

> The concepts of life and infinity are equiv-
> alents. In the Logic of Jena, Hegel thinks
> of infinity as a dialectical relation of the
> one and the many, but we can recognize
> in this logical dialectic the very idea of life.
> Reciprocally, life is this dialectic itself, and
> life forces the spirit to think dialectically.[25]

Thus, this linking of philosophy to life is in
effect a concern with life and *thought*, with

---

24. Jean Hyppolite, *Introduction to Hegel's
    Philosophy of History*, trans. B. Harris and
    J. B. Spurlock (Gainesville: UP of Florida,
    1996) 49.

25. Hyppolite, *Introduction to Hegel's Philosophy
    of History* 43. Cf. also Jean Hyppolite,
    "The Concept of Life and Consciousness
    of Life in Hegel's Jena Philosophy," *Studies
    in Marx and Hegel* (New York: Basic Books,
    1969) 3–21.

life as thinking, something that Foucault
also takes up, even in the very title of
the Chair he occupies at the Collège de
France, where philosophy gives itself over
to the history of systems of thought. Here,
too, Foucault comes after Hyppolite,
who, according to Foucault, did not see
himself as a historian of philosophy but
spoke rather of the history of philosophical thought, a distinction wherein one
can find "the singularity and scope of his
endeavour".[26] By insisting on this notion
of philosophical *thought*, Hyppolite was
insisting on

> that which, within any system—no matter
> how complete in appearance—overflows
> it, exceeds it, and puts it in a relation of
> both exchange and default with philo-
> sophy itself; philosophical thought was
> not for Hyppolite the intuition of a sys-
> tem, its unformulated intimacy; it was
> its incompleteness, the debt he could
> never repay, the space his propositions
> could never fill; that which, in its pursuit,
> always remains despite being taken up by
> philosophy.[27]

26. Michel Foucault, "Jean Hyppolite,
    1907–1968," *Dits et écrits*, vol. I (Paris:
    Gallimard, 1994) 780, my translation.
27. Foucault, "Jean Hyppolite, 1907–1968"
    780:

And thus, within this philosophical thought or philosophical thinking which Hyppolite would trace and outline and explore, one realizes through Hyppolite, philosophy itself

> is never actualized or present in any discourse or text; that, in fact, philosophy does not exist; rather it hollows out through its perpetual absence all philosophies, it installs within them the lack that they incessantly pursue, continue, disappear, follow and remain for the historian suspended and to be taken up.[28]

> . . . ce qui dans tout système—aussi achevé qu'il paraisse—le déborde, l'excède, et le met dans un rapport à la fois d'échange et de défaut avec la philosophie elle-même; la pensée philosophique, ce n'était pas, pour lui, l'intuition première d'un système, son intimité informulée; c'était son inachèvement, la dette qu'il ne parvient jamais à acquitter, le blanc qu'aucune de ses propositions ne pourra jamais couvrir; ce par quoi, aussi loin qu'il se poursuive, il demeure en reste par rapport à la philosophie.

28. Foucault, "Jean Hyppolite, 1907–1968" 780:

> . . . la philosophie n'est jamais actualisée ni présente dans aucun discours ni aucun texte; qu'à vrai dire la philosophie n'existe pas; qu'elle creuse plutôt de sa perpétuelle absence

Foucault, then, through Hyppolite, continues this questioning of philosophy, of the very presence of philosophy in and through the writing of history, which, in effect, describes philosophy's very condition of possibility, that is, those systems of thought that reveal thought's "machinery", its "discontinuous systematicities"[29] and trace at the very root of thought the elements of chance, discontinuity and materiality.[30] Foucault, after Hyppolite, radicalizes thought's relation to itself by radicalizing its relation to its historical manifestations. It is in this context that we can now better make sense of Foucault's claim to be producing "philosophical fragments", that is, fragments of philosophy within systems of thought whose ordering and deployment go beyond the synthesizing efforts of any single mind, even Hegel's.

But like Hegel, and like Hyppolite, Foucault knows that philosophy, if it is to

toutes les philosophies, qu'elle inscrit en elles le manque ou sans cesse elles se poursuivent, se continuent, disparaissent, se succèdent, et demeurent pour l'historien dans un suspens ou il lui faut les reprendre.

29. Foucault, "Discourse on Language".
30. This is especially evident in Foucault, *NGH* 367–91. We will return to this essay below.

continue philosophizing (and if philosophy is anything it is the effort to continue philosophizing as Socrates and
Nietzsche have shown us), must confront
the history that is its very condition of
possibility. Foucault, in his own work,
exemplifies Hyppolite's second Hegelian
theme, that of transforming, through
philosophical effort, any achieved or complete self-consciousness into a repeated
interrogation. This interrogation takes on
many forms throughout his career but situates itself fairly clearly and consistently at
a certain *level* of discourse that Foucault
calls *knowledge* (*savoir*), between opinion
and *scientific* knowledge (*connaissance
scientifique*).[31] In the document he sub-
mitted for the position at the Collège de
France, Foucault gives a brief description
of the "object" of investigation that gradually took shape through his specific concern with the interesting and seemingly
paradoxical question of how we might
have formulated the project of "knowing"
madness (which culminated, of course, in
his *History of Madness*). Through his concrete investigations of

---

31. For a good discussion of this distinc-
    tion, cf. Gary Gutting, *Michel Foucault's
    Archaeology of Scientific Reason* (Cambridge:
    Cambridge UP, 1989).

> how the mad were recognized, isolated,
> excluded from society, interned and
> treated; which institutions were destined
> to house and retain them—sometimes
> to care for them; which authorities pro-
> nounced them mad and according to what
> criteria; which methods were adopted for
> constraining them, punishing them, or
> healing them,

Foucault gradually came to discern the
delineation of what would become his
"object" of investigation: the "networks"
(*réseaux*) of knowledge invested "in complex institutional systems".[32]

But if this describes (at that point) his
"object" of investigation, and the level of
discourse at which he situated himself, it
is his *philosophical* questioning of it that
brings him back to Hyppolite. And Hegel.
We will recall the first inversion Hyppolite
effects with regard to Hegel's attempt to
conceive philosophy as a totality capable of
thinking itself, the idea of thought thinking itself through its very movement is to
have thought or philosophy conceive itself
as an unending task set against an infinite
horizon. It is within this context that one
must understand Foucault's claim that he
has in his work produced "*philosophical*

---

32. Michel Foucault, "Titres et travaux," *Dits et écrits*, vol. I 842.

fragments put to work in a historical *field* of problems". That is, I want to suggest that Foucault has taken up Hyppolite's—and Hegel's—challenge of making sense of history, of having this as philosophy's principal task with the proviso that philosophy understand itself as a *task* and not a result. Philosophy's purpose is not to describe or to understand an independently existing reality, nor is it to attempt to construct or constitute that reality; rather, it must make sense of its unfolding. Of course, for Foucault, that unfolding does not reveal or display or signal an increasing self-consciousness; or rather, he refuses this particular speculative move. Foucault, like Hegel, is concerned with thought, but unlike Hegel, he is not concerned with Spirit. Indeed, his rejection of Hegel is largely a rejection of the idea of Spirit and not a rejection of philosophy's task of making sense of history.[33] Foucault comes after

---

33. Having said that, he does later in his career appeal to the notion of "spirituality" as it relates to the care of the self that he contrasts with a "subjectivity" focused on self-knowledge and truth. Cf. his lectures published as *The Hermeneutics of the Subject: Lectures at the Collège de France, 1981–1982*, trans. Graham Burchell (New York: Palgrave Macmillan, 2005). I will take up the theme of the care of the self—in

Hyppolite, but he also comes after Marx and Nietzsche. After Marx, life "determines" consciousness and not the other way around, and after Nietzsche, life must be lived without God.

***

I am suggesting, then, that Foucault's insistent and creative attempts to *make sense* of history, that is, to render our world *intelligible* through an examination of its historical unfolding (or systematicites) should be seen as a continuation rather than a rejection of the Hegelian attempt to inhabit a reasonable world. I think it is important to do this because it helps us better appreciate how Foucault's work speaks to the "obscurities and difficulties" encountered when we attempt to work out a philosophy of history, understood as a reasoned account of our unfolding experience of the world that includes an appreciation of the correlativity of the past, present and future. It is in this context that I make the suggestion that we could, with profit, appreciate Foucault's various projects as an attempted *a-theistic theodicy* in that, like all theodicies, they refuse to give up the world to senselessness, to see it as without purpose and direction. Of course, Foucault's theodicy

---

connection with the question of what history is for—in Chapter Six.

is a-theistic in that it makes no claim to an ultimate purpose or direction for the world (hence Foucault's philosophical fragments). However, despite the death of God, the world does not sink into meaninglessness and purposelessness. On the contrary, what has happened is that meaning and purpose have been *released* from the dictates of any ultimate guarantor, any founding subjectivity. What we are faced with is a proliferation of purposes and meanings with no clear way of evaluating them. It is *this* situation that we need to make sense of: a world with proliferating meanings and purposes, not one that lacks meaning or purpose. (Even if we return to the "general view" of history discussed in Chapter Two, which would have it proceed "from domination to domination", we could see in these different forms of domination particular meaning and purpose.) This is the world that Foucault's thought tackles by trying to render it not meaningful (it is already rent with meaning) but *intelligible.*[34]

---

34. An a-theistic theodicy also suggests that, although we cannot be concerned with God's justice (which of course is the etymological significance of the word "theodicy"), the concern with justice does not automatically devolve to "Man" or human justice. Rather the concern is with

Another way to put this is to see Foucault's efforts as fitting squarely within what Leonard Lawlor has recently described as the "Hyppolite" middle, that is, the investigative space as delimited by Foucault between "a phenomenology of pre-discursive experience and an

---

the structural and systematic deployment of justices understood historically, those "installations of violences in systems of rules" discussed in Chapter Two. John McCumber, in a discussion I will take up in the next chapters when we look more closely at Foucault's appeal to the notion of power, makes a similar suggestion, contrasting Foucault's use of the notion of power, within the context of relating form and matter through a process of "designation", with Aquinas's approach. For the latter,

this designation of the matter of a thing was the effect of divine creation: God was the primary 'designator,' uniting form and matter in the *actus essendi*. Foucault calls the designator in question 'power,' and his conception of power therefore has something divine about it—or perhaps, since power is hardly God, 'demonic.' Foucault's genealogical work, aimed at revealing the nature of power, is at bottom an exercise in theodicy (or demonodicy). (John McCumber, *Philosophy and Freedom: Derrida, Rorty, Habermas, Foucault* (Bloomington: Indiana UP, 2000) 115) epistemology of philosophical systems",[35] which, following Hyppolite's *Logic and Existence*, is intent on keeping the focus on working out a logic of sense where "immanence is complete".[36] This phrase is in fact the last sentence of Hyppolite's commentary on Hegel's *Logic*.[37] It is followed by a concluding chapter which discusses

---

Rather than speak of the aim of revealing the "nature" of power, Foucault appeals to it in order to make better sense of history and better position his thought within history. More of this below.

35. Leonard Lawlor, *Thinking through French Philosophy: The Being of the Question* (Bloomington: Indiana UP, 2003) 12.

36. Lawlor 12; Hyppolite, *Logic and Existence* 176. Such a focus, according to Lawlor, characterizes all of what he calls "the great French philosophy from the Sixties" (Foucault, Derrida, Deleuze), with as its principal problem: "how to conceive, within immanence, the difference between logic and existence (the Logos and time), structure and genesis, thought and experience, the said and the unsaid, monument and soul, philosophy and non-philosophy" (Lawlor 12).

37. It may be worthwhile to give the final paragraph as a whole as it points to Foucault's discussion of the "inversion" of themes outlined above and which, I am arguing, opens up the space of his own thinking:

two directions for Hegel's *Logic*: one,
taken up by Feuerbach and Marx, which
"leads to the deification of Humanity",
and the other, taken up by Hyppolite himself appealing, though he does not name
him, to Heidegger, which "leans to the
Absolute's self-knowledge *across* man".[38]
This latter approach, rather than focus
on Man and the realization of Humanity
to be brought about by History, juxtaposes
the *Logos* (as expressed in language) and

> The logic of the concept corresponds to the
> major turn that transcendental logic represents
> in the history of philosophy. In a letter, Kant
> calls it his ontology and what is at issue indeed
> is in effect a new ontology since it replaces the
> world of essence, the being of Logic, with the
> logicity of being. By pushing the reduction of
> anthropology initiated by the transcendental
> to its limit, Hegel's speculative Logic is the
> deepening of this dimension of sense. Being is
> its own self-comprehension, its own sense, and
> the Logos is being positing itself as sense. It is,
> however, being which posits itself as sense, and
> this means that sense is not alien to being, is
> not outside of it or beyond it. This is why sense
> also comprehends non-sense, the anti-Logos; it
> is in itself just as much as it is for itself, but its
> in-itself is for itself, and its for-itself is in itself.
> The dimension of sense is not only sense, it is
> also the absolute genesis of sense in general,
> and it is self-sufficient. Immanence is complete.

38. Hyppolite, *Logic and Existence* 177.

Existence where the latter "defines man by the freedom of being-for-itself which is simultaneously always opposed to being-in-itself and always related to it" (historical existence as distinct from natural existence). Hyppolite immediately goes on to say (and I quote at length because of how this passage links up with the concerns raised in Chapter Two in connection with Heidegger):

> Man does not possess the freedom that allows him to wander from one determination to another or to be dissolved in abstract nothingness; rather, freedom possesses man. Nothingness is not then between the for-itself and the in-itself; it is the very nothingness of being or the being of nothingness. It opens to man, not the mere real negativity that makes history objective, but the dimension of the universal at the heart of which all sense is determined and engendered. Through this freedom, which Hegel says is immanent to all history, which Hegel says is the absolute Idea of history (and of course, equivocity is evident in the relation of the philosophy of history to the Logos in Hegel, and in this very term "freedom"), man does not conquer himself as man, but becomes the house (*la demeure*) of the Universal, of the Logos of Being, and becomes capable of Truth. In

this opening which allows the existents of Nature, and history itself, to be clarified, to be conceived, Being comprehends itself as this eternal self-engendering; it is Logic in Hegel's sense, absolute knowledge.[39]

Given what we have already seen in Chapter Two, through our juxtaposition of Heidegger's discussion of "truth" as it relates to Foucault's principle of rarity for comprehending or making sense of history, we can see here as well a broadening of the context of his particular approach to include the principle of *immanence*. And while such a principle can be stated fairly simply and straightforwardly as holding that, whenever one is considering the process of history, one should not appeal to anything outside of that process (a kind of *deus ex machina*) as governing it in order to account for its directedness (or the sense that it can be said to contain); or, stated positively, everything that we need to render the historical process more intelligible to us can be found *within* the historical process,[40] we can see how it arises

---

39. Hyppolite, *Logic and Existence* 187.
40. This is the way I formulated the principle in my "Moving Beyond Biopower: Hardt and Negri's Post-Foucauldian Speculative Philosophy of History," *History and Theory* 44.4 (2005): 60–61.

out of Hyppolite's particular reading of
the significance of Hegel's philosophical
endeavours.

***

I would like to examine this further by
returning to a number of key statements
made in Foucault's "Nietzsche, Genealogy,
History". As already mentioned in Chapter
Two, this text is often taken to be a key text
in understanding Foucault's conception of
history, and so it is. But it is also a text that
was included in a volume called *Hommage
à Jean Hyppolite* which I think is significant,
especially for those who read Foucault as
an "anti-Hegelian" philosopher insofar as
his "genealogies" are meant to be a rejection of the kind of speculative, teleological
philosophy of history that Hegel is typically
represented as offering us. Given that it is
an "homage" to Hyppolite's work, one can
assume that it will recognize the sophisti-
cation of that work, and will pay particular attention to its particular interpretive
strategies. And Foucault does indeed do
this, but indirectly, through a reading of
Nietzsche, with a specific focus on the
latter's concept of "genealogy" and how
this relates to the more general concept
of "history" (hence the title of the article
which, we will recall from our discussion
of the quote declaring his endebtedness to
Heidegger, Foucault claims to be the only

thing he ever wrote about Nietzsche). A closer examination of this text will allow me to clarify what I mean when I say that Foucault's work offers us an "a-theistic theodicy".

This article is ultimately about history, about the relevance of history as a mode of thought capable of questioning the actuality of our world.[41] This relevance is tested against Nietzsche's conception of something he calls "genealogy", which, Foucault tells us in the first section (there are seven in all), is an approach to history that distinguishes itself from another approach that sees history as an essentially linear development; rather than seeking in the past the "origins" of such a developmental process, genealogy reminds us that making sense of history is an operation "on a field of entangled and confused parchments, on documents that have been scratched over and recopied many times",[42] that history is in fact a many-layered thing, and that to understand its relevance, one's approach

---

41. For an excellent discussion of this essay as it relates to Hyppolite and to French philosophy generally, cf. Lawlor's *Thinking through French Philosophy*, especially the section entitled "Foucault's Three Great Concepts: Metaphysics, the Actual, and Genealogy," 15–20.

42. *NGH* 369.

must record the singularity of events outside of any monotonous finality; it must
seek them in the most unpromising places,
in what we tend to feel is without history—
in sentiments, love, conscience, instincts;
it must be sensitive to their recurrence,
not in order to trace the gradual curve of
their evolution but to isolate the different
scenes where they engaged in different
roles.[43]

Genealogy, then, is a specific approach
to history, one that in fact *extends* the scope
of history to include matters "we tend to
feel are without history". This is not specific to genealogy, of course. Much of
the thrust of contemporary historiography, especially the work of the *Annales*
school and the "new historians" that followed it, was towards the search for new
methods and new objects for studying the
past.[44] Foucault often contextualized his
own work within these historiographical

---

43. *NGH* 369.

44. Cf. the three volumes edited by Jacques
    Le Goff and Pierre Nora (the latter the
    editor responsible for the series that
    published *Discipline and Punish*) *Faire de
    l'histoire* (Paris: Gallimard, 1974). Some
    notable examples of new "objects" of his-
    tory include: fear, climate, culinary tastes,
    private life.

developments.[45] The specific appeal to *genealogy*, however, has more of a philosophical significance. One certainly can

---

45. A good example of this can be found in his "Return to History" in *EW* 2 423, where he criticizes, along lines similar to those adopted by Hayden White as discussed in the Introduction, traditional historiography as developed in the nineteenth century and appeals to new developments:

> History was a discipline by means of which the bourgeoisie showed, first, that its reign was only the result, the product, the fruit, of a slow maturation, and that this reign was thus perfectly justified, since it came from the mists of time; next, the bourgeoisie showed that, since this reign came from the dawn of time, it was not possible to threaten it with a new revolution. The bourgeoisie both established its right to hold power and warded off the threats of a rising revolution, and history was indeed what Jules Michelet called the 'resurrection of the past.' History assigned itself the task of bringing the whole national life back to life. This calling and the role of history now must be reconsidered if history is to be detached from the ideological system in which it originated and developed. It is to be understood, rather, as the analysis of the transformations societies are actually capable of. The two fundamental notions of history as it is practiced today are no longer *time* and the *past* but *change* and the *event.*

see in it an expression of a commitment, which Foucault shares with his contemporaries, as noted by Baugh and cited earlier, to an "anti-finalism, a denial of any ultimate telos that would allow one to overcome divisions and to understand them as interrelated moments of a fully realized 'totality'".

But in Foucault's case, this commitment is something more than a mere "denial". Already in Hyppolite's appreciation of Hegel's work, there is a questioning of a too-facile reading of Spirit's realization in and through history and that a reconsideration of the *Logic* involved reassessments of the unfolding of history in terms of its fully *immanent* process of "self-engendering". Might we not see in Foucault's appeal to genealogy here, in the context of honouring Hyppolite's work, a continued appreciation of such an immanent process? Might we not read the critique of the "search of origins" that Foucault's reading of Nietzsche emphasizes as a critique of a kind of *caricature* of history as a simple teleological picture of how something like "the present" came to be? Note that in trying to link the present to its "origins", one is thereby trying "to capture the exact essence of things, their purest possibilities, and their carefully protected identities; because this search assumes the existence of immobile forms that precede the external world of accident and succession".[46] To do this is not to take history seriously. It is in fact to do metaphysics and metaphysics is precisely what the genealogist refuses "to extend his faith in"; instead, if "he listens to *history*, he finds that there is 'something altogether different' behind things: not a timeless and essential secret but the secret that they have no essence, *or that their essence was fabricated in a piecemeal fashion* from alien forms".[47]

Again, if one pays attention to the context of this discussion, the genealogist, in his appeal to *history* as a critique of the *metaphysics of the timelessness of essences*, should be considered to have Hyppolite's Hegel as an *ally* rather than as an opponent or a target.[48] After all, the *Logic* involves a critique of the doctrine of essence that, in

---

46. *NGH* 371.

47. *NGH* 371; my emphasis.

48. Indeed, as the text makes clear in the final section—and in this it shows itself to be a commentary on Nietzsche and not Foucault's methodological manifesto— the target is Plato or what are called the "three Platonic modalities of history" which involve history as reminiscence or recognition, history as continuity and tradition and history as knowledge. Hegel, of course, takes up all of these themes but inverts them in his own way.

the end, cannot adequately capture the
movement of thought as it attempts to distinguish between appearance and reality; a
movement that, for Hegel, is best captured
in the self-movement of the Concept.
Indeed, no doubt Hegel would whole-
heartedly *agree* with the "genealogist" when
he affirms: "History is the concrete body of
becoming; with its moments of intensity;
its lapses, its extended periods of fever-
ish agitation, its fainting spells; and only
a metaphysician would seek its soul in the
distant ideality of the origin."[49]

But here we can also see how Foucault's
appeal to history (through Nietzsche
and "genealogy") begins—following
Hyppolite—to invert Hegel's. This appeal
to the "concrete *body* of becoming" is one
that, even if it accepts the self-movement
of thought as it attempts to *grasp* and take
up into philosophical comprehension
the non-philosophical (as we saw above),
insists on what might be called the "materiality" of this process, in effect inverting
the "ideality" that characterizes Hegel's
approach. This is where the appeal to
"genealogy" becomes most relevant, given
its twin task—discussed in sections three
and four of *NGH*—of tracing that movement's "descent" (*Herkunft*) and "emer-

---

49. *NGH* 373.

gence" (*Entstehung*).[50] Thus, if Hegel's thought makes sense of history by seeing how, despite the spent passions history so ostentatiously displays, it is actually animated by the *reconciliatory* movement it is philosophy's task to articulate and follow, then the inverted task of a genealogical appreciation of history, as it follows

> the complex course of descent is to maintain passing events in their proper dispersion; it is to identify the accidents, the minute deviations—or conversely, the complete reversals—the errors, the false appraisals, and the faulty calculations that gave birth to those things which continue to exist and have value for us; it is to discover that truth or being lies not at the root of what we know and what we are but the exteriority of accidents.[51]

We will see in detail Foucault's particular application of this inversion in the next part when we discuss both his early account of Reason's appropriation of madness, and then his genealogical account of the "birth" of the prison, that is, those movements of thought within which the

---

50. Both movements can be read as applications of what I have been calling the "principle of immanence" and of the "principle of rarity".

51. *NGH* 374.

notions of "discipline", "punishment" and "surveillance"[52] are deployed and whose "ideality" would have them play the role of guarantors of the value of "freedom" but whose "materiality" tells a potentially more significant story.

We will also see in that work the second task of a genealogical appreciation of history which, again as against the metaphysician who "would convince us of an obscure purpose that seeks its realization at the moment it arises", rather "seeks to *reestablish* the various systems of subjection: not the anticipatory power of meaning, but the hazardous play of dominations".[53] This, too, describes an inversion rather than a rejection of Hegel's project (which is not the metaphysician's; the purpose that realizes itself in history is not obscure: on the contrary, its realization in and through history is its increasing clarification as the purpose that it is, namely, the realization of the Idea of freedom). That is, as I will try to show, Foucault is not rejecting the notion that "freedom" is the "realization" of history, which is another way of saying that it "emerges" from the historical process (or, put otherwise, Hegel himself respects

---

52. The title of the work in French, of course, is *Surveiller et punir.*

53. *NGH* 376; my emphasis.

the principle of immanence). He is, however, inverting the theme of history as the *development of its Idea*, that is, what is to be sought in history is not *one* interpretation: the development of humanity; rather, "the development of humanity is a series of interpretations" and interpretation, as it emerges from history, needs to be understood as "the violent *or* surreptitious appropriation of a system of rules".[54] And the "role of genealogy is to record its history".[55] *Discpline and Punish*, for example, will record the surreptitious appropriation of the systems of rules of "justice".

The point of these inversions is to render our appreciation of history more *effective* by developing a "historical sense" that evades "metaphysics". Many think that Hegel, despite his own keen historical sense, does not altogether succeed in doing this; perhaps because, as Foucault would put it, his approach does not refuse "the certainty of absolutes".[56] Indeed, if Foucault claims to be engaged in producing philosophical *fragments*, it is because he does refuse this certainty, which includes the traditional historian's

---

54. *NGH* 378; my emphasis.

55. *NGH* 378.

56. *NGH* 379. Cf. the concluding chapter of Joseph Flay's *Hegel's Quest for Certainty* (Albany: State U of New York P) 1984.

reliance on "constants", which themselves serve as devices "for constructing a comprehensive view of history and for retracing the past as a patient and continuous development".[57] An "effective" history inverts the Hegelian theme of an appreciation of history as a process of "self-consolidation" that understands itself "as the ultimate goal of all discourse".[58] Instead, it affirms a principle of rarity which affirms that

> The world such as we are acquainted with it is not this ultimately simple configuration where events are reduced to accentuate their essential traits, their final meaning, or their initial and final value. On the contrary, it is a profusion of *entangled* events.[59]

But here is where I think it is useful to think that these "inversions" of Hegelian themes should be seen as in a sense continuing the basic work of philosophy as

---

57. *NGH* 380. Which, as pointed out above, is simply another way of denying the possibility of revolution, cf. "Return to History" in *Aesthetics, Method, and Epistemology: Essential Works of Foucault, 1954–1984*. Vol. 2. (New York: The New Press, 1998).

58. John McCumber, *Poetic Interaction: Language, Freedom, Reason* (Chicago: U of Chicago P, 1989) 306.

59. *NGH* 381; my emphasis.

making sense of history, but now through a keener sense of its entanglements. If such a "profusion of entangled events" is the *actuality* of our historical situation, our historical world, then it is the questioning of this actuality through an examination and (dis)articulation of those entanglements that allows us to think of Foucault's work as an attempted a-theistic theodicy. I do not insist on this term out of oxymoronic mischief but because I believe it captures something of the movement of Foucault's thought as it makes use of history and historiography. Indeed, associating the idea of theodicy with history, which is basic to Hegel's thought, is already to move theodicy in an a-theistic direction. Traditionally (and still today in analytic philosophy), theodicies concern themselves with the justification of evil in a world purportedly created by a benevolent and all-powerful God. (If there is evil, then God is perhaps good but not all-powerful, or all-powerful but not good.) However if, like Hegel, one thinks about what is manifest in the world without reference to a personal God (i.e., the personal attributes of goodness and potency), then what needs justification is not so much "evil" as it is senselessness. That is, sense must be made of that which appears as senseless. Hence, Hegel calls his philosophy of history the "true" theodicy. The senselessness that consideration of the past reveals, that "slaughter-bench on which the happiness of peoples, the wisdom of states and the virtue of individuals were sacrificed",[60] for Hegel is redeemed, not through passive contemplation from a divine standpoint, but through the active exercise of reason—of making sense—that history can also reveal when the passions that feed history are transfigured by philosophy into the contemplation of the process of development of the Idea of Freedom. The complaints that his view of history is too abstract and schematic miss the point of working out a philosophy of history whose task is to help us make sense of the world and not merely submit to it. Hegel tells us (to complete a quote introduced earlier) that:

> Philosophy concerns itself only with the glory of the Idea mirroring itself in the History of the World. Philosophy escapes from the weary strife of passions that agitate the surface of society into the calm region of contemplation; that which interests it is the recognition of the process of

---

60. Hegel, *Philosophy of History*, qtd. in Joseph McCarney, *Hegel on History* (London: Routledge, 2000) 199. McCarney provides a good discussion of Hegel's "theodicy" in the final chapter of this work, 195–220.

development which the Idea has passed through in realizing itself—i.e. the Idea of Freedom, whose reality is the consciousness of Freedom and nothing short of it.[61]

Clearly, Foucault's work does not seek to celebrate the grandeur of Hegel's vision. However, I am arguing that he does not in fact abandon it, or seek to replace it. Rather, he continues its "inflexion", started by Hyppolite, by refusing the speculative presumption of Philosophy with a capital "P" of escaping "from the weary strife of passions that agitate the surface of society into the calm region of contemplation" in order to have philosophy confront more directly history and the strife that characterizes it. I think this is how we need to understand Foucault's contribution to the *Hommage à Jean Hyppolite*: he has taken up a figure of philosophical thought— a practice dear to his teacher[62]—in this case, Nietzsche, and demonstrates how this figure's concept of genealogy can contribute to the task of having philosophy confront "the weary strife of history"

---

61. Hegel, *Philosophy of History* 457.
62. In the same year of the *Hommage*, a two-volume collection of Hyppolite's studies of various thinkers was published under the title *Figures de la Pensée Philosophique* (Paris: Presses universitaires de France, 1971).

rather than escape from it by showing that
history

> has a more important task than to be a
> handmaiden to philosophy to recount the
> necessary birth of truth and values; it should
> become a differential knowledge (connais-
> sance) of energies and failings, heights and
> degenerations, poisons and antidotes. Its
> task is to become a curative science.[63]

One sees immediately Foucault's own for-
ays into such "historical fields of problems"
as inspired by these genealogical considerations. But we will recall that his works
are not simply "historical treatises", even
if genealogically conceived, but are in fact
"philosophical fragments", that is, pieces
of philosophy, which following Hyppolite
(following Hegel), attempt to comprehend immanence as complete, only now
supplemented with a principle of rarity.

   In other words, through these inversions, I read Foucault's work as a continuation of Hegel's work by other means. His
also is a finite attempt to make sense of
history as an infinitely unfolding process.
However, the difference with Hegel is that
Foucault places himself more squarely
within that process as opposed to situating
himself at its end.

---

63. *NGH* 382.

But Foucault's work can be seen as a continuation of Hyppolite/Hegel even more precisely insofar as it is also (partly) motivated, like Hegel's philosophy, by the desire to make sense of (and realize) our "freedom". That is, rather than merely affirm or deny freedom, either treating it as a postulate or an illusion, his work shows how it is revealed, made manifest, through the working out of the intelligible structures of the world as they manifest themselves historically (i.e., through the "profusion of entangled events"). This is especially evident in his use of the notion of power-relations. It is the notion of power-relations that will (for a time) mediate the "endless task" of making sense of this world as it is set against its "infinite horizon". It is within the notion of power-relations that the unfolding of history is to be rendered intelligible. By understanding our attempts to make sense of the world within power-relations, Foucault is trying to situate our freedom in terms as concrete as the world as we experience it and struggle with it. Here, too, Foucault is following (but also subverting) the Hegelian understanding of history. That is, because Foucault is not concerned with Philosophy with a capital "P", and because he is not concerned with the relation of consciousness to Spirit, his account of freedom and the recognition of freedom take on a different form. Through this concept, he means to place the recognition of the possibility of freedom within the weary strife of history. That is the point of characterizing our relations as power-relations. A power-relationship, Foucault tells us,

> can only be articulated on the basis of two elements that are indispensable if it is really to be a power relationship: that the "other" (the one over whom power is exercised) is recognized and maintained to the very end as a subject who acts; and that, faced with a relationship of power, a whole field of responses, reactions, results, and possible inventions may open up.[64]

This is what I meant earlier when I said that Foucault wants to situate himself and his thinking more firmly within the unfolding of our attempts to make sense of the world. And this we do not do alone but with and against others, and to do so is to participate in power relations, to exercise power. But it is in and through this participation that we can truly recognize and realize our freedom because:

64. Michel Foucault, "The Subject and Power," *Essential Works of Foucault, 1954–1984,* vol. 3, ed. James D. Faubion, trans. Robert Hurley (New York: The New Press, 2000) 340.

> Power is exercised only over free subjects, and only insofar as they are "free". By this we mean individual or collective subjects who are faced with a field of possibilities in which several kinds of conduct, several ways of reacting and modes of behavior are available.[65]

Thus, there is no opposition between the notions of power and freedom or, rather,

> there is not a face-to-face confrontation of power and freedom as mutually exclusive facts (freedom disappearing everywhere power is exercised) but a much more complicated interplay. In this game, freedom may well appear as the condition for the exercise of power (at the same time its precondition, since freedom must exist for power to be exerted, and also its permanent support, since without the possibility of recalcitrance power would be equivalent to a physical determination).[66]

As I will try to show in the next part, Foucault is attempting to continue the project of recognizing and realizing the freedom that lies at the heart of our attempts to make sense of the world, but now understanding those attempts as "agonistic", the site of "mutual incitement and

---

65. Foucault, "The Subject and Power" 342.
66. Foucault, "The Subject and Power" 342.

struggle". This, according to Foucault, is the scene of history as we live and seek to understand it. Foucault writes:

> The history that bears and determines us has the form of a war rather than that of a language—relations of power, not relations of meaning. History has no "meaning", though this is not to say that it is absurd or incoherent. On the contrary, it is intelligible and should be susceptible of analysis down to the smallest detail—but this in accordance with the intelligibility of struggles, of strategies and tactics.[67]

Foucault's commitment to the intelligibility of the world is the same commitment that inspires all theodicies. And his efforts show us that, even if we live in an a-theistic world that can no longer promise an ultimate guarantee to our various attempts to make sense of it, we can still appeal to the guarantee that remains at the heart of all theodicies: that only careful attention to the actual world will reveal any sense it may contain.

With this in mind, we turn now to Foucault's histories.

---

67. Michel Foucault, "Truth and Power," *Power: Essential Works of Foucault, 1954–1984*, vol. 3 (New York: The New Press, 2000) 116.

PART B

The Histories

IV

Madness and the Cunning of Reason

Whoever looks at the world rationally will find that it in turn assumes a rational aspect; the two exist in a reciprocal relationship.

G. W. Hegel, *Reason in History*

Why are Foucault's histories so disconcerting? as Charles Taylor perspicuously pointed out in his influential essay already quoted.[1] We will recall that for Taylor himself, the principal reason (Taylor admits there may be others), is that "Foucault's analyses seem to bring *evils* to light; and yet he wants to distance himself from the suggestion which would seem inescapably to follow, that the negation or overcoming of these evils promotes a good."[2] Now, it is interesting that he should say this about someone who is engaged in writing *histories*. Histories tell

---

1. Taylor 152.
2. Taylor 152.

us about what happened in the past, reveal to us what is contained in the archive; that such investigations should bring something like "evils" to light should perhaps not be surprising. After all, human *res gestae* include some fairly odious deeds. But, of course, Taylor is not expressing surprise. He is concerned about the *disconcerting* quality of Foucault's histories, and they are indeed disconcerting in that they challenge our complacencies with regard to what we claim to know about the world and they confront us with the complicities that structure what is given us to do in the world. And he does this simply by having us confront our own historical archive! And it is precisely because of this that we return to them.

What is interesting about Taylor's remark is the way it points out that Foucault's work actually *undoes* something about our own self-understanding: it is dis-concerting; it challenges our *concerted* efforts to structure lives for ourselves, to put together *in concert* the kinds of conditions that are meant to enable us to lead meaningful lives.

But why? Why does Foucault aim at frustrating our concerted effort to provide the conditions for meaningful lives? Asking this question reminds us that historical investigations are not blindly undertaken, a mere laying bare of the contents of the archive that would some-how speak for itself. The very intelligibility of history depends on the articulation of the principled approach to its reconstruction. However, as I suggested in the Introduction, Foucault's approach is notable especially in the way that it is informed by a particular sensibility and that it is in connection with that sensibility that we need to look for the particular principles that ensure the intelligibility of the history he reconstructs.

The principle he both appeals to and challenges in his major work is the very principle of Reason itself, understood in the Hegelian sense as the self-developing realization of itself.

The recent publication of the complete translation of Foucault's *Histoire de la Folie à l'Age Classique*[3] helps us grasp this insofar as it leads us to reconsider what Foucault was attempting to do in this work. The complete translation[4] gives the reader a better sense of the "mass of documentation" (and we will recall that Foucault

---

3. (Paris: Gallimard, 1972), hereafter referred to as "*HF*".

4. Michel Foucault, *History of Madness*, trans. Jonathan Murphy and Jean Khalfa, ed. Jean Khalfa (London: Routledge, 2006), hereafter referred to as "*HM*".

affirms that *history* "is one way in which a
society recognizes and develops a mass of
documentation with which it is inextricably bound"[5]) that Foucault is working with
and through in a way that *Madness and
Civilization*[6] did not. Will explicit reference
to this mass of documentation reassure
readers of *Madness and Civilization* suspicious of Foucault's scholarly appreciation
of the historical record? Probably not.[7]

Part of the reason for this is that one
of the lasting features of Foucault's disconcerting approach is the way his histories challenge the historiographical
pretensions of all who appeal to the "historical record", in the way they have the

---

5. Michel Foucault, *The Archaeology of
   Knowledge*, trans. Alan Sheridan (New York:
   Pantheon, 1972) 7, herafter referred to
   as "*AK*".

6. Michel Foucault, *Madness and Civilization:
   A History of Insanity in the Age of Reason*,
   trans. Richard Howard (New York: Vintage
   Books, 1988). This is the translation of an
   abridged version of Foucault's original
   publication published by Plon in 1961,
   entitled *Folie et Déraison: Histoire de la Folie
   à l'Age Classique*.

7. The following paragraphs take up
   parts of the discussion of our, Beaulieu
   and Fillion's, review essay of the new
   translation.

historical record challenge itself. Here, the brief title *History of Madness* may be misleading. It can too easily lead the unsuspecting reader to think that the text is a history of a particular "object" called madness. What the text does, however, is somewhat more complex than that; part of the fascination exerted by this text is that it evokes something variously *called* madness, folly, insanity, precisely *not* as an object but as an Other to something else called Reason, and this, not in some kind of timeless opposition, but for a certain period and in a certain place (principally the seventeenth and eighteenth centuries in Europe). The (current) title of the French text (itself the original subtitle) makes this clear, as does the tripartite division of the complete text (a division not reproduced in *Madness and Civilization*). The focus of the text is "madness in the classical age". The first and third parts are contrastive and serve to frame the core discussion of the "classical age", which, for Foucault, presents us the archival figure of what he calls Unreason which itself serves as a contrast to the notion of reason itself. This division of the text, along with the introductory chapters to Parts II and III, should—somewhat paradoxically given the supplementary material—lead readers of *Madness and Civilzation* to appreciate the tentative and exploratory dimension of Foucault's text.

Indeed, the tentative and exploratory character is what makes *History of Madness* something other than a traditional work of history. From the latter, one could expect either an account of the different forms and shapes taken over time by some phenomenon now called "mental illness" or, on another register, a description of the genesis and development of the discipline of psychology. Foucault's approach is quite different. What distinguishes his work is the presumed vantage point from which certain changes in the perception of madness are recorded. In the preface to *Folie et Déraison*,[8] which Foucault later suppressed (but which is included, along with the 1972 preface that replaced it, in *History of Madness*), Foucault gave the impression that rather than write the story of how the mad have been perceived from the point of view of those who have formulated or articulated those perceptions, he would write about those formulations and articulations from the point of view of those perceived as such, from the point of view of the "mad themselves". Not, of course, to speak *for* them but to challenge what has been said

_____

8. As noted, this is the original title of Foucault's work, published by Plon in 1961.

about and done to those called "mad" by producing an "archaeology" of their *silence*.

As is well known, Derrida very early on questioned the cogency such a project, such a perspective. After all, what is a *history* but a discursive, *reasoned* account of the past? As he famously puts it:

> The misfortune of the mad, the interminable misfortune of their silence, is that their best spokesmen are those who betray them best; which is to say that when one attempts to convey their silence *itself*, one has already passed over to the side of the enemy, the side of order, even if one fights against order from within it, putting its origin into question. There is no Trojan horse unconquerable by Reason (in general). The unsurpassable, unique, and imperial grandeur of the order of reason, that which makes it not another actual order or structure (a determined historical structure, one structure among possible other ones), is that one cannot speak out against it except by being for it, that one can protest only from within it; and within its domain, Reason leaves us only the recourse to strategems and strategies.[9]

---

9. Jacques Derrida, "Cogito and the History of Madness," *Writing and Difference*, trans. Alan Bass (Chicago: U of Chicago Press, 1978) 36.

And generally critics have concurred with Derrida's view that Foucault's project of writing from the point of view of the mad or from some point of view outside of reason itself is impossible.[10]

But, I would suggest, this is not an accurate description of what Foucault is attempting to do in this work. Foucault is indeed writing a history and therefore is within the space of reason, articulating from within it a point of view that does reflect its own self-development. However, what he is attempting to do in what will later be called his "archaeological" approach is to adopt a point of view distinct from the *perspective* that "reason" has of *its own* explicit self-understanding; more specifically, his own perspective will be from that which "reason" silenced in *assuring* its own self-development and as evident in the archive. Todd May puts this quite nicely when he says that Foucault's history "articulates the various ways in which, once madness is established as such, the discourse on madness is structured. . . . The book is an archaeology of the historical structurings, the archives, of

---

10. Cf. Roy Boyne, *Foucault and Derrida:*
    The Other Side of Reason (London: Unwin
    Hyman, 1990).

reason in its monologue upon madness."[11]
He even goes so far as to say that, better
than Foucault's own early explicit expression of "drawing up" an archaeology of a
"silence",[12] one should see him as engaged
in

---

11. Todd May, *The Philosophy of Foucault*
    (Montreal & Kingston: McGill–Queen's UP,
    2006) 39–40.

12. Cf. the 1961 preface. In presenting what
    he is attempting to do, in contrast to what
    we do today with those we consider mad:

    on the one hand is the man of reason, who del-
    egates madness to the doctor, thereby authoriz-
    ing no relation other than through the abstract
    universality of illness; and on the other is the
    man of madness, who only communicates with
    the other through the intermediary of a reason
    that is no less abstract, which is order, physical
    and moral constraint, the anonymous pressure
    of the group, the demand for conformity.
    There is no common language: or rather, it no
    longer exists; the constitution of madness as
    mental illness, at the end of the eighteenth cen-
    tury, bears witness to a rupture in a dialogue,
    gives the separation as already enacted, and
    expels from the memory all those imperfect
    words, of no fixed syntax, spoken falteringly, in
    which the exchange between madness and rea-
    son was carried out. The language of psychiatry,
    which is a monologue by reason *about* madness,
    could only have come into existence in such a
    silence. (*HM* xxviii)

an archaeology of a *silencing*: of the forms
it has taken, the successive structures of the
discussions it has elicited, the practices of
experimentation and treatment to which

The next sentence is the one seized upon:
"My intention was not to write the history
of that language, but rather draw up the
archaeology of that silence." This notion
of a ruptured "dialogue" runs throughout
HM and I think one should see in it not
a romanticizing of the mad but rather an
expression of Foucault's modal sensibility
to the very concrete and real possibility of
their existence: that there are amongst us
those some of us designate as mad; some of
us who accept this designation; some of us
remaining indifferent; some of us responding to this designation by investing time
and energy in making something of the
designation, refining it, perhaps challenging features of it. What Foucault is intent
on showing is that these specific possibilities contrast with other distinct possibilities
that carry within them their distinct forms
of exclusion. But again, it is worth insisting
here that his sensibility to the way these
possibilities work themselves out in both
the theories and practices relating to what
is identified as mad grounds itself in the
free letting-be of possibility itself which
includes, *at that level*, those we call mad
and with whom we refuse—for the time
being—to engage in dialogue.

it has given rise. To put the point another way, it is not an archaeology of the mad; it is an archaeology of *us*, the ones who are caught up in reason.[13]

This notion of being "caught up in reason" is the one I would like to emphasize. Foucault, through his histories, shows how we are indeed "caught up in reason" in the precise sense Derrida noted in the quote above, where he reminds us "that one cannot speak out against it except by being for it, that one can protest only from within it, and within its domain. Reason leaves us only the recourse to stratagems and strategies." Here again, we can see why Foucault should refer to his work as "philosophical fragments within a historical field of problems".[14] The particular strategy he adopts in *History of Madness* is to target the workings of reason insofar as it sees itself as confronted by something that threatens it, something specifically identifiable in our history (during the "classical age", what in English is precisely called the "age of reason"; thus, his history is a challenge to

---

13. Todd May, *The Philosophy of Foucault* (Montreal: McGill–Queen's UP, 2006) 40.
14. Michel Foucault, "Questions of Method," in *Power: Essential Works of Foucault, 1954–1984.* Vol. 3. Ed. James Faubion (New York: The New Press, 2000) 224.

our own general self-understanding even
as it tracks the specificity of our relation
to madness).

Foucault calls this threat "*déraison*". The
"*dé-*" in "*déraison*" is from the Latin *dis-*,
which suggests a distancing, a separation
or a kind of lack or privation. The *dis-* of
course is also found in English; for example, in disrespect or disingenuousness or
disinterest. Something is missing, indeed
something very specific: respect, sincer-
ity or partiality. Given this indication of
a separation through lack and privation,
one might say that "*déraison*" would be
better translated as *dis*reason as opposed
to *un*reason. It is true, at least according
to the *Canadian Oxford Dictionary*, that the
un- prefix can indicate a lack or privation
when added to nouns, though more often
the prefix denotes an absence, as in for
example "unhappiness" or "uneducated".
The opposition is much more stark than in
words prefixed by *dis-*, the separation more
radical. Where there is unhappiness, there
is no happiness; the uneducated are without education. Whereas disrespect, while
it opposes respect, does so through a kind
of perverted appeal to respect; to be "unre-
spectful" would be simply to lack all respect,
to be *dis*respectful is also to deny respect,
but to do so while retaining the knowledge
of what respect means and demands.

My suggestion, then, is that Foucault's strategy of focusing on a specific figure of "disreason" (flanked as it is by the "madness" of the Renaissance and the "mental illness" that follows it) is meant to throw light not only on a particular period of history, but also to provide a kind of confrontation with a conception of history that understands itself as the sphere of reason's self-development. This Hegelian thematic of a historically self-developing reason through conflict is undeniable in *History of Madness*, something that Derrida noted as well. In the sentence immediately following the passage quoted above, Derrida writes:

> The revolution against reason, in the historical form of classical reason (but the latter is only a determined example of Reason in general. And because of this oneness of Reason the expression "history of reason" is difficult to conceptualize, as is also, consequently, a "history of madness"), the revolution against reason can be made only within it, in accordance with a Hegelian law to which I myself was very sensitive in Foucault's book, despite the absence of any precise reference to Hegel.[15]

---

15. Derrida 36.

As will be evident in what follows, it is indeed this conception of reason as manifested through its understanding of itself as progressive self-development that shapes Foucault's own project of thinking about Unreason. The way I would like to draw this out is by making use of one of Hegel's more famous characterizations of the way reason sees itself as operating in and through history: the cunning of reason. Rather than refer, as does Derrida, to "a Hegelian law" or to the "unsurpassable, unique, and imperial grandeur of the order of reason", Foucault is much more interested in tracking its *actual*, concrete operation, which Hegel tells us, requires *cunning*. Why cunning? Because, already in Hegel, there is a recognition of the tenuousness of reason's accomplishments, that it is threatened by those forces in the world that would deny it. Despite the caricature of Hegel's conception of history, reason's survival through its instituted accomplishments and self-development in the world is not some kind of automatic process somehow guaranteed to work out; reason's self-development is a function of its ability to progressively realize or actualize itself in and through the world, despite the obstacles the world presents (namely processes that appear to be devoid of reason, like war and conflict). The point that Hegel

is making in his *Lectures on the Philosophy of
World History* is the one that I insisted on in
my Introduction. If we are to make sense
of history (and to consider the possibility
that making sense of history can help us
make sense of our unfolding lives), then
we cannot blindly consider what has happened simply by "recording facts"; rather,
we are confronted with the need to see in
and through history the working out of a
principled developmental process (which
Hegel refers to as both Reason and Spirit).
Indeed, much of the point of Hegel's presentation of those *Lectures*[16] is to show how

16. I think it is an underappreciated feature
of Hegel's philosophical project that he
saw an important dimension of his own
"life-work" to be engaged in the practice
of lecturing, of teaching; that philosophy,
in this way, was a living, breathing activity.
On this point, cf. Jacques d'Hondt, *Hegel:
Philosophie de l'histoire vivante* (Paris: Presses
universitaires de France, 1966) and Terry
Pinkard, *Hegel: A Biography* (Cambridge:
Cambridge UP, 2000). He has come down
to us as the great systematic philosopher,
for some trying to enclose philosophy
within his own encyclopedic concerns;
and yet the attempt to frame philosophical
thinking encyclopedically can just as well
be understood within the context of this
teaching imperative of making knowledge
available for students to *consult* and

close attention to history, because of the attentiveness it brings to its examination, does not reveal a senseless process despite the wastefulness of much of what human beings have wrought in the past, but rather the working out of the universal Idea (of Freedom; we shall return to this later). What history reveals to us, Hegel writes, is that:

> Particular interests contend with one another, and some are destroyed in the process. But it is from this very conflict and destruction of particular things that the universal emerges, and it remains unscathed itself. For it is not the universal Idea which enters into opposition, conflict, and danger; it keeps itself in the background, untouched and unharmed, and sends forth the particular interests of passion to fight and wear themselves out in its stead. It is what we call the *cunning of reason* that it sets the passions to work in its service, so that the agents by which it gives itself existence must pay the penalty and suffer the loss. For the latter belong to the phenomenal world, of which part

---

assimilate in their own thinking. In this sense, his encyclopedic efforts are precisely the opposite of the kind of teaching that seeks to promote a doctrine and thus to "indoctrinate".

is worthless and part is of positive value. The particular is as a rule inadequate in relation to the universal, and individuals are sacrificed and abandoned as a result. The Idea pays the tribute which existence and the transient world exact, but it pays it through the passions of individuals rather than out of its own resources.[17]

What I would like to do here is show how this particular feature of reason—its use of cunning to realize itself—provides a framework for reading Foucault's *History of Madness* in the sense that such "cunning" is Foucault's focus as he tracks "reason's" self-development through the way it deals with what it perceives as the threat to its self-understanding that those perceived as mad possess. I do not pretend that this kind of reading of *History of Madness* is the only possible, or even most important, one for grasping what Foucault is all about. But it is, in my view, key to understanding Foucault's sense of *history* and the challenge his work presents. And it does contrast with another reading of Foucault, one perhaps closer to his own explicit sense of himself, that would emphasize not the

17. G. W. F. Hegel, *Lectures on the Philosophy of World History: Introduction*, trans. H. B. Nisbet (Cambridge: Cambridge UP, 1975) 89.

figure of Hegel, but that of Nietzsche and that would insist on the "untimely" character of his challenge to the philosophy of history. This reading would no doubt appeal to the—later suppressed—original preface which affirms that his investigation into madness—as what he calls a "limit-experience"—is an investigation into "the tragic itself" as Nietzsche understood it,

> having shown that the tragic structure from which the history of the Western world is made is nothing other than the refusal, the forgetting and the silent collapse of tragedy. Around that experience, which is central as it knots the tragic to the dialectic of history in the very refusal of tragedy by history, many other experiences gravitate.[18]

Already here, he identifies another such "experience" as requiring "the history of sexual prohibition"[19] and that the *History of Madness* he is proposing "will only be the first, and probably the easiest, in this long line of enquiry which, beneath the sun of the great Nietzschean quest, would confront the dialectics of history with the immobile structures of the tragic".[20] If I do

---

18. *HM* xxx.

19. *HM* xxx.

20. *HM* xxx.

not myself pursue this reading it is because, as I hope to continue showing, the texts themselves contain challenges to historical self-understanding that are better appreciated through other readings, other emphases, including Heidegger's insistence on relating truth to freedom and Hayden White's suggestion of the poetic prefiguration of the historical. Indeed, we might appeal to White's point in order to make sense of what is going on in Foucault's prefatory remarks. In his appeal to Nietzsche and to madness, Foucault seems to make a very broad, speculative claim about history-as-a-whole where he writes:

> The great *œuvre* of the history of the world is indelibly accompanied by the absence of an *œuvre*, which renews itself at every instant, but which runs unaltered in its inevitable void the length of history: and from before history, as it is already there in the primitive decision, and after it again, as it will triumph in the last word uttered by history.[21]

Well. It is passages such as this one that Foucault surely has in mind when he writes, later in *The Archaeology of Knowledge*, that one of the problems with *History of Madness* was that "it accorded far too great

---

21. *HM* xxxi.

a place, and a very enigmatic one too, to what I called an 'experience,' thus showing to what extent one was still close to admitting an anonymous and general subject of history".[22] Indeed, as I have argued throughout, Foucault takes history (as *res gestae*) too seriously to sustain this particular kind of speculative move.

Having said that, Foucault also understands that to take history seriously is not merely to open up the archive and let the facts speak for themselves and tell us "what happens in history". The facts only speak through us, through our attempts to understand them, and understanding them involves, if we follow Hayden White, a poetic prefiguration of their significance. With this in mind, it is interesting to consider the sentence that immediately follows the one quoted above referring to the triumphal absence running the length of history:

> The plenitude of history is only possible in the space, both empty and peopled at the same time, of all the words without language that appear to anyone who lends an ear, as a dull sound from beneath history, the obstinate murmur of a language talking *to itself*—without any speaking subject and without an interlocutor, wrapped up

22. *AK* 16; translation modified.

in itself, with a lump in its throat, collapsing before it ever reaches any formulation and returning without a fuss to the silence that it never shook off. The charred root of meaning.[23]

This passage, I would suggest, is much more evocative of a permanent concern in Foucault's sense of history, expressed logically in his commitment to a principle of rarity as discussed in the last chapter, but also as evidenced in his particular sensibility as this was discussed in connection with "The Lives of Infamous Men". This sensibility to his own prefiguration of the historical field is manifest here in his attempt to show how what we take to be history emerges and is shaped as specific and specified *possibilities* that themselves are not and cannot be exhausted in the *actual* "system of rules" that history installs as evidence of itself. Thus his evocation here of "words without language" (the possibility of language), "the dull sound beneath history" (the possibility of history, in the Heideggerian sense explored in the last chapter, the "free letting-be of disclosedness") "collapsing before it ever reaches any formulation" (the "installation of systems of rules" excluding possibilities as it realizes/actualizes itself). I emphasize here

---

23. *HM* xxxi–xxxii.

the notion of possibility because it seems to me to be a key element in what I take to be Foucault's keen *modal sensibility* (a sense of how the possible struggles through its contingent manifestations with the imposition of structures deemed necessary). Witness the very next paragraph which draws out the poetic prefigurative expressiveness he has just articulated, where he writes, "the perception that Western man has of his own time and space allows a structure of refusal to appear, on the basis of which a discourse is denounced as not being language, a gesture as not being an *œuvre*, a figure as having no rightful place in history".[24]

In what follows, then, I propose to examine some of the key moves in *History of Madness* that track the appearance of this "structure of refusal" within the text by singling out how this "perception" of what Foucault calls "Western man" can be seen as that exercised by the "cunning of reason" as expressed in Hegel's philosophy of history. And the principal feature that will be stressed is how the "cunning" of reason appropriates madness in order better to ensure its own self-development, or, put another way, to ensure its development as *history*. That is, I will emphasize in my read-

---

24. *HM* xxxii.

ing of *History of Madness* a basic *modal* point that Foucault expresses as follows: reason, as a structure of refusal,

> is constitutive of what is sense and non-sense, or rather of that reciprocity through which the one is bound to the other; it alone can account for the general fact that in our culture there can be no reason without madness, even though the rational knowledge that we have of madness reduces it and disarms it by lending it the slender status of pathological accident. *The necessity of madness* throughout the history of the West is linked to that decisive action that extracts a significant language from the background noise and its continuous monotony, a language which is transmitted and culminates in time; it is, in short, linked to the *possibility of history.*[25]

***

Foucault begins his *History of Madness* by directing our attention to the space left open by the disappearance of leprosy at the end of the Middle Ages; a space that, structurally speaking, beckons to be filled. Although he uses traditional historical language in his description of the reorganization of the finances of the now-defunct "leper colonies" and compares the French situation with simultaneous developments

---

25. *HM* xxxii.

in other parts of Europe, and even goes so far as to give a causal explanation for the retreat of leprosy (due to the end of the Crusades and thus contact with Eastern sources), his purpose is not to characterize this change as a particular "event" understood in the traditional historical sense where it would be a question of integrating it within an overall narrative. Rather, he points out that although the space is now empty, it still echoes with the values and images tied to the "figure of the leper", which are basically those of *exclusion*. In other words, the leper may be gone, but the structures and forms of his exclusion remain, right down to the "major form of a rigorous division, at the same time social exclusion and spiritual reintegration".[26]

In order to illustrate this "division", Foucault, in the first part of the book, which discusses the Renaissance period, contrasts what he calls the *tragic* experience of madness evidenced especially in many of the paintings of the period, like those of Bosch and Brueghel, with what he calls a *critical* experience of madness as expressed in literary and philosophical treatises.

Foucault maintains that there is considerable coherence between different paint-

---

26. *HM* 6.

ings illustrating the themes of madness
in the period. What they revealed was a
split between language and image, which
he claims is made evident, for example,
through the demise of gothic symbolism:
the symbols had lost their sense as well as
the whole discursive background which
guaranteed that sense. That is (and here
one should have Bosch's paintings in
mind), the sense was gone but the symbols remained, unanchored, unhinged
and

> little by little fell silent, ceasing to speak,
> to recall or instruct. The forms remained
> familiar, but all understanding was lost,
> leaving nothing but a fantastical presence;
> and freed from the wisdom and morality it
> was intended to transmit, the image began
> to gravitate around its own insanity.[27]

Cut loose from traditional forms of knowledge, the meaning of these paintings

> was no longer read in an immediate per-
> ception, and accordingly, objects ceased
> to speak directly: between the knowledge
> that animated the figures of objects and
> the forms they were transformed into, a
> divide began to appear, opening the way
> for a symbolism more often associated
> with the world of dreams. . . . But dreams,

---

27. *HM* 16–17.

senselessness and unreason could slip all too easily into this excess of meaning. Symbolic figures easily become nightmarish silhouettes.[28]

For Foucault, one must see in these "mad images. . . an expression of hidden Renaissance worries about the menacing secrets of the world, and it was those fears that gave these fantastic images such coherence and lent them such power".[29]

Now, contrast the darkness and disorder and fear evoked in these images with what one finds in the literary, philosophical and moral treatises of the period, which of course are the privileged venues for the self-expression of *reason*. What the former expressed with great dramatic, if uneasy, force, the latter characterizes as *folly*, which might be characterized as madness minus the fascination it exerts. That is, one finds in the writings of Renaissance philosophers an attempt to deal with the concern and worries provoked by consideration of the forces of madness to speak of them as expressive of something they called "folly", which itself speaks not of the secrets of the world, "but rather about man and the truth about himself that he

---

28. *HM* 17.
29. *HM* 21.

can perceive".[30] The threat to reason still exists, but in a move that will prove to be characteristic, that threat is internalized in a way that allows it to be better controlled, principally by refusing or rejecting its tragic dimension.

Let us examine how "cunning" this particular move is. First of all, reason accepts the fact that folly can and does, on occasion, "speak the truth"; but the purpose of this move is to tie folly *to* reason such that from now on "madness [or folly] and reason enter into a perpetually reversible relationship which implies that all madness has its own reason by which it is judged and mastered, and all reason has its madness in which it finds its own derisory truth".[31] Instead of being feared, folly is ascribed a *value* which consists precisely in reason's recognition of it as a sign of its *own* limitations. Reason assimilates folly into itself, and thereby triumphs over it, because "it places folly at the very heart of its own work, designating it as a movement in reason's own nature".[32] One can look at Bosch's paintings and rather than feel oneself confronted with a menacing, tragic experience of the world, one can gleefully

---

30. *HM* 23.

31. *HM* 29.

32. *HF* 46; my translation.

laugh at the absurdity of it. Reason has cunningly removed for us madness as a threat. Even more than this, reason has thereby better assured its own *self*-development. Foucault describes the result like this: "now the truth of folly (or madness) is nothing other than the victory of reason and its definitive mastery; for the truth of madness is to be within reason, to be a figure of reason, a force, almost a need so that reason can better assure itself".[33]

***

That was the Renaissance. As already mentioned, the focus of *History of Madness* is on the Classical Age or the Age of Reason. When characterized as an "Age" in traditional and pedagogical historiography, emphasis is placed on a—more or less—integrated development of key features of social life which include the growing importance of the explanatory models of the natural sciences in their appeal to mathematical reasoning (which implied an increasingly problematic relationship with ecclesiastical authorities); an increasingly market-driven economy of trade requiring the development of forms of statecraft that rendered much more complex the rule of

---

33. *HF* 47; my translation. "*car la vérité de la folie, c'est d'être intérieure à la raison, d'en être une figure, une force et comme un besoin momentané pour mieux s'assurer d'elle-même.*"

sovereign powers and the justificatory role
of notions of divine right; and a valorization of the individual as against the roles
defined by the traditional feudal hierarchi-
cal order, and along with this what might
be called a "principle of subjectivity" which,
captured in Descartes' *cogito ergo sum*, instituted a new way of relating to a world
increasingly described in terms of "objectivity", that is, not in terms of a traditional
order as sanctioned by ordained authority,
but rather through a knowing subjectivity.
That this was an Age of Reason meant that
all of these developments could be seen as
linked by the growing importance and use
of the powers of reasoning that was said
to belong to human beings in themselves,
however they might relate these powers to
conceptions of divinity.

Foucault's purpose in *History of Madness*
is not to take up or contribute to this traditional narrative by somehow placing
"madness" within it. Rather, his aim is to
show how the Age of Reason itself, in its
own self-understanding, constituted for
itself something he will identify as "unreason" as it deals with the threats posed to its
nascent order.

If the threat that haunted the Renaissance,
at least as evidenced in some of the paintings it produced, was more felt than articulated, more sensed than said, the threat at

the beginning of the Classical Age, the fear
that Foucault has us note is much more
concrete, much more palpable, as it takes
the form of a growing unruly crowd "where
peasants thrown off their land met desert-
ers and redundant soldiers, poor students,
the sick and the unemployed".[34] The disorderliness that all of these people manifest
invites a response and Foucault singles out
the Royal Edict of 1656, establishing the
Hôpital General, as a response to this general threat of disorder. One sees through it
the establishment of a new relation between
the sovereign and the people, between the
burgeoning nation-state and the identification of the individuals that make it up, an
establishment of a new system of obligation
between the idle (unemployed) and the
social order: "he had the right to be nour-
ished, but he had to accept the physical
and moral constraint of confinement".[35]
Confinement, with its wide and hetero-
geneous mandate, begins. According to
Foucault, who coupled it with the establishment of workhouses in England and
Zuchthaüser in German-speaking countries
(a coupling criticized by some historians, a
point I shall return to below), this represented a Europe-wide response to an eco-

---

34. *HM* 63.
35. *HM* 64; translation modified.

nomic crisis, though he insisted that it was in fact often repeated in times of crisis well into the eighteenth century.

The functioning of these "confining" practices was not restricted to periods of economic upheaval:

> outside of times of crisis, confinement took on another meaning, and its repressive aspects were soon paralleled by a second use. It was no longer simply a question of hiding away the unemployed, but now also of giving them work which could serve the interests and prosperity of all. The cycle was clear: in times of high wages and full employment, they provided a low-cost workforce, while in a slump they absorbed the unemployed, and protected society against unrest and riots.[36]

Foucault is quick to note, at this point, that this "economic" dimension of the issue should not be understood or evaluated in terms of the efficiency or efficacy of the response of "confinement". Such a linking of "efficiency" and "economic activity" would be anachronistic. The response here is to a disorderliness that is framed in specifically moral and ethical terms that placed value on work itself as work, not on productivity. Work was seen as a panacea,

---

36. *HM* 66.

as the rightful activity of "fallen man". It was not the fruits of labour that counted, but labour itself. The point that Foucault would like us to see and appreciate is that the idle have replaced the leper on the moral horizon, to be replaced in time by the insane; however, at this point, the "mad" are interned, not because they are mad but because they, like the others, are idle.

As mentioned above, some historians have criticized Foucault's use of this notion of "confinement" insofar as it leads him to treat in a single way the very different practices in different countries with regard to the treatment of the unemployed. While the "great confinement" in Paris might have occurred, to include the development of workhouses and *Zuchthaüser* as responses to local conditions as part of such a repressive movement is not warranted by closer attention to the historical record. This criticism of historians is echoed by many philosophical critics. For example, Cousins and Hussein offered this general assessment of *History of Madness* in their overview of Foucault's work:

> A central thesis of the book is that Classical internment was not based on what may now seem the ignorance of distinctions between sin, crime, poverty, misconduct

and physical and mental illness, but on a perception in which such distinctions were not pertinent, that is, their perception of species of "Unreason." And that the perception implicit in the Classical internment was clear and coherent. The first part of the thesis, which we regard as more important, does not require attributing coherence to the category of "Unreason," which is what Foucault seems to do in some general passages of the book.[37]

While this critique can be seen as echoing to some extent Foucault's self-critique cited above concerning how in writing *History of Madness*, he was "still close to admitting an anonymous and general *subject* of history",[38] I do not think it sufficiently appreciates the *principle* at stake here. For it is indeed *central* to Foucault's work on madness to identify the category of Unreason as this defines the basic *movement* of thought within the Classical Age as it constitutes itself as "Reason". In one of the general passages Cousins and Hussein are surely referring to, Foucault is quite explicit about what he is after. It is not only "now" that the principles governing the confinement of so many different kinds of

---

37. Mark Cousins and Althar Hussein, *Michel Foucault* (London: Macmillan, 1984).

38. *AK* 16; my emphasis.

people seem obscure to "us"; this was also the case at the end of the eighteenth century (that is, the end of the Classical Age) when John Howard toured the various places of "confinement" (prisons, gaols and hospitals):

> He was indignant at what he found, his philanthropic instincts shocked that common criminals were locked up with young men who had showed themselves to be spend-thrifts, or troubled the peace of their family, with vagrants or with the insane. His reaction was proof perhaps that a certain category of order in the classical age had lost its obviousness; suddenly confinement, which had sprung up with such rapidity and spontaneity across Europe, no longer seemed so obviously right. After 150 years, confinement appeared to be an ill-conceived blend of heterogeneous elements. Yet at its origins, *its unity must have been self-evident*, justifying the haste with which it was brought into effect. Between the varied forms that it took and the classical age there must be a *principle of coherence*, which it is wrong to ignore under the scandalous mask of the pre-Revolutionary sensibility. What was the reality targeted by the confinement of an entire sector of the population who almost overnight found themselves locked

up and banished far more rigorously than the lepers of the Middle Ages? We do well to remember that within a few years of its opening its doors, the Hôpital Général in Paris was home to more than 6,000 people, which was approximately 1 per cent of the population. For that to happen, a Europe-wide social sensibility must have almost imperceptibly taken shape, probably over many years beforehand, until suddenly it became manifest in the second half of the·seventeenth century. It was that sensi-bility that suddenly isolated the category destined to people these places of confine-ment. To our eyes, the population desig-nated to fill the space long left empty by lepers seems a strange amalgam, but what appears to us as a confused sensibility was evidently a clearly articulated perception to the mind of the classical age. And it is this mode of perception that needs to be addressed for any understanding of the sensibility to madness of the period we often term the age of Reason.[39]

I have quoted this passage at this length because it neatly captures what I take to be Foucault's approach to history (and, I am arguing, his contribution to our own sense of history), perhaps better than the

---

39. *HM* 54; my emphasis.

different methodological "innovations" (archaeology, genealogy, problematization) focused on by critics and defenders of Foucault's work. History, both as a field of investigation and as an intellectual engagement, is constituted through (different) *sensibilities* that, as they are taken up systematically in thought (through various discursive practices), articulate perceptions and give shape to particular mindsets that make sense of the world in particular ways. These mindsets and the perceptions they allow and, indeed, sanction and promote have evidently changed over time as sensibilities themselves have changed. What we see in this play of sensibilities and the mindsets that are constituted through the effort to make sense of and deal with a world is "the installation of systems of rules" we discussed in the last chapter, as particular forms of *errance*, particular forms of insistences that "adroitly forget and mistake [themselves] constantly anew". That is, when Foucault in this passage speaks of the "principle of coherence" that informs "a clearly articulated perception" which appears to us as a confused sensibility, he is in effect tracking a particular mode of *insisting* which we do not immediately recognize because of our own modes of insisting informed by different sensibilities.

Let me unpack some of these claims further before returning to *History of Madness* because of their importance for my general concern with the philosophy of history's relevance to our attempts to make sense of our unfolding lives.

As Hayden White reminded us in the Introduction, our relationship to something we call "history" is by no means straightforward and self-evident. We can see this even in our own personal appreciation of our own individual pasts. He reminds us that accessing the past from a present, either through memory or documentary interpretation or any other kind of "archival" work, is always poetically prefigured (for White, principally through the language we appeal to in our attempt— and desire—to make sense of the past). We can call this "poetic prefiguration" the particular sensibility that shapes our engagements, including the engagement to make sense of both the past and our unfolding lives.[40] As we engage the past,

---

40. And the claim I am making in this book is that the philosophy of history, as a particular engagement, attempts to see how making sense of the past helps us make better sense of our unfolding lives. It is possible that such an engagement will bear little fruit. But given that our unfolding lives, as unfolding, carry within them some

we do so through the particularities of
our sensibility; but insofar as we do so
engage, we articulate particular perceptions and appeal to particular principles of
coherence that mark our engagements as
attempts to make sense of the past.

Part of the value of Foucault's work
is that the impact it has on (some of) us
demonstrates in a powerful way how this
is so; how our sensibilities, as they engage
the world through their particular modes
of insisting, articulate principles of coherence governing perceptions that, in their
particularity, show themselves to be kinds
of "mistakings and forgettings", to use
Heidegger's language. However, rather
than continue to use Heidegger at this
point, I would like to take up again (and
will develop further in the next chapter)
the figure of Hegel in order to help us
make sense of this unfolding.

I cited as an exergue to this chapter a
famous passage from Hegel that insists
that "Whoever looks at the world rationally
will find that it in turn assumes a rational
aspect; the two exist in a reciprocal relationship." I think I have already shown,
and will continue in a moment to demonstrate further, how such a principle can be

---

kind of relation to the past, it makes sense
to try and see.

said to be at the heart of Foucault's *History of Madness*, insofar as in this work Foucault shows how "reason" ensures its own sense of itself, its own self-development, through its cunning appropriation of that which it perceives as posing a threat. But before returning to that demonstration, I would like to point out how Hegel's articulation of this basic principle animating his own work reflects what we have been discussing here. When Hegel refers to "Whoever looks at the world rationally", he is implying, of course, that not everyone does so look at the world, but more importantly for my purposes here, he is tying a rational approach to the particularity or specificity of a *perception*, which in turn (and in the terms we have been using) implies a prefiguring sensibility. In saying this, then, Hegel is actually articulating the principle of coherence arising out of his own sensibility to what a general consideration reveals, namely the expenditure of human passions, including "the historical consequences of their violence and the irrationality which is associated with them (and even more so with the good intentions and worthy aims)".[41] However, Hegel's sensibility to history does not confine him to

---

41. Hegel, *Lectures on the Philosophy of World History* 68.

simply *noting* such consequences, but commits him to *thinking* them; and it is this commitment to thought that points him not only to the consideration of passions spent but to the accomplishments of art, religion and philosophy and through that consideration to the articulation of a principle of coherence that *insists* on looking at the world rationally and thereby encounters a world that exhibits itself as rational.

Those who would immediately reject such a principle on the grounds of an alternative principle that would see the world as indifferent to such rational projections of course miss Hegel's point about the reciprocal relationship that animates our appreciation of the world. And this is a point that Foucault does *not* miss. Indeed, as my own reading of Foucault's *History of Madness* insists, it is remarkable the extent to which Foucault actually appreciates the reciprocal relationship between an organizing perception and a structured experience of the world that such a principle articulates. In fact, as I will continue to insist in my reading of Foucault's histories, there is in Foucault very much of Hegel's insistence on the reciprocity of perception and world, of principle and actuality, in a word, of the constitutive character of the *movement* of thought. A basic difference between Foucault and Hegel, though, is

that Hegel's appreciation of the work of
thought in its movement is, in the language
of commentators such as Robert Pippin,
strictly internalist in an "absolute" sense,[42]
that is, in the sense that, for Hegel, thinking about thought necessarily involves
thinking the whole, which, as thought or
thinking, can only be about itself, about
its own self-unfolding. Otherwise, it would
in fact be trying to think something outside of itself as in some sense determining it, which implies in this regard that
it is *not* thinking the very thing it is *trying*
to think, namely, its own ability to think
itself. Recognizing this "contradiction" is
one way Hegel describes the very movement of thought. Whereas Foucault does
not insist on attempting to grasp the movement of thought for its own sake (Foucault
does not attempt to develop a "science of
logic"), but is rather interested—and here
we note the Heideggerian influence—in
tracking that movement according to a
principle of "rarity", that is, as particular
manifestations within an open field.[43]

---

42. Robert B. Pippin, *Hegel's Idealism:
   The Satisfactions of Self-Consciousness*
   (Cambridge: Cambridge UP, 1989).
43. Another way to characterize the principle
   of rarity as referencing as it challenges
   Hegel's project is to see it as rejecting the
   "absolute standpoint" which, following

Foucault's point (or at least the point emphasized in this reading) is that this movement-of-thought-that-calls-itself-reason accomplishes its end (its self-consolidation, as it were) through dealing with that which is deemed threatening. The threat keenly felt by the Classical Age was the idleness apparent in parts of the population. That threat was dealt with through the act of actually confining people perceived in a *particular* way, that is, according to a particularity that Foucault is attempting to identify. That is, like Hegel, Foucault sees in the very notion of particularity a movement of thought determining its object. He notes that "confinement did not only play the negative role of exclusion; it also played a positive organizing role".[44] Foucault wants to show that

---

Joseph C. Flay's discussion, presupposes that "*the referents for the principle or ground of totality and for the principle or ground of intelligibility are one and the same*". *Hegel's Quest for Certainty* (Albany: SUNY Press, 1984) 252. The principle of rarity asserts that appreciation of the intelligibility of the world as it manifests itself historically does not in itself presuppose the sense we have of the totality of the world. In this way, the intelligibility of the past can radically contrast with our present experience of the world.

44. *HM* 82.

within this movement of confinement one
can begin to make out a reorganization of
values and norms which make the various
faces of those confined gradually take on
the same expression: the face of Unreason
as this appeared to the bourgeois family and its world.[45] That is, what Foucault
is describing then is not only "reason's"
response to an exterior threat (the idle
and unruly masses) but the articulation
of a perception of what might be considered a much more dangerous and subtle
interior threat (the transgressions within

---

45. This feature of the Classical Age, the role
     that families played in the (re)structuring
     and policing of the social field, is some-
     thing that long remained with Foucault
     and is captured in an interesting way in his
     archival presentation, with Arlette Farge, of
     the use of the "*lettres de cachets*" that families
     used when confronted with what was con-
     sidered as "disorderly conduct" and served
     as an indication of what was required of the
     forces of order, cf. *Le Désordre des familles.*
     Lettres de cachet des archives de la Bastille
     (Paris: Gallimard/Julliard, 1982). This
     book is also a good example of Foucault's
     continuing commitment not to speak for
     others and yet, at the same time, to give
     voice to that within himself that remained
     sensitive to the plight and lives of such
     others. Consider the interview with Arlette
     Farge, Foucault and Farge.

the family order). The result of confinement is the installation, as it were, of what
Foucault calls Unreason as a contrast to
what is deemed to be Reason and Order.
Unreason, which had previously been a
felt (and feared) dimension of the world,
is now *localized*, immobilized, held at
arm's length; it can now be watched over,
observed.

***

What we are made to see next is how,
within the structures of confinement (reason's response to the threat of unreason),
the mad are eventually singled out. The
Classical Age will call them "*les furieux*",
that is, those whose violence and disorderly
conduct is neither a result of sickness nor
crime. While this will certainly be enough
to confine them throughout the Classical
Age, insofar as it determines itself through
a moral sensibility that interns such misfits,
such an internment is *not* clearly justified
outside of such a moral sensibility.

If the mad, along with other misfits, are
excluded from the social order through
confinement, what happens *within* the
structures of that confinement? Within
these structures that, Foucault tells us,
are spaces of confinement somewhere
between hospitals and correctional institutions, that is, spaces watched over according to perceptions articulated *between* the

medical and legal articulations that establish them, the mad are singled out because
they fall through the cracks, as it were.
That is, the mad are, within the structures
of confinement, subject to a double alienation that will ultimately designate them
as "mentally ill". They are alienated from
the developing legal framework of society
because they are judged incompetent; at
the same time they are alienated from the
social framework insofar as their "scandal-
ous" behaviour is considered unacceptable. Neither a legal nor social subject, the
madman takes on a threatening singularity
that "reason" will need to respond to.

If *History of Madness* were to be understood as a more or less standard work of
history, as it sometimes is,[46] then it would
be read (and assessed) as an account of the
development of the modern conception of
mental health and mental illness. And this
account (if it were not to be merely a ram-
bling sampling of the historical record)
would generally be built around the
attempt to come as close as possible to the
necessary conditions that gave rise to and
permitted such a development. However,
to read the history of madness in this way
is to read it from a point of view that treats

---

46. Cf. J.-G. Merquior, *Foucault* (London:
   Fontana, 1985) 26–27.

the present, in the form of the established
contemporary (operative) conception of
mental health and mental illness (which
include its structuring debates and dissen-
sions) as the *stopping point*, as it were. The
novelty of Foucault's approach is precisely
not to describe the gradual development
and establishment of the contemporary
operative conception in order to make
sense of it, but rather to describe its (as it
turns out) discontinuous development and
establishment *over and against* something
other than itself, to which he gives the
general name of Unreason (*la déraison*),
here understood in a broader sense than
the "perception" developed within the
Classical Age.[47] The space Foucault occupies, which enables him here to propose
such an approach, is one that recognizes
that reason has not been completely successful in silencing "unreason". This is the
point of his periodic reference to names
such as Nietzsche, Nerval, Artaud and
Van Gogh. What he is doing when he lists
these names is to remind us that madness

---

47. A good discussion of the different senses
    and applications of the concept of "dérai-
    son" as it relates to madness ("la folie")
    can be found in Frédéric Gros, *Foucault
    et la Folie* (Paris: Presses universitaires de
    France, 1997) 52–53.

is not fully captured by reason's attempt to understand it; indeed "it" (madness) can never be fully captured, according to Foucault, insofar, he claims, as "the meaning of madness for any age, our own included, can never be covered entirely by the theoretical unity of a project: it lies instead in its torn presence".[48]

Indeed, I would argue that part of the force and lasting significance of *History of Madness* is the manner in which it reminds us of this "torn presence"[49] and, if Foucault proposes a history, it is as much a challenge to what we tend to expect of our histories as it is an attempt to account for it. Here again, Foucault displays for us what I have been calling his specifically *modal* sensibility in the sense that too often we expect our histories to tell us how the present came to be. Or, put another way, we expect history to give us an account of the processes that have led from point A to point B, where point B is a fixed conception of the present (for example, madness understood as various forms of mental illness). And while this appears to be more or less harmless in itself, it becomes less

---

48. *HM* 164.

49. I think this notion of a "torn presence" is at the heart of Foucault's commitment to a principle of "rarity".

so when the processes so described are
framed within a mode of thought that
would characterize them in terms of some
kind of necessity. Such an appeal to necessity, put crudely, would go something like
this: given these conditions, what occurred
was *bound* to happen, could not *but* happen. Historical "explanations" could then
be claimed and assessed according to the
degree of necessity they could be said to
demonstrate.

Now, Foucault is also concerned with
elaborating historical conditions: in this
particular case, the historical conditions
relevant to differing conceptions of madness, though unlike the traditional histories, he does not see in the past the slow
development of our current conception of
madness. Instead, by reminding us of the
figures of Nietzsche, Nerval, Artaud and
Van Gogh, he indicates, beside our current conception of mental illness, the existence of this other *possibility* of madness,
and it is within the space, as it were, of the
awareness of this "torn presence" that he
formulates his historical question: given
the *possibility* (and not the necessity) of a
conception of mental illness (which hardly
adequately grasps the figures of Nietzsche,
Nerval, Artaud and Van Gogh), what are
the *particular* conditions which have permitted its dominance? It is a description

of those conditions that make up the substance of *History of Madness*.

Let us return to the text. One of the things Foucault seeks to show in Part III is that the "isolation" of the mad did not, as the traditional story would have it, lead to their "liberation" but rather that their "liberation" was, in effect, a particular step in isolating their identification as "insane". In other words, the response to the "singular" threat of the mad became the articulation of the concept of *insanity*. That is, the isolation and specification of the madman permits the mutation and transformation of the notion of confinement (which loses its relevance) into that of the *asylum*.

The degree of difference between these institutional forms is perhaps best illustrated by the degree of danger each contains. Confinement is an attempt to remove the threat and force of Unreason, which in essence opposed the order and structure of the Classical self-conception of the world. The asylum, for its part, corrects "unreasonableness", the inversion of sense manifested by the mad and, in that sense, is not concerned with safeguarding the structures of the world per se; the concern rather is with correcting the "false" picture the insane have of the world. The threat posed by the mad is not overcome by forcibly suppressing the mad by confining them; they need simply to be supervised and their behavior controlled.

Interestingly, this became possible only once the threat was sufficiently reduced and isolated to permit such a move. What Foucault sets out to show is how this isolation was effected not by anyone in particular but by the very structures of confinement themselves, that is, those structures and the particular historical circumstances that permitted them.

To counter what has been called the reform "myth" of the treatment of the mad that would have it that at the beginning of the Modern Age (as distinct from the Classical Age) the mad were "liberated" from their chains and treated more humanely, Foucault discusses the prior "reform" of the practices of confinement themselves that occurred during the economic crisis between 1765 and 1770. The confinement of the mad did indeed become perceived as unjust, but "only *for the others*".[50] What is happening during this period is a reassessment of the "economic" and "social" character of the population as a whole, which includes a reassessment of the general attitude towards *poverty*. Briefly put, poverty is now too widespread to continue to be faulted

---

50. *HM* 401.

morally; its conceptualization shifts to the economic in such a way that confinement came to be seen as

> a clumsy error, and an economic one at that: there was no sense in trying to suppress poverty by taking it out of the economic circuit and providing for a *poor population* by charitable means... What was required was to palliate the high cost of products with cheap labour, and to make up for their scarcity by a new industrial and agricultural effort. The only reasonable remedy was to reinsert the population in the circuit of production, being sure to place labour in areas where manpower was most scarce. The use of paupers, vagabonds, exiles and émigrés of any description was one of the secrets of wealth in the competition between nations.[51]

But, of course, it couldn't merely be a question of dismantling *in toto* the structures of confinement. Distinctions needed to be made, especially between the useful and the useless poor, which translated into a distinction between "the positive element that was indigence, and the burden of sickness".[52] A further distinction was also being promoted, especially amongst those liberals

---

51. *HM* 409.

52. *HM* 411.

and economists who were gaining ascendancy in the period, where the "healthy poor" are put back into circulation, as it were, while the "sickly poor", rather than continue to be afforded public assistance through their "confinement" within hospitals and other institutions, were sent home to be with their families where

> in addition to the meticulous care they received at home, patients were not affected by the depressing spectacle of a hospital that was generally regarded "as a temple of death". The melancholy of the spectacle that surrounded them, the risk of contagion and distance from loved ones, were all factors considered to aggravate a patient's condition, and result in diseases that did not occur spontaneously in nature, but seemed creations of the hospitals themselves.[53]

In other words, everyone is released except for the criminals and the mad.

But this raises a key question: are the mad criminal or sick? Actually, the formulation of the question itself points to its eventual solution. The problem and the solution, according to Foucault, was this:

> Were the mad then to be treated simply as prisoners, and placed in a prison environ-

---

53. *HM* 415.

ment, or should they be treated as invalids
who had no relatives, and who therefore
needed a quasi-family environment created around them? ... Tuke and Pinel
combined both these approaches in defining the archetypal modern asylum.[54]

Because most commentaries focus precisely on this development as central to
the work, there is no exegetical need to
go into the details of the establishment of
the asylum by Tuke in America and Pinel
in France. (We will have occasion to discuss Foucault's own reassessment of his
views of *History of Madness* in his Collège
de France lectures, *Le Pouvoir Psychiatrique*,
when we turn to his increased interest in
thinking, less in terms of *reason* and that
which it excludes, than in terms of the
notion of power in Chapter Five.) In terms
of the cunning used by reason in order to
remove what threatens it and thereby better ensure its own self-realization, this last
development would appear to be the most
successful because the most subtle. This
is because the issue no longer revolves
around questions of reason and order but
concerns the rights and freedom of rational individuals. The subtlety of the new
situation is revealed in the fact that, so long
as Reason and Order were given prime

54. *HM* 427.

significance, Unreason and Disorder, as
their opposites, would always exist as an
underlying threat, their "suppression"
(i.e., confinement) notwithstanding.
However, once reason is intimately linked
with *freedom*, then the absence of reason
implies an absence of freedom. Thus, we
move from nature to freedom, or from the
animality of madness to the restraining of
the insane, or put more forcefully, from
chains to the straitjacket because now "in
madness, the experience was no longer of
an absolute conflict between reason and
unreason, but rather of a play—always
relative, always mobile—between freedom
and its limits".[55] What reason now creates is a carefully controlled environment
where the insane, under constant surveillance are allowed to "speak their minds",
as it were, but *to* reason. In other words,
reason—again cunningly—provides "a far
more effective means of mastering madness than its previous enslavement to the
forms of unreason. Confinement, in the
light of these developments, could offer
madness the luxury of liberty—as it was
now enslaved, and stripped of its deepest
powers."[56] Indeed, not only is madness
(or the *déraison* that has become insanity)

55. *HM* 439.
56. *HM* 443.

no longer capable of speaking other than for and to reason, but by being objectified (within the disciplinary matrix of psychology), madness enables reason to pursue an objective view of *itself* and its own continued self-development.

Or, to put it otherwise, in its concern with "mental health" (as progressively defined through its treatment of "mental illness"), reason allows itself to develop in such a way that it remains—in Hegel's language—"unscathed", that is, "it keeps itself in the background, untouched and unharmed, and sends forth the particular interests of passion [i.e. the mad] to fight and wear themselves out in its stead".

What Foucault has accomplished in this history—and indeed this is why many keep returning to this extraordinary book—is to cast archival light not only on the claims of reason's self-development, the ways in which the "universal emerges", but also on the "very conflict and destruction of particular things" that such emergence requires. The work reminds us how the development of reason to which we commit ourselves in various ways (through the processes of normalization that our actions insist upon) involve people—people like us—who, as Hegel put it, "must pay the penalty and suffer the loss".

Foucault's particular sensibility has us consider the question raised by this loss. That sensibility would lead him to track reason's self-development and point to a space of possibility that challenges it, the space left open by people like Nietzsche, Nerval, Artaud and Van Gogh, where "by the madness which interrupts it, a work of art opens a void, a moment of silence, a question without answer, provokes a breach without reconciliation where the world is forced to question itself".[57]

It is this particular sensibility and the work it inspires that will continue to urge us to look more closely at what exactly is involved in those views that would see in history a progressive realization of reason and invite us to problematize its claims to increasing our freedom.

---

57. Foucault, *Madness and Civilization* 288.
    I believe this translation is more faithful to
    the original: "*par la folie qui l'interrompt, une
    œuvre ouvre un vide, un temps de silence, une
    question sans réponse, elle provoque un déchire-
    ment sans réconciliation où le monde est bien
    contraint de s'interroger*". Foucault, *HF* 663.

V

A Contrastive History of Punitive Reason

They usually lie just on the outskirts of our cities, neither surrounded by trees nor shrouded in mist. On the contrary, were it not for the barbed wire fences, the occasional signs and the lookout tower, one might think that this compound of buildings was a school, or a home for the elderly, or perhaps even government offices, given the price of real estate in the city. But a closer look at the familiar architectural setting reveals its particularity: these buildings make up what has come to be called a penitentiary. The prison. We drive by, acknowledging its presence, the necessity of it. And then we do not give it a second thought.

The necessity of its presence? We are said to live in a free society. A free society is a society governed by the rule of law. Laws that are broken must not go unpunished. Punishment involves, normally, a fine and/or imprisonment. That is the logic of it, but where is the necessity? Why, to punish those who break the law, do we lock them up in prisons? And the question is not whether there are alternatives; fines alone are an example, community work is another. The question is rather: where does this idea come from, when did it arise? Not: why are there prisons, but: what is the problem for which the prison is a solution?

Is this a philosophical question? Or is it a historical question? Consider the title: *Surveiller et Punir: La Naissance de la Prison.*[1] The birth of the prison. Definitely a historical problem. But what about the main title: Do these words represent concepts? Or practices? A philosophical problem. So which is it: philosophy or history?

My examination of this work in this chapter will emphasize the manner in which it is indeed as Foucault claims it is: a philosophical fragment "put to work in a historical field of problems".[2] I have

---

1. (Paris: Gallimard, 1975). Published in the collection "Bibliothèque des histoires" under the direction of Pierre Nora. In English: Michel Foucault, *Discipline and Punish: The Birth of the Prison,* trans. Alan Sheridan (New York: Vintage Books, 1977), hereafter referred to as "*DP*".

2. Already quoted, Foucault, *Power* 224.

been suggesting throughout this book that it is useful and interesting to consider the production of Foucault's historical works as indeed "fragments" of an exploded—but nevertheless systematic—understanding of the course of history as the self-development of reason aimed at freedom: articulated most forcefully in Hegel's philosophy of history.[3] The last chapter, on the history of madness, presented a challenge to reason's self-developing conception by showing how that development seeks to assure itself through its attempt to *grasp* and "take up" the "torn presence" of madness. This chapter will continue to focus on this grasping movement understood as "reason", but now with specific reference to the *telos* or end of the movement understood as "freedom". *Discipline and Punish* will be read as a concrete, or "inverted", analysis of this general conception of our history.

---

3. As I argued in Chapter Three, despite Foucault's critical assessment of this conception of the relation between history and reason found in Hegel's philosophy of history, his work can be read as a kind of continuation of it inasmuch as it pursues an "a-theistic theodicy" bent on accounting for the intelligibility that manifests itself in history through the exercise and effects of power.

Although I am claiming that Hegel's speculative philosophy of history forms an important backdrop for understanding Foucault's "fragmentary" *philosophical* approach, his *historiographical* approach fits quite well with the "*nouvelle histoire*" being developed at the time. This is important in order to understand what he means when he says that he is placing these "fragments" within "a historical field of *problems*". *Discipline and Punish* is not a *narrative* account of "birth" and "rise" of the modern prison as it has taken its place in our institutional landscape. And in that sense *Discipline and Punish* can be seen as implicitly recognizing the distinction made in contemporary historiography between was has come to be called "*histoire-problème*" as opposed to "*histoire-récit*". Rather than simply posing itself as a narrative of past events, historiography recognizes itself as *problem-oriented*. As François Furet has pointed out,[4] such a recognition stems from four related developments. First, historians recognize that their object is not time as such, or even the past as a whole. The historian understands

---

4. *L'Atelier de l'histoire* (Paris: Flammarion, 1982) 76–77. English translation by Jonathan Mandelbaum, *In the Workshop of History* (Chicago: U of Chicago P, 1984).

that his treatment of his object is highly
selective, and that the significance of his
selections depends not on some hypothetical conception of the course of universal
history, but on the particular questions
he is asking. Thus, a history is judged less
on its alleged accuracy to certain "facts"
about what "really" happened, than on the
clear formulation of the problems it sets
out to solve. Second, historians are less
tied to events and their alleged effects and
concern themselves with conceptualizing
networks of significance that cut across
the period in question rather than linking them to a linear series leading up to
the present. This leads to the third point
concerning the historian's responsibility
for developing and "inventing" his own
sources that will enable him to answer his
questions. Finally, this intimate connection between the questions and problems
formulated by the historian and the development of sources meant to answer them
means that the conclusions reached carry
with them their own mode of verification.[5]

Discipline and Punish clearly falls within
this general pattern inasmuch as it is not a

---

5. All of this fits in quite nicely with
   Collingwood's claims for the "autonomy"
   of history with regard to the methods
   of the natural sciences.

narrative of the development of the prison but addresses this development as a "problem". It attempts to analyze the networks of significance surrounding the "birth" of the prison,[6] and it does so by examining not merely matters related to the prison, but matters relating to schools, factories and hospitals insofar as these are relevant to his analysis of what he calls, in his discussion of the importance of Dumézil's "structural" approach, "a transformable system and the conditions under which its transformations are carried out".[7]

But note how Foucault's "problem" is more *philosophical* than "historical" as the latter term is understood by the profession. Here is how he characterizes the book to a group of historians:

> What is "the birth of the prison" all about? French society in a given period?

---

6. The notion of the "birth" of the prison of course is making use of the genealogical notion of "emergence".

7. "Return to History," *EW* 2, 426. In a brief discussion of the importance of Dumézil's approach to historical analysis, Foucault illustrates how, "by showing the schema of transformation of the Irish legend into a Roman narrative, he also reveals the principle of historical transformation of the old Roman society into a state-controlled society".

No. Delinquency in the eighteenth and nineteenth century? No. Prisons in France between 1760 and 1840? Not even this. It is about something more subtle: the well-considered motives, the type of calculation, the "ratio" which was at work during the reform of the penal system when it was decided to introduce, though not without certain modifications, the old practices of imprisonment. In sum, it is a chapter in the history of "punitive reason" [raison punitive]. Why the prison? Why the reutilization of this discredited system of locking-up?[8]

Although Foucault doesn't exploit this expression of "punitive reason", I think it is significant that he uses it in this discussion with a group of historians. To call his book "a chapter" in the history of something called "punitive reason" both situates his work within a generally philosophical approach to history (a history of reason) and gives it its own specificity (focusing on it according to its specifically

8. From Michelle Perrot, ed., *L'impossible prison* (Paris: Seuil, 1980) 29–39. This translation (slightly modified: I translate "*raison punitive*" as "punitive reason" and not "punitive rationale") in Maurice Aymard and Harbans Mukhia, eds., *French Studies in History*, vol. II (New Delhi: Orient Longman, 1990) 327.

"punitive" character as evidenced in the unfolding of history). So Foucault continues his tracking of reason's self-movement, as it were, but now not in contrast to something called "unreason" but according to the particularity of its movement at a specific time such that it effected a basic *transformation* of the way we relate to ourselves as free beings, articulated now in terms of how power is exercised.

It is interesting to note how the movement of Foucault's own thought, from *History of Madness* to *Discipline and Punish*, is marked by this increasing preoccupation with the notion of power (which, of course, is in many ways his "claim to fame"). His first courses at the Collège de France indicate this movement. We have, in the first volume of his *Essential Works*, the summary statements of the courses he taught at the Collège up until 1982 (the last two years are not included). The first year's courses (1970–1971) were given the title "The Will to Knowledge" (which of course will also be the title of the first volume of his *History of Sexuality*). Although obviously Nietzschean in inspiration, I would like to suggest, following up on the Hyppolitian themes discussed in the last chapter of Part I, that this preoccupation with something called the "will to knowledge" can be read as an application of the principle of immanence to the self-movement of thought, but one which inverts the consolidating guarantee in its "absolute" Hegelian incarnation. That is, the self-movement of thought (the fact that thought is not "determined" by anything other than itself) continues to pursue knowledge as a kind of self-realization but now without the "absolute" guarantee at the heart of Hegel's philosophy (which itself served to replace a suspect foundationalism that insufficiently recognized its specifically historical realization). Foucault can be said to be pursuing this question in his development of the notion of *discursive practices* where

> one finds a type of systematicity which is neither logical nor linguistic [i.e. two ahistorical accounts of systematicity R.F.]. Discursive practices are characterized by the demarcation of a field of objects, by the definition of a legitimate perspective for a subject of knowledge, by the setting of norms for elaborating concepts and theories. Hence, each of them presupposes a play of prescriptions that govern exclusions and selections.[9]

Such discursive practices thus play the consolidating role that Hegel's absolute

---

9. Michel Foucault, "The Will to Knowledge," in *Ethics, Subjectivity and Truth: Essential Works of Foucault, 1954–1984*, vol. 1, 10.

knowledge sought to play, but without the ultimately unified character that the latter sought to articulate. It is this lack of any guaranteed self-consolidating unity that makes sense of Foucault's use of the notion of a "will" to knowledge in connection with discursive practices. That is, their manifest, historically determinable

> principles of exclusion and selection—whose presence is multifarious, whose efficacy is concretely demonstrated in practices, and whose transformations are relatively autonomous—do not refer to a (historical or transcendental) subject of knowledge that would invent them one after another or would found them at an original level; they point, rather, to an anonymous and polymorphous will to knowledge, capable of regular transformations and caught up in an identifiable play of dependence.[10]

The point to be emphasized in this notion is that, like the self-movement of Hegel's Concept, we are *caught up* in the historical movement of this "will to knowledge" as it defines different regularities and imposes specific kinds of constraint of what we are made to think, say and do. It is this continuing sense of being *caught up* in the

---

10. Foucault, "The Will to Knowledge" 12.

self-movement of systematic thought that invites consideration of the notion of power as it circulates within the consolidation of different practices. And such a consolidation of different practices in and through the exercise of power gives us an account of history that, I hope to show, helps us make better sense of how history relates to our unfolding lives.

***

I mentioned above that if and when most of us drive by a prison on the outskirts of our cities, we no doubt recognize the necessity of such institutions, but otherwise do not give their reality much thought. In saying this, I am of course speaking of a particular "we", that is, those people who have not had any direct dealings with what we can call, following popular television series, the "justice system". And the reason for this, presumably, is that the "we" in question are made up of what can be called "law-abiding" people. It is because of this "law-abidingness" that "we" can drive by prisons, acknowledge the necessity of them and then give them no (or relatively little) further thought.

This relative lack of thought concerning prisons exhibited by the law-abiding is curious and interesting. It is curious because, after all, any one of us, as we go about doing the things we do, may actually find ourselves in a situation in which we are charged and found guilty of an infraction of the law and face, as a penalty for that infraction, a prison term. Most of us, abiding by the law, won't; but we could. And this is what is interesting: even as we "abide" or believe ourselves to be "abiding" by the law, we can still stand accused and be found guilty and be sentenced to prison. This latter situation would, at least from our point of view, be considered an injustice. But it can still happen. And it does.

I mention this because one of the lasting effects of reading Foucault's *Discipline and Punish* is the realization of the extent to which the development of the prison within our society is linked to this relative indifference of the "law-abiding" citizen to that development and that this is a cause for concern insofar as both are indicative of the movement of history and relate directly to our unfolding lives. Or at least this is what my reading of *Discipline and Punish* will emphasize.

Foucault accomplishes this by writing about the prison in the first place, by discussing its "birth" within the particular context of our present, in a very specific way, one that resembles the kind of work historians do, but remains distinct. In response to questions put to him by a group of historians, he says the following:

In this piece of research on the prisons, as in my other earlier work, the target of analysis wasn't "institutions," "theories" or "ideology," but *practices*—with the aim of grasping the conditions which make these acceptable at a given moment; the hypothesis being that these types of practice are not just governed by institutions, prescribed by ideologies, guided by pragmatic circumstances—whatever role these elements may actually play—but possess up to a point their own specific regularities, logic, strategy, self-evidence and "reason." It is a question of analyzing a "regime of practices"—practices being understood here as places where what is said and what is done, rules imposed and reasons given, the planned and the taken for granted meet and interconnect.[11]

What Foucault examines in *Discipline and Punish* is a regime of practices that have constituted the prison and a "law-abidingness" that largely takes this regime for granted, and shows how they in effect "interconnect".

This use of the notion of practices provides a framework for the unfolding of our lives. We are engaged in many different practices, which means that we are

---

11. In G. Burchell et al., *The Foucault Effect: Studies in Governmentality* (Chicago: U of Chicago P, 1991) 75.

pursuing many different goals by engaging in many different kinds of regular behavior governed by many different kinds of norms (right and wrong ways of going about doing the things that we are engaged in doing). What, it can be asked, holds all of these various norms, goals and regularities together? One might want to say that it is the relative *coherence* of the different goals, norms and regularities that holds these various practices together. Note that this coherence itself should be understood on a different level than the practices themselves because it is not itself a function of goals, norms and regularities of the practices themselves but merely the manner in which these different practices are taken up together (stuck together, as it were).

We might consider this distinction by taking up the notion of the "law-abiding" person mentioned above, the one who recognizes the necessity of a justice system to deal with people who break the law, but otherwise does not think about it. Like everyone else, the "law-abiding" person is engaged in practices. In addition to the various practices such a person is engaged in, is such a person also engaged in a specific practice of "abiding by the law"? Is that a specific practice distinct from the goals, norms and regularities that make up her other practices? It is interesting to see what happens when one does consider "law-abidingness" as a practice, that is, in terms of its own specific regularities, norms and goal. What would be the regularities in abiding by the law as distinct from those regularities that compose other practices? Consider the practice of driving.[12] It includes in its regularities controlling the speed of the vehicle through acceleration and braking. The norms that inform those regularities can include speed limits if one is driving on public roads and not on speed tracks (or the *Autobahn*). Such speed limits are established in law and vary according to jurisdiction. To respect them is as much to abide by the law as it is to engage in the practice of driving. I suspect that most drivers respect them more out of the practice of driving itself, that is, according to the norms and regularities that govern the practice of driving, rather than *add* to their practice of driving, a practice of "abiding by the law". Though, of course, some drivers do: the ones that characteristically drive at the exact posted speed limit. Interestingly, at

---

12. I return here to Todd May's mode of describing practices in terms of their goal, norms and regularities as discusssed in Chapter One above.

least in the areas where I drive, such drivers are the exception rather than the rule. Most drivers drive slightly *over* the posted speed limit, within a variable range; this variability actually forms part of the practice of driving. It clashes, of course, with a practice of "abiding by the law", strictly speaking, but falls within a zone of tolerated "illegality", a notion Foucault stresses and to which we will return below.

But consideration of such clashes between our various practices (and the norms and regularities that govern them) and something like a practice of "abiding by the law" raises the interesting question of the *goal* of the latter. What *is* the "goal" of "abiding by the law" as a practice distinct from our other practices? A Kantian philosopher might say that, insofar as to abide by the law is to act in accordance with the law, and insofar as that law is autonomously and not heteronomously conceived, then the goal of the practice of "abiding by the law" would be to instantiate in one's actions one's full humanity. (Now, wouldn't that be an interesting bumper sticker for those drivers we encounter on the highway driving at *exactly* the posted speed limit?) For most of us, however, insofar as we might be engaged in the distinct practice of "abiding by the law", and not merely respecting the norms and regularities of other practices, the goal is less loftily simply *not to get caught.* That is, if reducing our speed, not jaywalking, declaring all of our sources of income and in my city actually refraining from playing street hockey in the street, form part of the distinct practice of "abiding by the law", then the goal of that practice is to avoid being charged with an infraction and eventually facing a penalty.

All of this suggests that it is indeed possible to consider "abiding by the law" as a distinct practice. But it also suggests that, as a practice, it is more or less incidental to the other practices we are engaged in, as these engage us in their own norms and regularities (driving a car, crossing the road, filing a tax return, playing street hockey). That is, "normally" we are engaged in our various practices and respect the various norms and regularities that are integral to them and it is only to the extent that these practices themselves clash with something called the "law" that we might be expected to engage in the distinct practice of "abiding by the law". It is for this reason that most of us, as I mentioned at the beginning of the chapter, if and when we do drive by a prison, are quite prepared to acknowledge the necessity of its presence, but are just as likely not to give it a second thought.

Foucault's book *Discipline and Punish* challenges us to reconsider this state of affairs, that is, to reconsider the way we actually take up our own practices, which include this practice of "abiding by the law", whose goal is to avoid being charged with an infraction and punished. He does this by examining, more closely than we are "normally" prepared to do, just what it is we are avoiding. The way he does this is by having us confront the practices we are engaged in by giving a genealogical account that traces their "descent" and accounts for their "emergence".

***

The claim is that our "law-abidingness" is a mode of avoiding "punishment" and that the two interconnect in specific ways that not only characterize our "present" but that the "present" also challenges. I think it is important, if one wants to measure the full weight of what Foucault is attempting to do in this work, to see how Foucault makes this particular claim within the context of what he calls "the history of the present", by which he means the tracing of those movements that constitute our "system of actuality"[13] as it manifests itself

---

13. This excellent expression, meant to clarify Foucault's notion of *dispositif,* is offered by Edward F. McGushin in his *Foucault's*

both through its constraining effects and through resistances to those effects. The expression the "history of the present" comes at the end of an important paragraph where Foucault situates his examination of the prison:

> In recent years, prison revolts have occurred throughout the world. There was certainly something paradoxical about their aims, their slogans and the way they took place. They were revolts against an entire state of physical misery that is over a century old: against cold, suffocation and overcrowding, against decrepit walls, hunger, physical maltreatment. But they were also a revolt against model prisons, tranquilizers, isolation, the medical or educational services. Were they revolts whose aims were merely material? Or contradictory revolts: against the obsolete, but also against comfort; against the warders, but also against the psychiatrists? In fact, all these movements—and the innumerable discourses that the prison has given rise to since the early nineteenth century—have been about the body and material things. What has sustained these

---

Askesis: An Introduction to the Philosophical Life (Evanston: Northwestern UP, 2007) 188–89. I will return to this in the next chapter.

discourses, these memories and invectives are indeed those minute material details. One may, if one is so disposed, see them as no more than blind demands or suspect the existence behind them of alien strategies. In fact, they were revolts, at the level of the body, against the very body of the prison. What was at issue was not whether the prison environment was too harsh or too aseptic, too primitive or too efficient, but *its very materiality as an instrument and vector of power*; it is this whole technology of power over the body that the technology of the "soul"—that of educationalists, psychologists and psychiatrists—fails either to conceal or to compensate, for the simple reason that it is one of its tools. I would like to write the history of this prison, with all the political investments of the body that it gathers together in a closed architecture. Why? Simply because I am interested in the past? No, if one means by that writing a history of the past in terms of the present. Yes, if one means writing the history of the present.[14]

As will be expected, I will insist, in interpreting this passage, on the continuing inversion of certain Hegelian themes concerning the intelligibility of the his-

---

14. *DP* 30–31; my emphasis.

torical process. The most obvious one, of
course, is the way the passage insists on
the *materiality* of the movements that compose the history Foucault is interested in
exploring, that is, the materiality of the
prison itself; this inverts Hegel's insistence
on the "ideality" of the movement of history (characterized in a number of ways,
but here, perhaps most relevantly, as a
self-overcoming through the negating of
the determinacies of an experience that
is on its own terms insufficient). But again
(I insist), this is an *inversion*, not a rejection, of the theme of the self-movement
of thought; indeed, Foucault here even
makes use of the "contradictory" character
of what the prison revolts "tell" us as a reason to appeal to the *history* of the prison
context itself. Thus, writing the "history
of the present" is engaging the present
through the tensions it manifests and articulating the movements that constitute it.

But if the movements that constitute
the present need to be understood historically, they are not to be understood as the
movements of something called Spirit realizing itself. Inverting this theme as well,
Foucault is intent on showing how what
realizes itself in the movements constituting and maintaining the "prison system" is
not Spirit's self-recognition, but a certain
a kind of *body* fashioned through what

he calls a "political technology",[15] that is, a particular combination of *power* and *knowledge* whose effects Foucault wants to trace. The prison captures (indeed, is a kind of *grasping*, a mode of conceptualizing the way we relate to each other), through the concentration of this combinatory effect of power and knowledge, the very movement of thought we are *caught up in* that is the history of our present. In Foucault's decision to work out the "history of *this* prison", the prison as it makes itself manifest through the prison revolts, Foucault is once again exhibiting his particular *sensibility* to the way our world manifests itself and attempts to work out the "difficulties and obscurities" that structure it. And here too we can see a kind of inversion of the Hegelian account of the logical movement of thought from singularity, through particularity, towards the universality of mutual recognition; Foucault begins with the apparent "universality" of the recognition of necessary consequences that must attend the breach of lawfulness, then moves to the particularity of a system of justice which, along with the development and use of prisons, "provides the mechanisms of legal punishment with a justifiable hold not only on offences, but

---

15. *DP* 30.

on individuals; not only on what they do, but also on what they are, will be, may be".[16] And through this examination of the particularity of the way justice unfolds in our society, Foucault achieves what he calls the objective of his book, which is

> a correlative history of the modern soul and of a new power to judge; a genealogy of the present scientifico-legal complex from which the power to punish derives its bases, justifications and rules, from which it extends its effects and *by which its masks its exorbitant singularity.*[17]

It is Foucault's own particular sensibility that led him to "take up" an investigation into the history of the "body of the condemned", but it is the way that he executes his project (no pun intended) that has us question our own relation to each other (through the prism of the way we go about punishing those who engage in practices that involve "unlawfulness"). Part of the force of what Foucault shows us is precisely how prisons concentrate the various social projects and political goals that characterize our present's general self-understanding. The prison demonstrates not how these projects have been successfully realized, or

16. *DP* 18.
17. *DP 23*; my emphasis.

for that matter how they have failed, but how such projects and practices actually and effectively both *take* shape within, and *give* shape to, the social body.

However, Foucault's analysis remains a *history* of the prison and not a metaphorical or microcosmic portrait of contemporary society. Foucault is not suggesting that our society is a prison. His focus on the prison, as quoted above, on its very *materiality*, on the way it constrains the movement of human bodies, shows it to be an "instrument and vector of power". That is, it reveals the political technology at work within our society both in its functioning and in its directionality (to produce what he will call "docile bodies" through processes of "normalization"). And in that sense it is a history that challenges the sense we have of history as about a past distinct from the present but in some way leading up to it, and by so leading up to it, in some sense thereby *explaining and justifying* our present. Foucault's history challenges this sense of history that would suggest that the present had to turn out the way it in fact has; its genealogical purpose is to underscore the present as a contingent matter of fact. He traces the contingent relations that have combined and that, at times, have been radically transformed. Indeed, the real force of Foucault's genealogical investigation into the prison is to have us confront the radical transformation of the practice of punishment into an exercise of power over human bodies that occurred at the end of the eighteenth century and consolidated itself in the nineteenth century. His graphic archival *contrastive* description of the manner in which certain types of wrongdoers were at one time tortured in public and at another locked up in prisons imply radically different configurations of relations of power: the power of the sovereign to exercise absolute force is not the power of the State to establish widespread systems of surveillance and control.

Such radically different configurations of relations of power are hardly accounted for by appealing to some kind of quantitative increase in the "humanity" that the system of justice displays towards those who break the law. In fact, behind such an appeal (with its continuist and developmental assumptions) to an "increased humanity" as responsible for the reduction in the severity with which punishment is meted out on human bodies, one finds in effect a "change of objective".[18] Tracing and accounting for this change of objective will be Foucault's principal task as he attempts to give a better account of the

---

18. *DP* 16.

intelligibility of the deployment of what, as we saw above, he had occasion to call "punitive reason".

***

In my reading of Foucault's *History of Madness*, I emphasized the manner in which he gave an account of reason's self-consolidation or self-assurance through its cunning appropriation of the threat posed by something he called "unreason". That work ended with the consolidation of the nineteenth-century asylum. And the triumph of reason over madness (as posing a threat to its self-development) this consolidation celebrated also concealed its "exorbitant singularity" in a similar appeal to an "increasing humanity" in the treatment of those who have lost their "reason". This is perhaps most poignantly captured in the use of the straitjacket to restrain those who might harm themselves or others. It is, of course, a piece of technology designed according to a conception of "restraint" that connects the notions of reason and freedom (free movement) characteristic of the nineteenth century (as distinct from the governing conceptions of reason in the Classical Age) and operates within the wider structures of a transformed system of confinement.

Confinement was to operate like a permanent measuring of madness, a constant
series of readjustments in response to the
changeable nature of its truth, restraining
only inside the limits within which freedom alienated itself: "Humanity, justice
and good medicine dictate that only the
mad who risk genuinely harming others
should be locked up; the only patients
who should be restrained are those who
otherwise risk harming themselves." The
justice that was to reign inside asylums
would no longer be that of punishment,
but that of truth: there was to be an exact
measurement of the exercise of liberty and
of its restrictions, and as rigorous a confor-
mity as possible between constraints and
the alienation of liberty. And the most concrete form of this justice, its most visible
symbol, was no longer to be the chain—an
absolute, punitive restriction that "invari-
ably wounds the flesh it rubs against"—but
the new, soon-to-be-famous straitjacket, "a
close-fitting canvas shirt, which constrains
and contains the arms", designed to progressively hinder movements as their violence increased. The straitjacket should
not be seen as the humanization of chains,
or as the progress towards "self-restraint".
A process of conceptual deduction leads
to the straitjacket, showing that in madness, the experience was no longer of

an absolute conflict between reason and
unreason, but rather of a play—always relative, always mobile—between freedom and
its limits.[19]

In *Discipline and Punish*, Foucault is
returning the same problematic of a
radical transformation evidenced in the
archive in the way we relate to (some of)
ourselves, but now not in the figure of
the mad, but in the figure of the criminal
and the delinquent, and shows us how the
story we tell ourselves about the increasingly "humane" treatment of those figures
hardly captures the dynamics of what is
actually being effected by the practices
governing such treatment.

But before turning to a reading of those
dynamics, it is interesting to note what
Foucault says about his own conceptualization of the asylum in the *History of Madness*
in the first lecture of his course, *Le Pouvoir
Psychiatrique*.[20] This course took place in

---

19. *HM* 439. As Mathieu Potte-Bonneville
     points out, the agitation of the mad is what
     tightens the hold of the straitjacket, which
     loosens when "reason returns". *Michel
     Foucault, l'inquiétude de l'histoire* (Paris:
     Presses universitaires de France, 2004) 45.

20. Michel Foucault, *Le pouvoir psychiatrique*
     (Paris: Seuil/Gallimard, 2003); English
     version, *Psychiatric Power, Lectures at the*

1973–1974, a year before the publication
of *Discipline and Punish*. As the title of the
course indicates, this is the period when
he becomes interested in making use of
the notion of power in his analyses and he
tells us in the first lecture that the reason
for this was his dissatisfaction with some of
the assumptions that guided his work on
madness. With hindsight, he feels that he
was still working on the level of "representations", with the "images" or "perceptions"
of madness as these informed the development of different "fantasies" (*fantasmes*)
and knowledges and were the "origin" of
a number of practices. In the course he
proposes for that year, which he characterizes as a "second volume" to the *History of
Madness*, taking matters up where the latter left off, he wants to introduce a new
approach, one not based on something
like the perceptual representations that
thought gives itself "which inevitably refers
to a history of mentalities, of thought" but
rather, "from an apparatus (*dispositif*) of
power".[21] The appeal to the notion of an
"apparatus of power" is meant to enable
us to grasp (*saisir*) a discursive practice "at

Collège de France, 1973–1974, trans. Graham
Burchell (New York: Palgrave Macmillan,
2006). Hereafter referred to as "*PP*".
21. *PP* 13.

precisely the point where it is formed".[22] In the next paragraph, he admits that this appeal to the word "power" remains somewhat enigmatic and will need to be explored more fully, but presses on with the notion that he is after: the point of formation of discursive practices, where strategies and tactics are deployed which are productive of certain kinds of "assertions, negations, experiments, and theories, in short [involving a whole] game of truth".[23]

We are reminded here of our discussion in Chapter Two of the manner in which "truth" is set up in the Heideggerian language of the free letting-be, which turns out to be a form of "erring", that is, the installation of systems of rules. And, indeed, the considerations raised in Chapter Two continue to be relevant to the critique Foucault is here making of his earlier work. He considers three notions that he appealed to (either "implicitly or explicitly") in the *History of Madness* which he now considers to be "rusty locks".[24] The

22. *PP* 13.

23. *PP* 13, translation modified. "*Comment cet aménagement du pouvoir, ces tactiques et stratégies du pouvoir peuvent-elles donner lieu à des affirmations, des negations, des experiences, des theories, bref à tout un jeu de la vérité?*" *Le pouvoir psychiatrique* 15.

24. *PP* 14.

first is the one most relevant to our discussion here and concerns the notion of violence.[25] If he made use of such a notion in that earlier work, it was because he was struck (again, an example of how Foucault allows his work to be guided by his particular sensibility) by the great appeal made to "physical force" by the reformers Pinel and Esquirol, a fact papered over by their "hagiographers", and which led him to question the view that attributed those reforms to a "humanism", given that "his entire practice was still permeated by something like violence".[26] But now, he rejects his own appeal to the notion of violence because of its connotations of a kind of irregular, passion-filled, reckless (*déchaîné*) power; this he thinks is dangerous because it leads us to suppose that "good power, or

---

25. The other two are his use of the notion of the "institution", which he seeks to replace with the notion of "tactic", and the notion of the "family", which he seeks to replace with the notion of "strategy". In a word, he is replacing what he calls a "psycho-social" vocabulary with a "pseudo-military" one, which he admits may not move him further ahead, but "we will try to see what we can do with it". (*PP* 16) This pseudo-military vocabulary will stay with him for a number of years.

26. *PP* 14.

just simply power, power not permeated by violence, is not physical power" while on the contrary he wants to claim that "what is essential in all power is that ultimately its point of application is always the body. *All power is physical, and there is a direct connection between the body and political power.*"[27] In addition, the notion of violence, and its association with passion and recklessness, leads us away from a close examination of the way power actually operates through "a rational, calculated, and controlled game".[28]

This is an important point for Foucault. The contrast he sets up in *Discipline and Punish* between the spectacular mode of punishment exhibited in the Classical Age and a mode of punishment that is "the most hidden part of the penal process"[29] that follows it is not, despite (indeed because of) its shock value, a contrast between "brutality" and "humanity". Both modes of punishment, he is intent on showing, display a meticulously reasoned approach. And yet both modes of punishment are radically different. The book attempts to make sense of this transformation which he captures in an unde-

---

27. *PP* 14; my emphasis.
28. *PP* 14.
29. *DP* 9.

niable way by having us recognize "the disappearance of torture as a public spectacle",[30] that is, "the disappearance of the tortured, dismembered, amputated body, symbolically branded on face and shoulder, exposed alive or dead to public view", in a word: "The body as the major target of penal repression disappeared."[31] If, today, any of us "abide by the law" out of a fear of being caught and being punished, that fear is not fueled by the contemplation of physical agony. On the contrary, according to Foucault, in this radical transformation, punitive practices became much more discreet (*pudique*) where they "no longer touched the body, or at least as little as possible, and then only to reach something other than the body itself".[32] But such discretion should not be read as a wavering in the determination to punish, and to punish decisively. Foucault reminds us of the invention of the guillotine, which captures the whole transformation (understood as a "double process: the disappearance of the spectacle and the elimination of pain"):[33] "Death was reduced to a visible, but instantaneous event. Contact

---

30. *DP* 7.
31. *DP* 8.
32. *DP* 11.
33. *DP* 11.

between the law, or those who carry it out, and the body of the criminal, is reduced to a split second."[34]

But, then, what is this "something other than the body itself" that the law is attempting to "reach" through punishment? Well, obviously, if not the body, then the soul. If punitive practices no longer seek to impress themselves, quite literally, on the body, it is because they have changed their focus and seek instead to impress themselves "in depth on the heart, the thoughts, the will, the inclinations".[35] But this shift in focus has far-reaching consequences in the manner in which punitive practices are executed, resulting in a very different "system" of justice. As Foucault writes:

> Certainly the "crimes" and "offences" on which judgment is passed are juridical objects defined by the code, but judgment is also passed on the passions, instincts, anomalies, infirmities, maladjustments, effects of environment or heredity; acts of aggression are punished, so also, through them, is aggressivity; rape, but at the same time perversions; murders, but also drives and desires.[36]

---

34. *DP* 13.

35. *DP* 16.

36. *DP* 17.

Thus, the disappearance of torture in the practice of punishment signals something much more concrete than "an increase in humanity": a whole new systematic approach to justice, where "the sentence that condemns or acquits is not simply a judgment of guilt, a legal decision that lays down punishment; it bears within it an assessment of normality and a technical prescription for a possible normalization".[37] And this new "system" is constructed through a "whole machinery" that, in effect, "creates a proliferation of the authorities of judicial decision-making and extends its powers of decision well beyond the sentence",[38] powers that not only judge particular actions but initiate processes of "cure" and of "normalization".

This "machinery" focused on the "soul" of the criminal, then, actually brings us back to the body in the sense that "this entry of the soul on to the scene of penal justice, and with it the insertion in legal practice of a whole corpus of 'scientific' knowledge" is actually, when examined more closely, "the effect of a transformation of the way in which the body itself is invested by power relations".[39]

---

37. *DP* 20–21.

38. *DP* 21.

39. *DP* 24.

It is quite "normal", then, that most of us do not fear being punished by the law as we go about our business, that is, as we engage our practices in terms of their norms, goals and regularities; it is normal because those practices themselves are structured by systems of constraint that, in fact, for a large part "normalize" what we think, say and do. This, in effect, is what *renders* our behaviour "lawful". What Foucault wants to show us is that such "lawful" behaviour is in fact illustrative of the operation of a certain system of power relations. This becomes evident when we look more closely at what happens when behaviour becomes "unlawful". But what is meant by "looking more closely" is considering historically the system at work as a transformation. This is required because the ways in which power is exercised cannot be made "evident" simply by trying to understand our practices as we are currently engaged in them (indeed, *because* we are currently engaged in them); nor will they be made "evident" simply by presenting an argument. They will be made evident by means of a historical *contrast* sustained through the tracing of a radical transformation.

***

How should we make sense of this radical transformation? Because it is a transformation that affects the body, it is at the level of the body that one should look. The mode of punishment of the Classical Age, for all of its ferocity in the agony and suffering it put on display, remained a *technique* of punishment, where "a whole economy of power is invested"[40] and which was carefully measured along a spectrum of pain from the suddenness of decapitation to the drawn-out spectacle of being drawn and quartered. The pain the guilty had to suffer was administered according to the gravity of the crime and the point of making a spectacle of it was to show the power of the king marking his subjects, both the victim and those gathered to witness to it.

> It was the task of the guilty man to bear openly his condemnation and the truth of the crime that he had committed. His body, displayed, exhibited in procession, tortured, served as the public support of a procedure that had hitherto remained in the shade [the establishment of guilt; RF]; in him, on him, the sentence had to be legible for all...the procession through the streets, the placard attached to the back, chest or head as a reminder of the sentence; the halts at various crossroads, the reading of the sentence, the *amende honorable* performed at the doors of the

---

40. *DP* 35.

churches, in which the condemned man solemnly acknowledged his crime....exhibition at a stake where his deeds and the sentence were read out; yet another reading of the sentence at the foot of the scaffold; whether he was simply to go to the pillory or to the stake and the wheel, the condemned man published his crime and the justice that had been meted out to him by bearing them physically on his body.[41]

This is a political ritual where the sovereign manifests his power over his subjects and reminds them that any crime is a direct attack on the sovereign himself and the whole point of the spectacle "is not so much to re-establish a balance as to bring into play, as its extreme point, the dissymmetry between the subject who has dared to violate the law and the all-powerful sovereign who displays his strength".[42] This, of course, is why *Discipline and Punish* opens with contemporary descriptions of the *supplice* of Damiens, someone who quite literally tried to kill the king, as it showcases the ultimate manifestation of the power of the sovereign: "A body effaced, reduced to dust and thrown to the winds, a body destroyed piece by piece by the infinite power of the sovereign consti-

---

41. *DP* 43.
42. *DP* 48–49.

tuted not only the ideal, but the real limit of punishment."[43]

Indeed, the next thing Foucault does is to show the effective limits of this mode of punishment. As a spectacle, it is something that needs to be put together and performed. Not all performances succeed in what they aim at. The same applies here. And like all spectacles, success is measured by the way the audience reacts. As Foucault says, "In the ceremonies of the public execution, the main character was the people, whose real and immediate presence was required for the performance."[44] The reaction sought was, of course, terror and awe before the power of the sovereign. But the role played by the people was not merely reactive; their presence as witnesses was meant to confirm the power of the sovereign, that is, "they must be made to be afraid; but also…they must be the witnesses, the guarantors, of the punishment, and. . . they must to a certain extent take part in it".[45] Thus, the people had an ambiguous role to play in this ritual expression of the sovereign's power; supposed to suffer its mark along with the guilty, they were the warrant of

---

43. *DP* 50.

44. *DP* 57.

45. *DP* 58.

the justice of the condemnation. And the people took this role seriously, so seriously in fact that

> it was on this point that the people, drawn to the spectacle intended to terrorize it, could express its rejection of the punitive power and sometimes revolt. Preventing an execution that was regarded as unjust, snatching a condemned man from the hands of an executioner, obtaining his pardon by force, possibly pursuing and assaulting the executioners, in any case abusing the judges and causing an uproar against the sentence—all this formed part of the popular practices that invested, traversed and often overturned the ritual of the public execution.[46]

But further, these public executions could take on a kind of festive character because, in gathering around the scaffold, the crowd sought not only "to witness the sufferings of the condemned man or to excite the anger of the executioner: it was also to hear an individual who had nothing more to lose curse the judges, the laws, the government and religion".[47] The spectacle could take certain aspects of "the carnival, in which rules were inverted,

---

46. *DP* 59–60.
47. *DP* 60.

authority mocked and criminals transformed into heroes".[48] And perhaps most
importantly, in terms of the transformation Foucault's account is attempting to
make sense of,

> the terror of the public execution created
> centers of illegality: on execution days,
> work stopped, the taverns were full, the
> authorities were abused, insults or stones
> were thrown at the executioner, the guards
> and soldiers; attempts were made to seize
> the condemned man, either to save him or
> to kill him more surely; fights broke out,
> and there was no better prey for thieves
> than the curious throng around the
> scaffold.[49]

In a word, what was meant to be a performance displaying the solemn and awesome
power of the sovereign became occasions
for a generalized *disorder* that made something of a mockery of its intended function
and indeed, for the authorities responsible for the performance, the whole affair
began to appear to them as a kind of political danger inasmuch as

> the people never felt closer to those who
> paid the penalty than in those rituals
> intended to show the horror of the crime

---

48. *DP* 61.
49. *DP* 63.

> and the invincibility of power; never did
> the people feel more threatened, like
> them, by a legal violence exercised without
> moderation or restraint[50]

thereby constituting a kind of "solidarity
of a whole section of the population with
those we would call petty offenders"; and it
was precisely "the breaking up of this solidarity that was becoming the aim of penal
and police repression".[51]

What I think needs to be emphasized
in these descriptions—something that is
not sufficiently done in the literature on
Foucault that wants to grasp his work in
terms of a kind of *theory* of power—is the way
they track the *movement* of people engaged
in various practices, but with a particular
emphasis on the way some of them (let
us call them "authoritative") have as their
explicit purpose the constraining or directing of movements that appear threatening
to certain ("authoritative") self-conceptions
about the way things are or should be.
Foucault is certainly appealing to a *concept* of
power—the forceful constraining of bodily
engagements—but rather than have such a
concept contribute to a general theory, he
uses it to better make sense of an unfolding
world (that is, a world that does not display

50. *DP* 63.
51. *DP* 63.

a fixed structure given that it has a past that contrasts with its present and shows itself to be contingently constituted).

What we can see in the descriptions offered in *Discipline and Punish* resembles what we saw in *History of Madness*: the manner in which certain kinds of "reasonable" discursive practices constituted themselves by controlling or attempting to control something that came to be seen as a threat to that "reasonableness", as it were, and that, in so doing, Foucault shows us, these practices *consolidate themselves* and take on a certain systematicity. This is why I have been insisting on reading Foucault according to the Hegelian thematic of a history of reason as self-development. Foucault, of course, differs from Hegel, in that he is particularly interested in tracking its actual movement at the level of *bodily resistance* to what might be called its excesses. And no doubt the lasting significance of Foucault's work, especially *Discipline and Punish*, is the way it shows how such "excess" can be present in ways not immediately evident.

***

The second part of that work shows how the "impossibility" for us today to contemplate a mode of punishment that would publicly torture and destroy the bodies of criminals is not a matter of something like an "increased humanity" that we somehow

now possess, but rather is indicative of a
shift in the manner in which the power to
punish was effected.

What the notion of an "increased humanity" actually refers to, historically speaking,
is an attempt to "soften" (*adoucir*) the mode
of punishment because the mode of putting it on public display ceased to be seen
to be effective. Many factors contributed
to this assessment, some of which were discussed above (e.g., the threat of generalized disorder that tended to manifest itself
during the staging of public executions).
Included among them was the fact, "uncovered through the study of legal archives",
that crimes themselves were losing something of their violence inasmuch as

> one observes a considerable diminution in
> murders and, generally speaking, in physi-
> cal acts of aggression; offences against
> property seem to take over from crimes of
> violence; theft and swindling, from mur-
> der and assault; the diffuse, occasional,
> but frequent delinquency of the poorest
> classes was superseded by a limited, but
> "skilled" delinquency.[52]

In a word, the period of penal reforms,
which discursively appealed to more
"humanity", was one marked by a "gen-

---

52. *DP* 75.

eral movement" that "shifted criminality
from the attack of bodies to a more or
less direct seizure of goods; from a 'mass
criminality' to a 'marginal criminality',
partly the preserve of professionals".[53] The
point, of course, was to "install" discourses
of reform within the concrete contextual
coalescence of practices of the time that
Foucault tends to describe as "mechanisms", in order to emphasize the manner
in which different parts need to be seen as
functioning together, in this case, the practices of crime and of justice.

> ... the shift from a criminality of blood
> to a criminality of fraud forms part of
> a whole complex mechanism, embrac-
> ing the development of production, the
> increase of wealth, a higher juridical and
> moral value placed on property relations,
> stricter methods of surveillance, a tighter
> partitioning of the population, more effi-
> cient techniques of locating and obtaining
> information: the shift in illegal practices is
> correlative with an extension and a refine-
> ment of punitive practices.[54]

Thus, while reformers were *calling* for
a different, more "humane" mode of
punishment rather than the "excessive"

53. *DP* 76.
54. *DP* 77.

spectacular one in place, their *actual* concern was with "an excess that was bound up
with an irregularity even more than with an
abuse of the power to punish".[55] That is,
the "criticism of the reformers was directed
not so much at the weakness or cruelty of
those in authority, as at a bad economy of
power".[56] In terms we often hear today, the
system had become "inefficient". Foucault
insists on this point, showing that the
reform was something that "was not prepared outside the legal machinery and
against all its representatives; it was prepared, for the most part, from within, by
a large number of magistrates and on the
basis of shared objectives and the power
conflicts that divided them".[57]

This last point is important to emphasize, especially if we are to take seriously
the notion of being "caught up" in the discursive practices that structure the historical field, of being "caught up" in history.
We will discuss the impact this has on our
conception of "critique" in the next chapter, but we can say here that tracking the
shifts and changes in history through what
people have done (*res gestae*) means taking
into account both what they take themselves to be doing and the effects of what

---

55. *DP* 78.

56. *DP* 79.

57. *DP* 81.

they do as what they do is "taken up" in the interplay of the various discursive practices at work in a given present. Close attention to those practices is what is required because it is within and through them that the world takes on the particular shapes that it does. In a word, the intelligibility of history is a function of the intelligibility of the practices human beings engage in as they respond to the particular constraints they face in their unfolding lives.

And this, of course, includes the intelligibility of practices not afforded official sanction in the predominant discourses of legitimate conduct. Here as well, *Discipline and Punish* proves to be especially interesting in the attention it pays to those practices that constitute forms of *illegality*. It is largely as a response to the changing character of those practices that reforms of punishment actually took place such that their primary objective became

> to make of the punishment and repression of illegalities a regular function, coextensive with society; not to punish less, but to punish better; to punish with an attenuated severity perhaps, but in order to punish with more universality and necessity; to insert the power to punish deeply into the social body.[58]

---

58. *DP* 82.

Indeed, the success of such reforms, that
is, the force of consolidation they exhibit,
can be measured by the extent to which
the various practices that human beings
engage in at a given time have taken the
shape of something like a social *body*, that is,
something, an intelligible whole, that can
be made to do something (for example,
generate wealth).

Most of us simply take for granted that
we are each of us "individuals" and that,
taken together, we form "societies", social
wholes that have distinct features, and
that some such relation holds universally
(human beings form distinct societies
made up of distinct individuals). But from
a practice-based approach, such a view of
the composition of social wholes is quite
particular, such that, if we look more closely
at the practices that people engage in, we
will see such a social "whole" is indeed the
scene of a number of battlegrounds (hence
Foucault's appeal to a grid of intelligibility
that made use of more "war-like" conceptions of political and historical development leading him to invert "Clausewitz's
proposition and say that politics is the
continuation of war by other means"[59]).

---

59. Michel Foucault, "Society Must Be
    Defended," *Lectures at the Collège de France
    1975–1976*, trans. David Macey (New York:
    Picador, 2003) 15.

That is, the engagement in various practices is not a smooth process but very often involves various modes of coercion.

The point of making use of the notion of power and power-relations is not to over-dramatize social life, but rather to conceptualize it in the dynamic terms characteristic of *history*, where the ways human beings relate to each other show changes and transformations. Rather than speak of "society" then, Foucault makes use of the concept of *regime* in order to capture the particularities of the manner in which a social order constitutes and consolidates itself through different modes of coercion of those bodies that make the order a "social" one (as opposed to "natural" one). That is, these bodies need to be coerced or constrained in particular ways because there is no guarantee that their movement or comportment will accord with what the regime deems important, thus generating a particular social order or *ordering* of those practices that engage human beings.

If we return then to *Discipline and Punish*, we can see how it is devoted to describing the consolidation of a particular *disciplinary* regime which contrasts with a social ordering structured around sovereign, spectacular power which is no longer showing itself to be adequately responsive to the movements of human beings through their practical engagements. Sovereign, spectacular power operated in a mode that not only tolerated a number of "illegal" practices (that is, practices upon which it did not exert its particular mode of spectacular coerciveness), but did so in a way that allowed them to take on their own particular shape, one which had "in a sense its own coherence and economy".[60] In a regime (the *Ancien regime*) that was in fact structured around a system of privileges for the higher orders, that is, one in which the "least-favoured strata of the population did not have, in principle, any privileges", these least-favoured nevertheless

> benefited, within the margins of what was imposed on them by law and custom, from a space of tolerance, *gained by force or obstinacy*; and this space was for them so indispensable a condition of existence that they were often ready to rise up to defend it; the attempts that were made periodically to reduce it, by reviving old laws or by improving the methods of apprehending, provoked popular disturbances, just as attempts to reduce certain privileges disturbed the nobility, the clergy and the bourgeoisie.[61]

---

60. *DP* 82.
61. *DP* 83; emphasis added.

This description, of course, underscores the idea that social orders are in some sense "battlefields" where opposing forces are pitted against each other and in tension, their relations flaring up on occasion into explicit confrontation.

The historical shift of a regime of sovereign, spectacular power to a regime of disciplinary power can be traced according to Foucault to what he attempts to show is "a crisis of popular illegality"[62] where, for example,

> all the tolerated "rights" that the peasantry had acquired or preserved (the abandonment of old obligations or the consolidation of irregular practices: the right to free pasture, wood-collecting, etc.) were now rejected by the new owners who regarded them quite simply as theft

which, put more generally, resulted in a situation where the "illegality of rights, which often meant the survival of the most deprived, tended, with the new status of property, to become an illegality of property. It had then to be punished."[63] Further, this new status consolidated itself in the development of commerce and industry, that is,

---

62. *DP* 84.
63. *DP* 85.

> the development of ports, the appearance
> of great warehouses in which merchan-
> dise was stored, the organization of huge
> workshops (with considerable quantities
> of raw materials, tools and manufacturing
> articles, which belonged to the entrepre-
> neurs and which were difficult to super-
> vise) also necessitated a severe repression
> of illegality

and "presupposed a systematic, armed intolerance of illegality".[64]

In a word, then, given the changing practices in the production and distribution of wealth and the effect these changes had on the different kinds of practices engaged by different social strata, including new forms of illicit ones (theft, smuggling, counterfeiting, for example), there was a shift in the practice and function of punishment where the "right to punish has been shifted from the vengeance of the sovereign to the defence of society".[65] Now, its purpose is not the spectacular affirmation of the power of the sovereign who has been injured by the crime, rather "the injury that a crime inflicts upon the social body is the disorder that it introduces into it: the scandal that it gives rise to, the example that it gives, the incite-

---

64. *DP* 85.
65. *DP* 90.

ment to repeat it if it is not punished, the possibility of becoming widespread that it bears within it".[66] Thus, the new "order" taking shape is one that consolidates itself through the way it responds to the threat of disorder.

Thus, *Discipline and Punish* continues the strategy already present in *History of Madness* where Foucault insists on seeing the consolidating efforts of something like "reason" (here we are dealing with "punitive reason"), not from its own self-developmental perspective, but from the manner in which it manifests itself through its response to something that poses a threat to it. And it is interesting to note how, in *Discipline and Punish* as well, the notion of "cunning" is invoked. For example, Foucault writes of the new "microphysics of power" that reaches out "to ever broader domains" in the following way:

> Small acts of cunning endowed with a great power of diffusion, subtle arrangements, apparently innocent, but profoundly suspicious, mechanisms that obeyed economies too shameful to be acknowledged, or pursued petty forms of coercion—it was nevertheless they that brought about the mutation of the punitive system, at the threshold of the contemporary period. Describing

66. *DP* 92.

them will require great attention to detail: beneath every set of figures, we must seek not a meaning, but a precaution; we must situate them not only in the inextricability of a functioning, but in the coherence of a tactic. They are the acts of cunning, not so much of the greater reason that works even in its sleep and gives meaning to the insignificant, as of the attentive "malevolence" that turns everything to account. Discipline is the political anatomy of detail.[67]

One can obviously read Foucault's genealogical intentions in such a passage; but one can also see a continued *inversion* of a basic Hegelian theme of reason's self-deployment and an application of what I have been calling a principle of immanence, which sees in our reasoning efforts, not some grand scheme of progressive self-realization, but the very concrete, very particular efforts of tactical responses to unfolding situations that are seen to pose particular threats or risks (not reason's own self-motivated self-deployment, as it were, but a responsive self-deployment in view of a perceived threat or risk to itself).[68]

***

67. *DP* 139.
68. As mentioned in my discussion of Hyppolite in Chapter Three, I am not in

Thus, if "punitive reason" takes on its particular disciplinary shape from the eighteenth century on, it is because it (re)constituted[69] and consolidated itself around a series of tactics it developed as it responded to an unfolding situation of disorder. It is in this context that I would like to discuss the notion of "panopticism", no doubt the most famous chapter of *Discipline and Punish*. It begins with a discussion of the measures taken at the end of seventeenth century "when the plague appeared in a town".[70] The response to the plague is one of a radical imposition of *order* on a very threatening situation; one that, in effect, produces "a segmented, immobile, frozen space. Each individual is fixed in his place. And, if he moves, he does so at the risk of his life, contagion or punishment."[71] It is an order of thorough *surveillance*,[72] which

---

this study concerned with how well these "inversions" actually properly appreciate Hegel's philosophy. My claim is that the Hegelian reference helps us understand, not Hegel, but Foucault's appreciation and use of history.

69. Through the reform of punitive practices we have been discussing.

70. *DP* 195.

71. *DP* 195.

72. And of course Foucault's work in French has the title: *Surveiller et punir*.

organizes itself around the threat posed to the town by the plague. Foucault is keen on underlining this point:

> The plague is met by order; its function is to sort out every possible confusion: that of the disease, which is transmitted when bodies are mixed together; that of the evil, which is increased when fear and death overcome prohibitions. It lays down for each individual his place, his body, his disease and his death, his well-being, by means of an omnipresent and omniscient power that subdivides itself in a regular, uninterrupted way even to the ultimate determination of the individual, of what characterizes him, of what belongs to him, of what happens to him. Against the plague, which is a mixture, discipline brings into play its power, which is one of analysis.[73]

It is within this experience of the plague at this particular time, in terms of this kind of particular response, that the disciplinary mode of constraining and consolidating a variety of different human practices takes shape. As Foucault puts it, "The plague as a form, at once real and imaginary, of disorder had as its medical and political correlative discipline."[74]

---

73. *DP* 197.
74. *DP* 198.

It is thus within this "medical and political" *form*, both imaginary and real, that the notion of "panopticism" is to take its place; that is, this latter notion needs to be understood against the backdrop of the historical experience of the "plague-stricken town, traversed throughout with hierarchy, surveillance, observation, writing; the town immobilized by the functioning of an extensive power that bears in a distinct way over all individual bodies—this is the utopia of the perfectly governed city".[75] I say this in order to emphasize that the fact that, at the heart of this study, is a sensibility to the self-movement, not of concepts, but of individual *bodies* and the manner in which that movement is constrained. Foucault chooses to discuss Bentham's Panopticon not because it is an appropriate metaphor but because of its conceptual function of articulating a kind of principle of intelligibility: the way modern power grasps our bodies by individualizing them. That is, if the plague-stricken town effected a *fixating* of bodies meant to control their movement, the Panopticon describes a technology that will *shape* that movement by individualizing it. Within that technology, as an "architectural figure",[76] "The

---

75. *DP* 198.

76. *DP* 200.

crowd, a compact mass, a locus of multiple exchanges, individualities merging
together, a collective effect, is abolished
and replaced by a collection of separated
individualities."[77] And what is fascinating about the Panopticon is how it clearly
illustrates the way this division of a crowd,
or a group, or of a mix of human beings
into separate individualities is maintained
through a kind of self-identification with
the power that separates, that is:

> He who is subjected to a field of visibility,
> and who knows it, assumes responsibil-
> ity for the constraints of power; he makes
> them play spontaneously upon himself;
> he inscribes in himself the power relation
> in which he simultaneously plays both
> roles; he becomes the principle of his own
> subjection.[78]

Once this system of self-subjection is put
in place, that is, is made to operate, then it
opens up a space for experimentation on
the *individual* bodies that are caught up in
it. In other words, the "Panopticon was also
a laboratory; it could be used as a machine
to carry out experiments, to alter behaviour, to train or correct individuals".[79]

---

77. *DP* 201.
78. *DP* 202–03.
79. *DP* 203.

Indeed, as a general principle, or a general figure of a certain political technology (a mode of exercising power over bodies), the "panoptic schema" can be called upon whenever "one is dealing with a multiplicity of individuals on whom a task or a particular form of behaviour must be imposed"[80] and thus one see its relevance to places like hospitals, workshops, schools and prisons.

It is this *productive* capacity of the "panoptic schema" that Foucault seeks to underscore as it constrains the activities and practices people find themselves engaged in. Thus the movement of a disciplinary mode of reasoning meant to deal with disorder which was instantiated in the plague-stricken town, which itself serves as a kind of model or ideal of its functioning, is in fact *amplified* through its panoptic applications and moves from its *reactive* function (to the threat posed by the plague, i.e., disorder) to a more productive function whose "aim is to strengthen the social forces—to increase production, to develop the economy, spread education, raise the level of public morality; to increase and multiply".[81]

---

80. *DP* 205.
81. *DP* 208.

At its most general level, then, Foucault is attempting to describe the consolidating self-movement of thought that characterized the eighteenth century as the development of "disciplines" as "techniques for assuring the ordering of human multiplicities".[82] This consolidating movement of thought was taking place at a particular "historical conjuncture" which saw a "large demographic thrust" combined with the "growth in the apparatus of production",[83] and it shaped that conjuncture through the various disciplines "in order to extract from bodies the maximum time and force",[84] surely, but more importantly did so through what Foucault insists is "the unitary technique by which the body is reduced as a 'political' force at the least cost and maximized as a useful force".[85]

It is in this *historically defined* context that Foucault would have us consider our self-conception as autonomous individuals engaged in various practices and in fact as "law-abiding". Foucault would like us to see that the juridical framework that "ideally" structures our various practices is actually grounded in the movement

---

82. *DP* 218.
83. *DP* 218.
84. *DP* 220.
85. *DP* 221.

of particular forms of reasoning focused on techniques of coercion that "work in depth on the juridical structures of society in order to make the effective mechanisms of power function in opposition to the formal framework that it had acquired".[86] Or, put even more forcefully, Foucault is showing us that

> although the universal juridicism of modern society seems to fix limits on the exercise of power, its universally widespread panopticism enables it to operate, on the underside of the law, a machinery that is both immense and minute, which supports, reinforces, multiplies the asymmetry of power and undermines the limits that are traced around the law.[87]

For the purposes of this study, what needs to be underlined here is that this is the context within which our lives unfold, that in our particular forms of "law-abidingness" we are supporting a particular kind of order, historically constituted and maintained through particular technologies of power, most evident in the manner it which it "punishes" those who contravene its order, but one which has "a certain policy of the body, a certain

---

86. *DP* 222.
87. *DP* 223.

way of rendering groups of men docile and useful".[88] The question and concern Foucault is raising for us through this genealogy of the prison, is the extent to which our own self-conceptions of our unfolding lives are taken up, indeed, are caught up, in this disciplinary mode of constraint, in

> the growth of the disciplinary networks, the multiplication of their exchanges with the penal apparatus, the ever more important powers that are given them, the ever more massive transference to them of judicial functions; now, as medicine, psychology, education, public assistance, "social work" assume an ever greater share of the powers of supervision and assessment.[89]

In a word, throughout these various processes of normalization, is there any sense in which we can continue to call these lives our own? Are we then truly caught up, even through our self-conscious activities, through our engagement in our practices, as suggested in Chapter Two, in a historical process taking shape within different

---

88. *DP* 305; translation modified; "*une certaine politique du corps, une certaine manière de rendre docile et utile l'accumulation des hommes*" *Surveiller et Punir* 312.

89. *DP* 306.

"systems of rules" that merely proceed from domination to domination? Is that what history ultimately shows us?

VI

From History as Self-Awareness to Self-Wariness through History

What kind of sense of history does one retain after having read *Discipline and Punish*? Many no doubt see in this history of the prison a kind of metaphor of our world: we are imprisoned in our discursive regimes whose ordering function is to normalize us through a constant policing of our engagements in our practices; this regime, operating through a specific conjunction of power and knowledge, shows itself to be ever ready to correct deviations and anomalies in the name of rendering everyone docile, useful and productive. One might call this the "claustrophobic" reading, and it provokes any number of reactions: from despair, to disbelief and rejection, to a desire to revolt or simply to break free. The "claustrophobic" reading lends support to the general view of history, discussed in Chapter Two, that sees it as proceeding from domination to domination through its violent installation of systems of rules.

I have been suggesting throughout this book a different reading, one that sees Foucault's work as pursuing what I have called an "a-theistic theodicy", one that pursues while inverting Hegel's commitment to seeing *reason in history,* because only an attentive consideration of the historical forms that our engagements with each other and the world take will reveal to us the free beings that we are. My reading, then, shares with the "claustrophobic" reading a yearning to be free of constraints that would imprison us, but perhaps unlike it, I think that such yearning is best expressed through a commitment to making sense of history, rather than in some sense breaking free of it.

Foucault's commitment to seeing reason in history is of course very different from Hegel's in that he does not see in its self-movement the reconciliatory gesture that Hegel promotes. Indeed, he shows himself to be very suspicious of such a gesture, where the grasping character of the self-movement of conceptual thought gathers into itself its various others as moments of its own self-development, the whole of which would take on the form of an "absolute" self-identity. This, of course, is why I suggest his work describes a kind

of "*a-theistic*" theodicy. It eschews any reference to an *ultimate justificatory context* for
making sense of history; Foucault restricts
himself to what history has shown itself
actually to "justify" in its unfolding. This,
it seems to me, is the way we should make
sense of his claim to be producing "philosophical fragments" through his histories.
They are "fragments" because they refuse
the "absolute" context that something like
Hegel's philosophy sets out to provide.
Foucault's histories can be read as committed refusals, as it were, of the systematic
whole that Hegel attempted to provide by
showing, *through his histories*, the fragmentary character of reason exposed as the
self-deployment of self-consolidating *systems of thought* in which certain kinds of
disorderliness (the mad, the unlawful, our
desiring selves) are taken up and made
sense of.

But what of the commitment to ourselves as free beings that ostensibly drove
Hegel's systematic appreciation of history
(that we should see in history the self-realization of the idea of freedom)? How does
this commitment relate to Foucault's fragmentary appreciation of such constraining
movements as those of a "punitive reason"
whose policing function increasingly nor-
malizes our engagements with each other
and the world?

It is at this point that most defenders of Foucault's thought will appeal to his notion of *resistance* as key to understanding Foucault's genealogical commitment to freedom, reminding us that there is no power without resistance. But beyond this rather abstract claim, what so many find salutary in Foucault's work is the way, as Todd May has put it, "that kind of resistance which arises in micropolitical domination, is articulated in the specific struggles in which it arises".[1] What May, and others receptive to Foucault's genealogical efforts, are interested in is the *space* that Foucault opens up for intellectual critique, as opposed to an overall theoretical critique which aims at universality. For it is within those spaces that intellectual efforts may prove to be more responsive to actual demands and constraints.[2] As May writes,

1. Todd May, *Between Genealogy and Epistemology: Psychology, Politics, and Knowledge in the Thought of Michel Foucault* (University Park, PA: Penn State UP, 1993) 118. The next few paragraphs are selected from my "Freedom, Responsibility, and the 'American Foucault'," *Philosophy & Social Criticism* 30.1 (2004): 115–26.

2. W. E. Connolly's extension of Foucault's insights in this regard is especially illuminating, cf. *The Ethos of Pluralization* (Minneapolis: U of Minnesota P, 1995) xv,

"The task of the intellectual is no longer to pronounce the truth of the revolt against a power both sovereign and repressive; it is to analyze specific forms of domination and to participate alongside—not above—those who are resisting those forms."[3] The genealogist's task is not one of denunciation and identification, but of *documentation*; that is, "the genealogist documents oppression and domination, patiently detailing their emergence and descent, in order to be able to offer the oppressed one of a number of tools they will need in their struggle against the more insidious forms of modern domination".[4] His work is to be judged not by the truth of its affirmations, but by its relevance to micropolitical struggles. At its core, then, on this view, Foucault's work is concerned with freedom understood as "a concrete project of change from specific forms of domination to alternative courses of behaving and acting in which the relationships of power are more tolerable".[5]

---

where he develops the idea that intellectual work can "strive to cultivate an ethos of critical responsiveness to political movements that challenge the self-confidence and congealed judgments of dominant constituencies".

3. May, *Between Genealogy and Epistemology* 118.
4. May, *Between Genealogy and Epistemology* 119.
5. May, *Between Genealogy and Epistemology* 119.

And, of course, this does seem to accord with Foucault's stated intentions both at the end of *Discipline and Punish*—where the final paragraph states that "At this point I end a book that must serve as a historical background to various studies of the power of normalization and the formation of knowledge in modern society"[6]—and in the projected studies that were to make up his *History of Sexuality.*

However, as is well known, this is not the path his published work will ultimately follow.[7] Instead of continuing on the genealogical path he set out for himself in the mid-seventies, his last works turn to Greek

---

6. *DP* 308.

7. Of course, we now have the publication of Foucault's courses at the Collège de France during the hiatus between the publication of the first volume of the *History of Sexuality* in 1976 [1978 for the English translation] and the subsequent publication of the last two volumes in 1984. The focus here, however, will not be on tracing the evolution of Foucault's thought as evidenced in these courses, but in discussing what his actual publication record says about the concern he brings to the relevance of history as a mode of making sense of our lives. For an excellent discussion of these courses, cf. Edward F. McGushin, *Foucault's Askesis: An Introduction to the Philosophical Life* (Evanston: Northwestern UP, 2007).

and Roman practices of self, which seem at some remove from the engaged critique of power relations inaugurated by his genealogical approach. Although the change of tone and subject matter of Michel Foucault's last two volumes of his *History of Sexuality*[8] has caused much discussion and reconsideration of his work as a whole,[9] what has been little discussed is the way

8. Michel Foucault, *Histoire de la sexualité, t. 2, L'usage des plaisirs* (Paris: Gallimard, 1984) (in English: *The Use of Pleasure*, trans. by R. Hurley (New York: Pantheon, 1985), hereafter referred to as "*UP*"); and *Histoire de la sexualité, t. 3, Le Souci de soi*, Paris, Gallimard, 1984 (in English: Michel Foucault, *The Care of the Self*, trans. R. Hurley (New York: Pantheon, 1990), hereafter referred to as "*CS*").

9. The debate is often characterized in terms of whether or not there is a "return of the subject" in these works. What is meant by the phrase is whether or not Foucault is finally recognizing that, in order for his analysis to be effective, he cannot rid himself of the concept of a grounding subjectivity, in the Kantian sense of a condition for the possibility of experience. Cf. Luc Ferry and Alain Renaut, *French Philosophy of the Sixties: An Essay on Antihumanism*. Trans. Mary H. Cattani. Amherst: U of Massachusetts P, 1990; and Alain Touraine, *Critique de la modernité* (Paris: Fayard, 1992) 193ff.

these works shed light on Foucault's conception of the relation between ourselves and history, and between the past and the present in ways that enrich, in my view, a strictly genealogical approach (that is, one concerned with the "emergence" and "descent" of what we find ourselves committed to in our practices). A very general and widespread criticism of Foucault is that his work, specifically in its genealogical form, although clearly evaluative in its unmasking of incipient forms of modern power (or so the story goes) does not in itself provide the normative framework that would justify and ground such evaluations. Indeed, not only do we encounter this objection in critics like Taylor, Habermas, Merquior, Grumley and Dews,[10]

---

10. Jurgen Habermas, *The Philosophical Discourse of Modernity*, trans. F. G. Lawrence (Cambridge: MIT Press, 1987); Charles Taylor, "Foucault on Freedom and Truth," in *Philosophy and the Human Sciences: Philosophical Papers 2*, (Cambridge: Cambridge UP 1985); José G. Merquior, *Foucault* (London: Fontana, 1985); John E. Grumley, *History and Totality: Radical Historicism from Hegel to Foucault* (London: Routledge, 1989); Peter Dews, *Logics of Disintegration: Post-Structuralist Thought and the Claims of Critical Theory* (London: Verso, 1987).

but also in such sympathetic readers as Dreyfus and Rabinow. On the last page of their important study on Foucault, they write:

> It might seem that if Foucault wants to give up one set of dangers for another, he owes us a criterion of what makes one kind of danger more dangerous than another. Foucault is clear that he cannot justify his preference for some dangers over others by an appeal to human nature, our tradition, or universal reason. His silence on this matter, while consistent, is nonetheless a source of confusion.[11]

However, the confusion here does not stem from Foucault's work as such, but from certain assumptions about the function of philosophy. To say that Foucault "owes us" criteria and must "justify" his preferences, presupposes a view of philosophical activity as precisely that: the formulation and articulation of criteria and justifications for evaluating between "good" and "bad" and "true" and "false". Clearly, Foucault, insofar as he wishes to continue Nietzsche's project, rejects such a view of

---

11. Hubert L. Dreyfus and Paul Rabinow, *Michel Foucault: Beyond Structuralism and Hermeneutics*, (Chicago: U of Chicago P, 1983) 264.

philosophy; but, what is more important
for our purposes, he rejects it in terms
of and by means of his historiographical
practice. The question I would like to ask
here is the extent to which his last works
modify his historiographical practice in
ways that clarify his overall approach and
appeal to history as a way to help us make
sense of our unfolding lives.

***

Alasdair MacIntyre, in a critique of what
he calls the "program of genealogy" as a
rival version of specifically moral inquiry,
makes the following comment:

> . . . the question arises as to whether what
> even Foucault's partial implementation
> of that program may not have revealed is
> that the successive strategies of the genea-
> logist may not inescapably after all involve
> him or her in commitments to standards
> at odds with the central theses of the
> genealogical stance. For in making his
> or her sequence of strategies of masking
> and unmasking intelligible to him or her-
> self, the genealogist has to ascribe to the
> genealogical self a continuity of deliberate
> purpose and a commitment to that pur-
> pose which can only be ascribed to a self
> which cannot but be conceived as more
> and other than its disguises and conceal-
> ments and negotiations, a self which just

insofar as it can adopt alternative perspectives is not itself perspectival, but persistent and substantial. Make of the genealogist's self nothing but what genealogy makes of it, and that self is dissolved to the point at which there is no longer a continuous genealogical project.[12]

The point MacIntyre is making is an interesting one. It is not so much (although it is for MacIntyre) that a unified project supposes a unified self, but that a unified project, as it is reworked and reformulated, supposes that certain standards "are independent of the particular stages and moments of the temporary strategies through which the genealogist moves his or her overall projects forward".[13] MacIntyre claims that in the very reworking of one's project, if that project is to remain intelligible both to oneself and to others, appeals to certain independent standards must be recognized. But this raises the question: "can genealogy, as a systematic project, be made intelligible to the genealogist, as well as to others, without some at least tacit recognition being accorded to just those standards and

---

12. Alasdair MacIntyre, *Three Rival Versions of Moral Inquiry* (Notre Dame, IN: U Notre Dame P, 1990) 54.

13. MacIntyre 55.

allegiances *which it is avowed aim to disrupt
and subvert*"?[14] Would not such recognition
undermine the very nature of the project?
Why continue to be a genealogist if one
ultimately must appeal to the same standards? Why not join the traditional project of defining, articulating and justifying
common standards and allegiances?

A few things might be said in response to
this critique. First of all, the focus seems to
be on something called "the genealogist"
pursuing an overall project, as opposed to
the genealogies themselves, which, after
all, are specific forms of historical inquiries. Do we have to consider Foucault *as*
a genealogist? In producing genealogies,
does one thereby become a genealogist
(*someone* who produces genealogies)? Is
not the point of producing genealogies
the production of genealogies (and not
genealogists)?

But what, then, of the *project* of producing genealogies? Here a response might
be that Foucault's *principal* (as opposed to
overall) purpose is not to disrupt and subvert our particular, contingent standard
and allegiance, but to disrupt and subvert
precisely that *mode* of thinking that constructs out of the appeal to certain defini-
tions and articulations of standards and

---

14. MacIntyre 55; emphasis added.

allegiances particularly oppressive forms
of self. As Karlis Racevskis has suggested, it
is the intellect itself that Foucault attempts
to subvert so that we might create a space
for "the liberation of man from the images
that have contributed to subjugate him in
the name of various ideals and interests".[15]

However, what is interesting about both
the critique and these responses is that
they do raise the question of the self and
the way it relates to the kinds of histories
we produce, the kinds of account we give
of the past, both in terms of the past itself
and in terms of its relation to the present,
that is, it raises the question, identified in
Chapter One, of what history is *for*.

The suggestion throughout this book
has been that if Foucault can and should
be read as rejecting a teleological, subject-
centred conception of history, it is less
a theoretical challenge to a particular
philosophical tradition (stemming from
German idealism), than a practical challenge to the predominant way in which
philosophers and historians of ideas conceive and practice history. By doing this,
Foucault is virtually alone amongst contemporary thinkers in following through

---

15. Karlis Racevskis, *Michel Foucault and the
    Subversion of the Intellect* (Ithaca: Cornell UP,
    1983) 166.

on his rejection of such subject-centred philosophies of history by not attempting a theoretical justification of those criteria of significance that would render history intelligible; rather, he seeks to explore and articulate the actual operation of various criteria of significance and selection already hard at work in the variety of processes that configure both the past and the present. (These criteria are especially evident—or made so with the help of Foucault's genealogical inquiries—in our prisons, asylums and ambiguous attitudes towards sex.)

More importantly, for our purposes here, Foucault draws out the philosophical implications of such a practice (and concomitant conception) of history. If criteria of significance, indeed of intelligibility itself, are historically constituted and if history itself is best described in terms of a variety of different processes whose configurations depend on the questions they allow to be asked, then the picture of history as a process of ever-increasing rationality or increased self-consciousness (presupposed by the demand for criteria of significance) cannot remain unquestionable or unquestioned. Indeed, even the rather innocuous idea that more historical knowledge can only lead to better self-awareness becomes problematic when history becomes a question of the various knowledges that have been produced, the kinds of awareness they promote, right down to the very selves that are thereby constituted.

Which brings us to the last two volumes of the *History of Sexuality*. What I would like to do through an examination of these two texts is to show how the ultimate function of Foucault's historical analysis is to provide us with a critical self-knowledge (of ourselves and the present) that I call *self-wariness* (as opposed to self-awareness, the principal concern of traditional philosophy of history). Rather than a substantive self-knowledge, his type of historical analysis can be seen as providing a critical self-knowledge, a knowledge that can show the different ways our "selves" have been constituted and constructed, and thus providing a contrast with the way they constitute themselves in the present. As Foucault has said:

> Among the cultural inventions of mankind there is a treasury of devices, techniques, ideas, procedures, and so on, that cannot exactly be reactivated, but at least constitute, or help to constitute, a certain point of view which can be very useful as a tool for analyzing what's going on now—and to change it.[16]

---

16. Dreyfus and Rabinow 236.

Thus, further, this idea of self-wariness leads not only to a critical self-knowledge but also to action, not by prescribing any particular course, but by grounding itself in possibility. Here, too, Foucault's understanding of history challenges the more traditional conception that sees its task as that of discerning the necessary conditions of that which it investigates. The problem with this approach is that that which is investigated must already be defined and in some sense complete. However, history itself insofar as it issues into a self-constituting present, denies us such completion; therefore, rather than seek necessary conditions, Foucault's histories spell out conditions of possibility. And by pointing out the possibility of various configurations, one thereby implies the possibility of other possibilities; and it is in the very possibility of these other possibilities that one recalls the freedom at the heart of our insistent forms of forgetfulness that buttress our practical engagements.

***

Why, in his last works, did Foucault turn to Antiquity? This is the question that most commentators ask when confronted with the last two volumes of the *History of Sexuality*.[17] Foucault had occasion to

---

17. This is especially true in France. Aside from the works mentioned above, see also

respond to this question in various interviews,[18] but perhaps the most pertinent response for our purposes is to be found in *The Use of Pleasure*, where he writes:

> After all, what would be the value for the passion for knowledge if it resulted only in a certain amount of knowledgeableness and not, in one way or another and to the extent possible, in the knower's straying afield from himself? There are times in

---

Mario Vegetti, "Foucault et les anciens," *Critique* 471–72 (1986): 925–32; Maria Daraki, "Le voyage en Grèce de Michel Foucault," *Esprit* 100 (1985): 55–83; Henri Joly, "Retour aux Grecs: Réflexions sur les 'pratiques de soi' dans *L'usage des plaisirs*," *Le Débat* 41 (1986): 100–20.

18. Probably the most cited is the interview conducted by Dreyfus and Rabinow, published as an afterword to their work on Foucault and entitled "On the Genealogy of Ethics". Cf. also "An Aesthetics of Existence," "The Return of Morality" and "The Concern for Truth", all interviews reprinted in Michel Foucault, *Politics, Philosophy, Culture: Interviews and Other Writings, 1977–1984* (London: Routledge, 1990); as well as "The Ethic of Care for the Self as a Practice of Freedom," *The Final Foucault*, ed. James Bernauer and David Rasmussen (Boston: MIT Press, 1988) 1–20.

life when the question of knowing if one
can think differently than one thinks, and
perceive differently than one sees, is abso-
lutely necessary if one is to go on looking
and reflecting at all.[19]

This is an important statement; indeed,
in a sense, it provides a key to understanding this "turning" to the Greek experience
of ethics. The point to note is that it is the
experience of ethics that is of interest to
Foucault and not principally the fact that
it is of Greek and Roman origin.[20] In fact,
then, objections such as that put forward
by Daraki that Foucault misrepresents the
Greeks,[21] or again that he overestimates
the value of Greek "freedom",[22] or even

---

19. *UP* 8.

20. Of course, the choice is not arbitrary
    either. The point is that it provides an
    important perspective on our contempo-
    rary experience of ethics. As he explains
    in "The Return to Morality":

    Trying to rethink the Greeks today does not
    consist in setting off Greek morality as the
    domain of morality par excellence which one
    would need for self-reflection. The point is
    rather to see to it that European thinking can
    take up Greek thinking again as an experi-
    ence which took place once and with regard
    to which one can be completely free. (249)

21. Daraki 72.

22. Vegetti 928.

yet that he undervalues a potential Greek "feminism"[23] within that experience of ethics, are in some sense beside the point, because they misunderstand the particular use Foucault is making of history. He does not turn to Ancient history in order to find a pre-modern normative foundation. Indeed, as we saw above, he does not see the philosophical use of history to be one of establishing criteria and justifying norms. Foucault understands philosophy as an activity and not as the elaboration of a doctrine or theoretical construct. This is the reason his philosophical questions have consistently been connected to historical research; his histories do not merely serve as illustrations of his "theory". As he himself puts it:

> There is always something ludicrous in philosophical discourse when it tries, from the outside, to dictate to others, to tell them where their truth is and how to find it, or when it works up a case against them in the language of naïve positivity. But it is entitled to explore what might be changed, in its own thought, through the practice of a knowledge that is foreign to it.[24]

---

23. Joly 113.
24. *UP* 9.

Thus the appeal to history; it takes us away from our all-too-familiar world and serves as a contrast to our current engagements. He once again insists, however, that although he is clearly "doing" history in these works, they are not to be considered the works of a "historian", by which he means that their primary task is not to tell us something about the past, although they remain keen to the latest historiographical developments. In other words, these works are clearly works of historical research but they are presented philosophically, from philosophical motives. Foucault calls them a philosophical exercise whose "object was to learn to what extent the effort to think one's own history can free thought from what it silently thinks, and so enable it to think differently".[25]

While this continues to show why Foucault consistently attaches his philosophical questions to historical ones, it still does not tell us why Foucault now chose the Greeks and Romans. Is Foucault— a professor at the Collège de France for some time now—simply paying his dues and returning to the canon? Foucault, whose work until then had consistently restricted itself to a certain periodization of history (the Renaissance, the Classical

---

25. *UP* 9.

Age, the Modern Age), insists that by distancing himself from this periodization he was able to get a better perspective on what he had consistently been trying to do (which he now characterizes as a "history of truth"), that is, "analyzing, not behaviors, or ideas, nor societies and their 'ideologies', but the problematizations through which being offers itself to be, necessarily, thought—and the practices on the basis of which these problematizations are formed".[26] This analysis of problematizations is how Foucault characterizes his current genealogical approach, or what he also begins to explicitly characterize as "historical ontology",[27] and it is important to remember that genealogy, for Foucault, "means that I begin my analysis from a question posed in the present".[28] He writes:

---

26. *UP* 11.

27. Foucault, "On the Genealogy of Ethics". It is here that he gives a description of genealogy as "historical ontology" in general and the *History of Sexuality* in particular as "an historical ontology in relation to ethics through which we constitute ourselves as moral agents" (Foucault, "On the Genealogy of Ethics" 237).

28. Foucault, "The Concern for Truth" 262. Put in these terms, the question posed in the present for these works is why the lifting of sexual prohibitions does not

... in raising this very general question, and in directing it to Greek and Greco-Roman culture, it occurred to me that this problematization was linked to a group of practices that have been of unquestionable importance in our societies: I am referring to what can be called the "arts of existence." What I mean by the phrase are those intentional and voluntary actions by which men not only set themselves rules of conduct, but also seek to transform themselves in their singular being, and to make their life into an œuvre that carries certain aesthetic values and meets certain stylistic criteria. These "arts of existence", these "techniques of the self", no doubt lost some of their importance and autonomy when they were assimilated into the exercise of priestly power in early Christianity, and later, into educative, medical, and psychological types of practices. Still, I thought that the long history of these aesthetics of existence and these technologies of the self remained to be done, or resumed.[29]

It is clear from this passage that the concern with the concept of an "art of existence" is the main goal of the proposed

---

resolve the question of ethics. Cf. Foucault, "The Concern for Truth" 263.

29. *UP* 10–11.

history, but not because Foucault wishes to retrieve an Ancient practice, nor is his history meant to describe, as Dreyfus and Rabinow put it, "an attractive and plausible alternative". Foucault explains:

> I am not looking for an alternative; you can't find the solution of a problem in the solution of another problem raised at another moment by other people. You see, what I want to do is not the history of solutions, and that's why I don't accept the word "alternative." I would like to do genealogy of problems, or problématiques. My point is not that everything is bad, but that everything is dangerous, which is not exactly the same thing as bad. If everything is dangerous, then we always have something to do. So my position leads not to apathy but to a hyper- and pessimistic activism.[30]

Here we see again how what I have called the idea of wariness is connected to the idea of history. The kinds of history Foucault writes help keep us on our guard, keen to the dangers of seductive solutions and unspecified promises which we normally and unthinkingly accept as valid, self-evident or matter-of-course. The self-wariness he promotes through his

---

30. Dreyfus and Rabinow 231–32.

histories is an awareness of a self that is not "the source of self-assertion and exclusion but the target of a questioning through which people might start to depart from the historical limits of their identifications, taking their particularities as so many historical specificities".[31] In other words, its prescriptivism is primarily negative and connected to the political character Foucault emphasized in his earlier work. That is, the ethical considerations of the last two volumes of the *History of Sexuality* are intimately linked to the political concerns of the first volume, inasmuch as they are directed, as James W. Bernauer has pointed out, to "an effort to get at a form of becoming a subject that would furnish the source of an effective resistance to a specific and widespread type of power".[32] This is done, through the study of history,

---

31. John Rajchman, *Truth and Eros: Foucault, Lacan, and the Question of Ethics* (New York: Routledge, 1991) 108. This is essential reading for a proper appreciation of Foucault's later work. John Rajchman has also written an excellent overview of Foucault's work in his *Michel Foucault: The Freedom of Philosophy* (New York: Columbia UP, 1985).

32. James William Bernauer, *Michel Foucault's Force of Flight* (Atlantic Highlands: Humanity, 1990) 166.

by producing "a de-familiarization of the 'desiring man' who lies at the root of our willingness to identify with the form of individual subjectivity constituted for us in the modern period".[33] In other words, the point and purpose of history is to enable us to become self-wary in such a way that the identities "we" (as identified) recognize are loosened such that "we" (considered anonymously) can grasp them for "ourselves" autonomously and independently. But we are getting ahead of ourselves.

***

First, I would like to examine how Foucault effects this "de-familiarization" in *The Use of Pleasure*. Note that this is something that must be done because otherwise what happens is that most histories simply read backwards from the present in order to classify the experience they set out to recount. Here Foucault is consistently using the methods present in the earlier works of not looking for "precursor" ideas but looking instead at the formulation of different problems.[34] However, by going

33. Bernauer, *Foucault's Force of Flight* 166.
34. For this aspect of Foucault's historiographical methodology and its indebtedness to Gaston Bachelard and Georges Canguilhem, cf. Gary Gutting, *Michel Foucault's Archaeology of Scientific Reason* (Cambridge: Cambridge UP, 1989).

back to the Greeks, Foucault is not only seeking to trace the genealogy of the configurations of relations that continue to have a hold on us. He is not merely trying to identify them. He wants in effect to allow us the opportunity to "disengage" ourselves from them. This is the purpose of "de-familiarization".

Thus Foucault turns to the Greeks, who have pride of place in our culture's self-understanding and yet whose practices are in so many ways unfamiliar; especially those practices revolving around sex. The point is, unfamiliarity also presupposes familiarity and, as it turns out, Foucault is intent to focus as well on the continuities surrounding the self-understanding of sexual practices between the Greco-Roman world and the Christian world. Note that Foucault is interested in the self-understandings that define those practices and not the practices themselves, which, as has long been observed, differ substantially. from both those of the early Christians as well as those considered acceptable today. However, just to note some of the major points of difference between pagan sexual practices and Christian ones: They usually revolve around such notions as the nature of the sexual act, where it is connected to sin and the fall for Christians and given positive connotations for the pagans;

other practices revolve around notions of monogamy and fidelity, as well as chastity. And finally, of course, the acceptance and even valorization of homosexuality in the pagan world is often contrasted with the (until recently) unconditional exclusion of it in Christianity. The general character of these comparisons usually leads to the conclusion that while Christianity seems obsessively concerned with sexual practices, the Greeks appear to be largely indifferent.

However, Foucault argues that this appearance of indifference stems from the fact that sexual practices for the Greeks were neither codified nor monitored in the same way that such practices were to be within Christianity. They were nevertheless discussed, and evoked similar concerns. For example, monogamy and fidelity were encouraged because there was a fear that unreproductive sex had negative effects on a given individual (i.e., involved "spending" too much of one's vital energy). As well, homosexual practices were of course accepted, but the image of the effeminate and flaccid male was also current and carried with it clear negative connotations. And, finally, there was a clear valorization of sexual abstention (one need only think of Socrates) and its connection with the achievement of truth and wisdom.

Thus, we see here important continuities between the attitudes towards certain sexual practices.

So much for continuity and familiarity. What is so *different* (i.e., discontinuous and unfamiliar) about the Greek attitudes towards these sexual practices is that they are not presented as a set or rules for the relation between the sexes but are rather "an elaboration of masculine conduct carried out from the viewpoint of men in order to give form to their behaviors".[35] And, furthermore, this elaboration does not take the form of a set of prohibitions or interdictions but rather as, for the individual male, a "stylization of an activity in the exercise of its power and the practice of its liberty".[36] Here, the purpose for studying the Greeks becomes exceptionally clear inasmuch as the effect of de-familiarization reaches its peak. And yet, again, such a de-familiarization contains within it an element of familiarity (otherwise it would not be described as unfamiliar, but as incomprehensible or unrecognizable) in that the problematization of sexual practices in connection with this notion of "stylization" is describable in terms of an individual's personal freedom,

---

35. *UP* 22–23.
36. *UP* 23.

autonomy and self-mastery; notions definitely familiar to "our" self-understanding.

The concept that holds together the
twin poles of familiarity and unfamiliarity, continuity and discontinuity, is that
of problematization. The interest in the
problematization of sexual practices for
Foucault is that it opens up a new conceptual dimension of moral or ethical reflection and activity. While morality and ethics
usually involve discussion concerning codes
and conduct, Foucault's problematizing
approach brings out a third dimension
which he calls the self-constitution of the
subject vis-à-vis these codes and the conduct required of them. That is, this third
dimension involves the individual's choos-
ing to conduct himself according to the
prescriptions of the code. In other words,
within any given code, and within the conduct it prescribes, "there are different ways
to conduct oneself morally, different ways
for the acting individual to operate, not
just as an agent, but as an ethical subject of
this action".[37] Thus, one might say, there
is an internalization effected between the
code and the conduct, and this internalization is what one would call the "moral subject". The moral subject is thus something
constituted.

---

37. *UP* 26.

An individual is not merely related to the—in this case "moral"—world (via codes) but also to himself, and this is not simply in terms of self-awareness but in a practical and constitutive sense. Or, as Foucault puts it, there is no particular moral action

> that does not refer to a unified moral conduct; no moral conduct that does not call for the forming of oneself as an ethical subject; and no forming of the ethical subject without "modes of subjectivation" and an "ascetics" or practices of the self that support them.[38]

And Foucault of course sets as his task the examination of this third dimension of practices of the self found in Antiquity surrounding the problematization of pleasure, desire and sex.

Rather than go in great exegetical detail—I refer the reader directly to the text, for Foucault's stylistic flourishes are at a minimum and his clarity is exceptional—I would simply like to draw out the major features of this "art of existence" Foucault is describing and connect it with the goal of what I have been calling "self-wariness".

Sex is a problem for the Greeks, but not the sexual act in itself. That is, the sexual

---

38. *UP* 28.

act is not classified in any particular way and details about it are not normally discussed. One might say that sexual acts are a matter for concern, but "when they were the subject for questioning, what was at issue was not the form they assumed, it was the activity they manifested. Their dynamics was much more important than their morphology."[39]

There is, within Greek sexual activity, a general unity between act, desire and pleasure (a unity which, Foucault notes, Christianity will dissociate). That is, the Greeks were not confronted with the problem between the desire for sex, the sexual act itself and the pleasure one gets from it (it is not a matter of lack and satisfaction). What we have instead is the problem of force. That is, it is a question of the force (of nature) that unites the three terms. The problem of sexual activity (and not the act considered in itself) concerns the dynamics of the triad act-pleasure-desire, which itself is analyzed in terms of two variables : 1. quantity, or more precisely, intensity (homosexuality, for example, is not so much abnormal or unnatural as it can be excessive); and 2. the role or polarity, that is, the positioning, of the free adult male (women, slaves and boys were considered

---

39. *UP* 42.

as objects, not as partners, and therefore moral concern was not extended to
them).

Immorality, then (for men, since this
morality is for and by men), revolves
around the notions of excess and passiv-
ity. The sexual act, being natural, is valued;
but it remains a matter of moral concern
because it is, like all natural things, a force
and a force that must be controlled. The
question becomes: how is this control to
be effected? Not from above, nor from
without, but from within. What Foucault
calls the "use" ("usage", chresis) of pleasure has to do, not with what is permitted or forbidden, but rather with what is
a matter "of prudence, of reflection, and
calculation in the way one distributed and
controlled his acts".[40] The moral criteria
involved in the use of pleasure cannot be
codified or tabulated beforehand but is a
matter of an individual's assessment of his
need, an opportune moment, as well as
regard for that individual's status. This is
not to say there are no general laws that
the individual must also take into account.
The laws of nature and the city and
indeed of religion cannot be disregarded.
However, they serve as the context, or
background, of the actions of a particular

---

40. *UP* 54.

individual, and not as a code or a model to be adopted. Foucault writes:

> The few great common laws—of the city, religion, nature—remained present, but it was as if they traced a very wide circle in the distance, inside of which practical thought had to define what could rightfully be done. And for this there was no need of anything resembling a text that would have the force of law, but rather, of a techne or "practice," a savoir-faire that by taking general principles into account would guide action in its time, according to its context, and in view of its ends. Therefore, in this form of morality, the individual did not make himself into an ethical subject by universalizing the principles that informed his action; on the contrary, he did so by means of an attitude and a quest that individualized his action, modulated it, and perhaps even gave him a special brilliance by virtue of the rational and deliberate structure his action manifested.[41]

In this important passage we see how Foucault plays off the familiar with the unfamiliar. He describes a context in which moral or ethical conduct is individualized in a way that is alien to the present's

---

41. *UP* 62.

universalizing approach to morality, revealing morality's historical dimension that in effect relativizes its universalizing pretensions. Thus, an individualized and individualizing approach becomes intelligible and perhaps even desirable; but even more importantly, it underscores its possibility.

But this does not mean that Foucault thinks that the Greek approach is a solution to present concerns. As we have seen, he explicitly denies this on the simple grounds that the problems of the present cannot be resolved by using the solutions of the past. (If history teaches us anything, it teaches us that.) But that does not mean the past therefore has nothing to offer the present. On the contrary, because the past has provided solutions to its problems, and to the extent that its problems share certain similarities with present ones (and they must, otherwise we would be unable to recognize them as problems), what the past has to offer is a contrast and a vantage point from which to view the present's "self-entanglements", that is, the way the self is presently constituted.

The present's view of the self is entangled with notions of freedom, autonomy and truth. The Greek experience of sex— the subject of Foucault's history—reveals another self entangled in related notions of freedom, self-mastery and truth. His first volume showed how, in trying to untangle the knot tying together the notions of freedom, autonomy and truth (the knot might be called "the repressive hypothesis"), the knot was only tightened further (talk leading to talk and only talk). Thus, rather than getting entangled further, Foucault turns to past knots which he can untangle because he is not completely tied to them. The knot freedom-autonomy-truth is not the same knot as freedom-self-mastery-truth. The latter he can and does untangle. And he does so, as mentioned above, by examining the "use of pleasure" divided in the triple distinction of desire-pleasure-act. The virtuous "use of pleasure" in Greek experience does not involve the proper ordering or balancing of the triple distinction; the virtue needed for the proper ethical "use of pleasure" revolves around the notion of self-mastery, which is connected to the notion of freedom, not in the sense of the former leading to the latter, but in the sense of the one being constituted by the other. That is, self-mastery is necessary in order to be and remain free. Freedom is here understood as "a certain form of relationship of the individual with himself".[42] The opposite of

---

42. *UP* 92.

freedom on this view is not a natural deter-
minism or a divine will but a kind of slavery; the opposite of self-mastery would be
self-enslavement (*esclavage de soi par soi*).
This freedom then is not a freedom from
all constraints (the kind of freedom called
for by the repressive hypothesis, i.e., a "liberating" freedom) but "a power that one
brought to bear on oneself in the power
that one exercised over others".[43] As well,
in this ethical perspective, self-mastery is
also constitutive of truth inasmuch as the
truth of the self is not seen as the elucidation and revelation of inner desire, but
rather is conceived constitutively as the
"*mode of being* of the moderate subject".[44]
Thus, the goal or ideal of such an ethical
perspective is as follows: "The individual
fulfilled himself as an ethical subject by
shaping a precisely measured conduct that
was plainly visible to all and deserving to
be long remembered."[45] One might say
that this ethical perspective of the self—as
opposed to being the inner truth that must
be universalized in theory as is the case in
the present—must be constitutively exter-
nalized in practice in order for such a self
truly to *be* a self, that is, in order to be free

---

43. *UP* 93.
44. *UP* 89; my emphasis.
45. *UP* 91.

and autonomous. This is what Foucault calls the "aesthetics of existence" characteristic of the Greek experience.

Historically specific and thus capable of being untangled, Foucault shows how the knot of Greek experience has at least one string tied to the present, namely "that some of the main principles of our ethics have been related at a certain moment to an aesthetics of existence"[46]; and that the possibility thus exists for an ethics based on an individual's creating a work of art out of his or her life. Thus, rather than proposing a return to the Greek triad of freedom-self-mastery-truth, Foucault seems to be arguing for a new triad one might describe as freedom-*creativity*-truth. This would be a new "aesthetics of existence", where one's *life* is to be one's work of art. It is within this creative possibility that a new relation between freedom and truth resides.

Note that Foucault is arguing for a creative life and not a creative self as in, for example, the radical freedom of the existentialist self. Foucault is careful to distinguish himself from a view such as Sartre's:

> From the idea that the self is not given to us, I think that there is only one practical consequence: we have to create ourselves as works of art. In his analyses of

46. Dreyfus and Rabinow 236.

Baudelaire, Flaubert, etc., it is interesting
to see that Sartre refers the work of creation to a certain relation to oneself—the
author to himself—which has the form of
authenticity or inauthenticity. I would like
to say exactly the contrary: we should not
have to refer the creative activity of some-
body to the kind of relation he has to himself, but should relate the kind of relation
one has to oneself to creative activity.[47]

And thus the need for the particular
kind of historical analysis Foucault offers.
It shows the different (creative) ways individuals have related to themselves, thereby
challenging the supposed necessity of
current predominant ones. While all of
this is rather upbeat and positive, challenging the prevailing sense of necessity
does not by itself remove the effective
constitutive relations individuals have to
themselves. Foucault is pointing to a possibility, not a reality. The reality is that
most individuals are bound and tied to
particular "selves" that leave little room
for creativity, indeed, selves that are normalized as self-monitoring "individuals"
in the sense described in *Discipline and
Punish*. This is because most individuals
do not see their relation to their "selves" as
a creative activity, but as something to be

---

47. Dreyfus and Rabinow 237.

uncovered, discovered, recovered and ultimately obeyed. This is the sense of self that
Foucault is combating, the idea that one's
life should be devoted to discovering one's
true self. These are the selves Foucault is
wary of (thus the need for and function of
self-wariness rather than self-awareness).
History shows that the relation to self has
taken on many forms, demanding of the
individual things like submission, obedience or renunciation. Amongst these possibilities, there is one to which Foucault
pays particular attention in his last work; it
is a self that calls for careful concern, and
it is this concern for self that I would like
to consider next.

***

To recapitulate: the self constitutes itself
through its relating to itself. This is the
fundamental claim of the last two volumes
of the *History of Sexuality.* The self is not a
given, it is constituted through a set of practices within a given historical context. The
self is thus a historical object (practice),
subject to change and transformation.
Historical analysis and research enables
us to identify those practices constitutive
of different kinds of relation to self, and
does not therefore provide the self with an
identity (as some would have history do).
The point that Foucault is making is that
the self is not the product of a particular

activity in the sense that the product can be detached from the activity; the self is the activity. The self is constituted by a set of practices but it is not those practices; rather it resides in the way those practices are taken up. But taken up by whom? The answer is: by particular individuals.

In order to be clear about this point, I would like to introduce an idea suggested by my reading of much contemporary historiography and its efforts to distinguish itself from sociology (inasmuch as sociology is much more "theory-driven" than history is). The idea is that of the anonymous individual. This is the term I give to all those individual human beings who people the historical process and are the subject matter of historical reconstructions and yet remain unnamed. That is, they are the individuals that historians refer to when they speak of peasants and warriors, doctors, teachers and lawyers or vagabonds and bandits. The idea of an anonymous individual is a historical concept and not a sociological one, inasmuch as the primary reference is to the actual flesh and blood individuals who were peasants, doctors, criminals and so forth. Put another way, although the subject matter of both these disciplines may be the same—the activities of these people—the reference is not. For sociology, the reference is to the function and role of the activities themselves; for history, the reference is to the (past) lives of human individuals. Sociology has as its goal the explanation of social behaviour; history the task of describing past human lives. The results of sociological investigations are destined for various administrative and governmental uses; historical investigations are undertaken with the view of achieving a particular kind of "self-knowledge".

I would like to use this concept of the anonymous individual in order to distinguish between the concrete (i.e., bodily) individual human being and his or her self.[48] The attempt to distinguish them is not meant to say that there are individuals out there who are not also selves, or selves that are not individuals. Rather, the distinction is to help us understand the different elements involved in the way human beings relate, not only to the world and others, but to themselves as well. Indeed, the

---

48. One might want to say that the distinction is simply between the social, cultural, symbolic properties of human beings as opposed to their physical and biological ones. However, since this is a problem of *historical* reference, appeals to biology and physics are not really helpful. The distinction is not between the physical and mental but between *real* and hypothetical or ideal.

distinction I am trying to make is implicit in the very expression: one's relation to oneself. The "one" here refers to the individual considered anonymously related to that same individual considered as a specifiable self with specific characteristics. And the relation is one of "identity" when there is no conflict or gap between the individual considered anonymously and the individual considered as a particular self. That is, the self is complete, such that the individual is totally identified with it and does not distinguish himself from that self (or there are no evident occasions where this distinction is made). However, more often than not, and perhaps today more than in the past, an individual can distinguish himself from that self and consider himself "anonymously", that is, independently of the different roles and functions he is "said" to have and which make up his sense of self. And to the extent that he can do this, the relation he has to himself is no longer one of identity but instead becomes problematic and a matter for concern.

This brings us to the third volume of Foucault's history of sexuality, *Le Souci de soi*, usually translated as *The Care of the Self.* The use of the term "care" to translate "*souci*" is to a certain extent quite appropriate, given that the work does deal with medical texts devoted to what today we would characterize as "health care". However, "*souci*" can also be translated as "worry" and "concern", as in having concerns or worries about some matter.

Both senses are reflected in Foucault's work inasmuch as an increasing concern for the self displayed in late Antiquity— that is, concern for what was seen as the self's "fragility"—led to the preoccupation (another word for *souci*) by doctors and moralists in their writings to develop a careful practice of examination and care for one's self. This care and concern found expression in the writings of those doctors and moralists explicitly concerned with sexual matters and what they thought was a sign of the "immorality and dissolute ways"[49] of their society. However, what is interesting and remarkable (and directly relevant to the present's concerns) is that:

> ... this desire for rigor expressed by the moralists did not take the form of a demand for intervention on the part of public authority. One would not find in the writings of the philosophers any proposal for a general and coercive legislation of sexual behaviors. They urge individuals to be more austere if they wish to lead a life different from that of "the throngs"; they do not try to determine which measures or

---

49. *CS* 39.

punishments might constrain everyone in a uniform manner.[50]

We see here again the anti-universalist focus of Foucault's analysis. He considers these writings of the moralists and philosophers of late Antiquity and their call for austerity precisely because they are not proposing a blueprint or model to be applied or constructed; they are, rather, addressed to individuals. Foucault is aware that this appeal to individuals is often seen as reflecting the more general weakening of the social and political structures characteristic of late Antiquity. Unstable periods are characteristically said to give rise to this kind of "individualism" where people retreat into their private lives where things can more readily appear under control.

However, this kind of "explanation" is historically suspect. Lumping together different phenomena under the rubric "the rise of individualism" serves only to obscure matters that need to be carefully distinguished. The term "individualism" can describe what Foucault calls different "realities". He writes:

Three things in fact need to be distinguished here: 1) the individualistic atti-

---

50. *CS* 40.

tude, characterized by the absolute value
attributed to the individual in his singularity and by the degree of independence
conceded to him vis-à-vis the group to
which he belongs and the institutions to
which he is answerable; 2) the positive
valuation of private life, that is, the importance granted to family relationships, to
the forms of domestic activity, and to the
domain of patrimonial interests; 3) the
intensity of the relations to self, that is, of
the forms in which one is called upon to
take oneself as an object of knowledge and
a field of action, so as to transform, correct,
and purify oneself, and find salvation.[51]

Note that Foucault calls what he is
describing here different "attitudes". This
of course is connected with the kind of
"ethics" we discussed in the last section
that dealt not with codes and practices
principally but with the *way* in which codes
were understood and practices undertaken. The same applies here. Foucault
acknowledges immediately that these different "attitudes" need not be mutually
exclusive, although different periods in
history can be seen as characterized by the
predominance of one or the other. For
example, he uses ancient warrior societies as exemplifying the first; nineteenth

51. *CS* 42.

century bourgeois society the second; and
certain early Christian ascetic movements
as typical of the third.

The point of making these distinctions
is to show that the period he is describing,
while obviously fitting in a general way with
the third "attitude" described above, displays a specific kind of "individualism"—if
one can even call it that—which revolves
around the general idea of a "*culture de soi*".
Foucault argues that this idea reaches far
back in Greek culture and is characterized
by the general principle that one should
take care of oneself (*prendre soin de soi-
même*). One finds it in Xenophon, Plutarch
(when discussing the Spartans) and of
course in Plato's Socrates. It is the guiding
principle of what Foucault calls the "art
of existence" of the period he is describing, and in the course of its development
it had taken on a very general sense which
Foucault summarizes as follows:

> . . . the principle of care of oneself became
> rather general in scope. The precept
> according to which one must give attention
> to oneself was in any case an imperative
> that circulated among a number of differ-
> ent doctrines. It also took the form of an
> attitude, a mode of behaviour; it became
> instilled in ways of living; it evolved into
> procedures, practices, and formulas that

people reflected on, developed, perfected, and taught. It thus came to constitute a social practice, giving rise to relationships between individuals, to exchanges and communications, and at times even to institutions. And it gave rise, finally, to a certain mode of knowledge, and to the elaboration of a science [*savoir*].[52]

Thus, if one still wants to call this "care or concern for the self" an individualism, then it is certainly not the kind of individualism characterized by autonomy and independence as in the first model; nor by the retreat into privacy typical of the second; nor even is it properly applied to the third model of purification and salvation. If we describe these "individualisms" as the relation *one* (considered anonymously) has with *oneself*, then the first identifies the self with the will, the second with the private enjoyment of one's possessions and the third with one's purified soul. As distinct from these, Foucault describes a relation to oneself as the care one gives to a fragile and vulnerable body in need of constant attention. In other words, it is something that takes a great deal of time and effort. The point of considering the self as a fragile body emphasizes that the relation to the self is not something that is sought

52. *CS* 45.

after as a goal, or an end, as a prize, or discovery, but is rather a continuous process.
It is not the culmination or point or object
of all other activities but relates to the way
those activities are undertaken; it is not the
focal point but the centre of those activities. The concern for self should be seen
principally as

> a change of activity: not that one must
> cease all other forms of occupation and
> devote oneself entirely and exclusively to
> oneself; but in the activities that one ought
> to engage in, one had best keep in mind
> that the chief objective one should set for
> oneself is to be sought within oneself, in
> the relation of oneself to oneself.[53]

The interest of this relation to self is
that, while still connected to the ethics of
self-mastery, there is what Foucault calls an
"*infléchissement*", a bending, a slight change
of direction or accent. What we have at this
point is a unique situation where the self
is poised, as it were, between a complete
immersion and identification within given
practices and an abstract universalism.
The Care of the Self is devoted to the historical analysis of this new attitude towards
the self which has the individual poised
between concrete identification and uni-

---

53. *CS* 64–65.

versal appeal. Probably the best example Foucault gives of this dislocation from embedded practices or relating oneself to oneself is most evident in what he calls the "political game", that is, in political practices. He argues that the dismantling of the city-states and the growth of empire is not best described in terms of a decline of civic life and political elites and a retreat or withdrawal into self. The important point is that the extension of the Empire required changes in "the conditions of the exercise of power"[54] in the sense that the administrative reach had to be adjusted to a widened Empire. Thus what we see is not the decline and decadence of a civic elite, but rather we are confronted with "the search for a new way of conceiving the relationship that one ought to have with one's status, one's functions, one's activities, and one's obligations".[55] In other words, the new political realities required a different understanding of oneself as a political actor. Given the wider circumstances (and unfamiliar ones) in which "one" had to act politically, "one" became more acutely aware of the outward signs of function and role (uniform, habits, gestures) and, concomitantly, one became increasingly aware

---

54. *CS* 83.
55. *CS* 84.

and concerned with that which was not connected to these functions and roles. Or, to put it another way, one became increasingly aware of, and concerned with, the nature of one's relation (as an individual considered anonymously) to these roles and functions. And once this step is taken, then the whole relation one has with oneself is rendered problematic. Indeed, the attitude one has towards one's own acts becomes problematic. That is, one's status and position no longer dictate what "one" is to do. That status may be responsible for the general outline of one's situation, but it is the individual who is responsible for the actions "one" undertakes. Put in terms of political action, the individual exercising power "has to place himself in a field of complex relations where he occupies a transition point. His status may have placed him there; it is not his status, however, that determined the rules to follow and the limits to observe".[56]

Again, it is important to note that in describing this particular relation to self, Foucault is not proposing an ideal to be adopted or even emulated. This would be to miss the point of historical analysis. What he is doing is describing a historical possibility that neither finds its *raison d'être* in

---

56. *CS* 88.

what came before nor in what followed. It is
the familiarity and the unfamiliarity of the
period in question and we are not meant
to subsume it into a uniform and linear
process. *The Care of the Self*, like Foucault's
other histories, is set up precisely to make
the contrast evident. He contrasts the "*culture de soi*" of late Antiquity with the earlier
model of self-mastery discussed in *The Use of
Pleasure*. He also makes frequent references
to the future relation to self characteristic
of early Christianity (the subject matter of
the unpublished *Les Aveux de la chair*) in
order to contrast it with the period in question. In his conclusions to *The Care of the Self*,
he takes up the themes discussed in detail
in the book and emphasizes the continuity
and discontinuity of the period in question.
He writes:

> A certain style of sexual conduct is thus
> suggested by this whole movement of
> moral, medical, and philosophical reflec-
> tion. It is different from the style that had
> been delineated in the fourth century, but
> it is also different from the one that will be
> found in Christianity. Here sexual activity is
> linked to evil by its form and its effects, but
> in itself and substantially, it is not an evil.
> It finds its natural fulfillment in marriage,
> but—with certain exceptions—marriage
> is not an express, indispensable condition

for it to cease being an evil. It has trouble
finding its place in the love of boys, but the
latter is not therefore condemned as being
contrary to nature.[57]

The interest of Foucault's work, then, is
the way it describes a period that is poised
between the aesthetics of self-mastery and
an abstract moralism where the concrete
bodily individual is nothing and the "soul"
everything. The interest of the period,
however, is not in its character as a *threshold*, a watershed between what came before
and what comes after, in the continuing
story of something called the "self". This
character of being a threshold or a watershed is not specific to this particular period
but is rather characteristic of *any* period
inasmuch as it is considered as a present,
situated between a past and a future. In
other words, any present, considered in
itself, is a threshold between the past and
the future. Rather, the interest of *The Care
of the Self* is the particular relation to self it
describes: the care and concern for a fragile self, one not grounded in unquestioned
and unquestionable practices, and yet one
still constituted in its relations to self and
others. It is this historical (and therefore
real) *possibility* that is of interest.

***

---

57. *CS* 239.

But what, exactly, is meant by the phrase "historical possibility"? (Especially if we recognize that the point is not to revive and relive the past in any practical sense.) The notion of possibility here is contrasted with that of necessity inasmuch as history teaches that current practices do not express ahistorical essences or necessary features of human "being", but express rather contingent configurations of relations. This includes those relations in which individuals relate to their selves as selves. The purpose of the type of historical analysis Foucault proposes—the exploration of different historical "possibilities"—also serves as the basis for a certain wariness vis-à-vis the constitutive functions that make up the relation between the individual and his or her self; a wariness, that is, based on the contingent character of those relations and directed to the appearance of necessity, and perhaps more importantly, to the appeal to necessity.

However, the notion of possibility can be contrasted with the notion of actuality as well. That is, if one recognizes that the actual world is a contingent matter of fact, that is, that it could have turned out differently than it actually has, then one is saying that the actual world is only one possibility amongst many possibilities (or one set or configuration of possibilities amongst many). Yet, actuality is not *merely* one set of possibilities amongst others for the simple reason that it is not a *mere* possibility but an actual one. Actuality is, as it were, actualized or real possibility as opposed to possibility considered as such.[58] This gives actuality or the actual world or the real world a kind of distinctiveness and concreteness that merely possible worlds do not possess.

What does this have to do with Foucault's approach to historical possibility? The distinctiveness of the actual world raises the question of why this particular set of possibilities was actualized and not some other set. And the question is normally answered by looking to the antecedent conditions which "led up" to this particular set of actualized possibilities. This way of answering the question further distinguishes actuality from other possibilities because only actuality is tied in a more or less clear way to its antecedent conditions whereas mere possibilities remain "open" and unconnected to anything real. What this does, in effect, is provide the tempta-

---

58. For the connections between actuality, possibility and necessity, cf. Hegel's *Science of Logic*, trans. A. V. Miller (Atlantic Highlands: Humanities, 1969), the section on "Actuality," 541–53.

tion to remove actuality from the realm of possibility altogether and place it within the realm of necessity. The purpose here, of course, is not to say that actuality or the actual world necessarily, that is, by means of a necessary process, came to be what it in fact is; but that because it is what it is, then it is reasonable to ask why this is so, and to do this one is said to go back and ascertain the necessary conditions that permitted the actual set of possibilities to be the ones that were, in effect, actualized. Thus, history becomes the inquiry of what it is in the past that made the present possible, that is, actual, that actualized possibility that it is.

This is where Foucault comes in. I have noted that Foucault rejects the view of history that sees the present as the culmination of the past. Now we can clearly see why: this approach has the effect of removing the present from the realm of possibility by giving it the character (and illusion) of necessity. It is true that the present can be described as an actualized set of possibilities and it is also true that actualized possibilities differ from *mere* possibilities by the simple fact of their actuality. However, it is not true that actual or present possibilities are the only *real* ones. Reality is not exhausted by actuality. At least, not if the idea of a "historical reality" makes sense.

The problem is that the idea of "actualized possibilities" is ambiguous. It could
refer to possibilities that *have been* actualized. Or it could refer to possibilities
that currently *are being* actualized. Stating
things this way, however, clears up matters considerably. Possibilities that have
been actualized obviously refer to the past;
while possibilities that are being actualized
clearly refer to the present. Here we see the
problem with the view of history that sees
the present as the culmination of the past:
in doing so it in effect treats the present as
though it were past, that is, as something
that has been actualized. Thus, its point
of departure is not the "real" present—a
set of possibilities currently being actualized—but an "imaginary" present, one
that is deemed complete. However, one
can only find possibilities that have been
actualized in the sense of "completed"
in the past. Possibilities that are currently
being actualized are being actualized in
the various practices that make up the
present, including of course the practice
of historical analysis.

Foucault's mode of historical analysis—
the exploration of historical possibilities—
is designed to respond to this ambiguous
and complex situation. He analyzes historical possibilities that *have been* actualized—
for example, Greek and Roman practices

of self—in a way that reveals the connections (and disconnections) those possibilities have with possibilities that *are currently being actualized*, that is, modern practices and relations to the self, characterized in terms of relations of power and processes of normalization. However, because there are certain connections between the two sets of possibilities (those that *have been* and those that *are being* actualized) and because the latter are still "open" in the sense of being ongoing, then, history does not only tell us about the past, but helps and indeed provides the tools for restructuring the present, not from scratch, nor from some point outside of it, but from within its ongoing process. The actualized possibilities of the past, through historical analysis, offer perspectives on the possibilities being actualized in the present.

It is for this reason that the suspicion characteristic of Foucault's approach is neither gratuitous nor destructive. It is, one might say, a specific characteristic of historical analysis, especially if one considers historical analysis as the play between the familiar and the unfamiliar. We can now also characterize this "play" as expressing the two senses of "actualized possibilities": present configurations are familiar while past configurations are unfamiliar, on the

one hand, and on the other, past possibilities can be made intelligible, thus familiar,
and can then enable us to see present possibilities from a different perspective, thus
rendering them unfamiliar.

* * *

If we are to sum up our discussion, then,
what Foucault provides in the last two volumes of his *History of Sexuality* is a response
to the present and to our self-understanding by offering a contrastive perspective
from which to view them, thereby suggesting the possibility of moving beyond them.

   The Use of Pleasure described a possibility
of one's relation to oneself as characterized by the triad of freedom-self-mastery-
truth that contrasts with the present triad
freedom-autonomy-truth. Thus while the
present is familiar with the idea of the
self freely related to its own truth, it is
not through the mode of self-mastery but
through the mode of an autonomous relation to the universal. The point of contrasting the two is to reveal the possibility
of creativity implicit in the mode of self-
mastery; creativity, that is, vis-à-vis the codes
and rules regulating conduct, and thus of
introducing this possibility of creativity into
the open (because currently ongoing) possibilities being actualized in the present.

   The Care of the Self, for its part, described
the possibility of a mode of caring and con-

cern for the self—contrasting it with the present's "technological" approach to the self[59]—and thereby introduced the notion of a fragile self, one in need of constant attention. Thus, according to Foucault, if one is to entertain or practice a freely creative or creatively free relation to one's self as truth, then one should also take care to account for the fragility of that self and its truth. At least, this is what Foucault's historical analysis appears to suggest. The exploration of historical possibilities that *have been* actualized are thus turned into possibilities that join those that *are currently being* actualized in the present.

Here we see the positive role of the concept of self-wariness that has been a focus of this presentation of Foucault. The wariness it advocates is not only directed towards the imposition of particular selves such that complete identification is attained, but is also directed to the protection and sustenance—not of this or that particular self—but of the possibility of freely and creatively relating to self. And the only guarantee of this possibility, at least within the possibilities currently being actualized in the present, is the continuous exploration and analysis of historical possibilities,

---

59. Cf. L. H. Martin et al., *Technologies of the Self* (Amherst: U of Massachusetts P, 1988).

for it is by means of history that one can,
through the contrast between the familiar
and the unfamiliar it offers, disconnect
oneself from one's self and one's present,
and open up a space for what Foucault has
called "the undefined work of freedom".

CONCLUSION

The Indefinite and Undefined Work of Freedom as History

Neither a postulate nor a presupposition, freedom is the work of history. This is the basic claim of the philosophy of history as I understand it. Turning one's attention to history—to the fact that our existences take place within the temporal unfolding of the past, the present and the future—involves considering the changing shapes the world has taken as the distinct sphere of our own becoming. And that distinctiveness lies in its being freely taken up as human beings continue to be born into the world. However compelled we may be to do what we find ourselves doing, that compulsion is never simply a given: it is taken up and made sense of, if not always wholly by ourselves, then by the others that sustain the space within which what we do happens.

I have not argued in this book that Foucault himself is explicitly making this

claim. He has not been presented as proposing a philosophy of history. He seems
to have been content with having his work
oscillate between the claims of historical
investigation and those of philosophical
elucidation, thereby creating a unique
interrogative space that continues to inter-
pellate us. But I have sought to show that
his work does help us get a clearer view of
this basic claim of the philosophy of history. Given the philosophical underpinnings explored in Part A and given certain
key features of the histories explored
in Part B, his work places us in a better
position to make sense of history and to
account for ourselves as free.

Foucault connected his own sense of
freedom, of our free being, to the critical *work* of a philosophical ethos that sets
itself the task of testing the limits of what
is given us to think, say and do.[1] As I mentioned when I first introduced the expression that forms the title of this book, it is
because Foucault ties the notion of freedom to this critical *work* that I think a
more appropriate translation of "*indéfini*"
is *indefinite* rather than *undefined*, in the
sense that it is a kind of work that must be
taken up ever anew, that it has no term or
end, that it is in being indefinitely engaged

---

1. Cf. "What Is Enlightenment?" *EW* 1 315–19.

that our freedom manifests itself, however
fleetingly. Of course, the fact that freedom should merely manifest itself, and
fleetingly at that, within our busy engagements and commitments, within what we
are given to think, say and do, also points
to its "undefined" character, that is, its
lack of definition, or at least of a definition that would fix it once and for all. One
might say, then, that the "indefinite work
of freedom" Foucault calls for, on the one
hand, emphasizes the Hegelian sense of
history as an unfolding process we need
to make sense of and which makes sense
of us (and thus appeals to the principle of
immanence); while, on the other hand, as
"undefined", recalls Heidegger's reminder
of the "free letting-be" at the heart of
our engagement in the world (and thus
appeals to the principle of rarity).

I think the connection Foucault makes
between a critical work of engaging with
the limits that are *given* to us (in a self-
consolidating discursive present) with the
freedom that lies at the core of *all* of our
engagements is important for the speculative philosophy of history. It reminds
us that the historical realm, the realm of
our engagements with the world and with
each other, is a distinct one which can
never be fully *known* because, in its temporal unfolding, it remains constitutively

incomplete: the past it considers arises out of present concerns which, as ongoing, point to a future. Thus, the speculative philosophy of history is less an attempt to *know* something—the pattern, the process, the meaning of history—than one of *situating* our engagements within this intelligibly changing realm we call history.

John McCumber, in a variety of places but perhaps most relevantly here in his work *Reshaping Reason: Toward a New Philosophy*,[2] argues that taking time more seriously is philosophy's most urgent task. Philosophy needs to recognize the radically temporal character of reasoning, whose task it is, precisely, to *situate* us in our unfolding relation to the world; indeed, freedom itself should be understood as a *situating* that is shaped by our

---

2. (Bloomington: Indiana UP, 2007), hereafter referred to as "*RR*". His excellent works also explore the issues raised in this book, including the importance of thinking Hegel and Heidegger with and against each other, cf. *Poetic Interaction: Language, Freedom, Reason* (Chicago: U Chicago P, 1989); *Metaphysics and Oppression: Heidegger's Challenge to Western Philosophy* (Bloomington: Indiana UP, 1999) and *Philosophy and Freedom: Derrida, Rorty, Habermas, Foucault* (Bloomington: Indiana UP, 2000).

reasoning efforts. He offers useful tools (indeed, the title of the second chapter is "Enlarging the Philosophical Toolbox") to help in that situating. He also offers in the first chapter an interesting discussion of time that helps us better grasp our relation to its unfolding. Rather than speak of time simply in terms of three tenses—the past, the present and the future—he suggests we need to consider the way we situate ourselves within its *six* dimensions, by which he means the following: we need to consider and distinguish two pasts, two presents and two futures when we think about our actual experience of time, phenomenologically speaking (the way time *seems* to us). He suggests this because the notions of the past, the present and the future, all have dimensions that are "largely unknowable and so ineffable" and because of this, they largely go unacknowledged; and yet they are part of our experience and in fact "are quite accessible to attentive common sense".[3]

First, he distinguishes between "the past", which references everything that has taken place before now, and the "usable past", which refers to the sense we make of select parts of it. Note that the whole past is in fact unknowable as a whole and

---

3. *RR* 34.

yet it exists as a check on that which we end up claiming about the past within our "usable past". That is, as we organize and put together a "usable past" out of the vast openness of the past itself, that which gets constructed and organized still gains its sense from that openness which is itself unknowable. This is an important point because it *situates* what it means to "know" something. What we can "know" of the past is part of constructing and organizing a relation to the past (that makes it "usable") such that it in effect becomes something "knowable" (because constructed and organized in specific ways). However, the knowledge thereby gained can also be challenged and transformed by appealing to more and other features of "the past", which of course means constructing and organizing it differently. Thus, "knowing" is a kind of *shaping* within the "unknowable": the past is shaped into a usable past which, insofar as it is used, is sustained by a continued relation to the past as such. Anyone can test this by simply considering his or her own past, which as a whole is unknowable, but in that very ineffability, nevertheless sustains any sense that one has of having been. (Consider that relation in the context of, say, finding out that you were adopted. Your relation to both pasts becomes evident to you as you try to re-situate your sense of yourself.)

Similarly, we relate to two futures, or to two senses of the "future": the predictable future and the unpredictable future. The same idea applies here. We shape and organize our relation to the future through an assessment and prediction of a variety of outcomes, and many of those assessments and predictions turn out to be accurate. But not all of them. Again, like the past, the future as a whole is unknowable and ineffable and frames our efforts to deal with it through the possibility of those efforts being undone. The point of distinguishing between the two senses of both the past and the future is to mark the difference that sustains the relation between them in our unfolding lives and this is *not* wholly encapsulated in our practical efforts to create for ourselves a "usable past" and a "predictable future". As McCumber writes:

> The predictable future and the future in itself are as different from one another as the usable past and the past in itself, and for the same reason: we create the predictable future in order to know and to do other things, while the future in itself is neither made nor known by us. A genuinely temporalized thought must respect

the difference between these two sorts of futures.[4]

And respect as well the two sorts of past.

As one would expect by now, McCumber also talks about two sorts of present, which he describes as follows:

> There is an incredibly large set of things which are actually happening, just in my vicinity, at any given moment, far too large to be known and therefore constituting a "present in itself," and there is also the "presentable" present, the set of things of which I actually become aware—or had better become aware—in the course of my life.[5]

These six dimensions of our temporal being—a usable past and the past in itself, a presentable present and the present in itself, a predictable future and the future in itself—give, in their interplay, the context of our unfolding lives. This is the whole that we find ourselves dealing with; it is the whole within which we *situate* ourselves. It is interesting to note how emphasizing this six-dimensional temporality can be seen as a form of the application of the two principles we have identified as inherent in Foucault's work: The principle of

---

4. *RR* 37.

5. *RR* 37.

immanence insists on the temporal character of our reasoning efforts within an unfolding historical field that faces a presentable present through its creation of a usable past and a predictable future such that the "knowledge" we have of the world is one that emerges from our interaction with the world. However, because the consolidation of those efforts takes place also within a present in itself arising out of a vast past in itself and confronting an unknown future in itself, it is also subject to a principle of rarity that sets up our relation to our consolidated relation to "truth".

This seems to me to argue for the continuing relevance of the speculative philosophy of history whose task it is to seek to grasp this complex whole from within its very unfolding. However, following McCumber, we should say that such a "grasping" should now be seen as a kind of *situating* as opposed to a *fixing* of the sense of history, "sense" here meaning less its "significance" than the "direction" it promotes (or insists upon). This *situating* is in fact a mode of responding to demands being made by the particular constraints of a particular present, arising out of a specific past and facing an indeterminate future. It is an exploration of existing possibilities, those which *have been* actualized and those *currently being* actualized in an unfolding present (as discussed in Chapter Six).

To recognize ourselves as *situating* beings—that is, to see this as a fundamental task we are called upon to undertake, as McCumber shows us—is to recognize ourselves as *historical* beings, being born of, subject to, but also responsible for, history which includes the knowledges established within that historical experience. This reference to knowledge brings us back to Foucault's contribution to an appreciation—through his own application of the principles of immanence and rarity—of our historicality. His thought is often summed up as a reminder of the *contingency* of the structures of knowledge and the systems of constraint that give shape to our unfolding lives, and that in this recognition of contingency there are the seeds of a possible freedom to think otherwise or differently from the ways we are made to think presently. For example, Stuart Eldon writes, "For what Nietzsche, Heidegger and Foucault share is a realization that the structures of knowledge that are taken as absolutes at a particular time are contingent, and that they must be examined historically."[6]

---

6. Stuart Eldon, *Mapping the Present: Heidegger, Foucault and the Project of a Spatial History* (London: Continuum, 2001) 23.

I think we need to be careful not to get things backwards, however. There is a sense that what is being affirmed here is that we need to realize that things, ultimately, are contingent and that once we realize this, we can demonstrate it through historical examination which will then confirm the openness within which we exist, suggesting a realm of possibility hitherto covered over. However, the basic claim I would make (basically following Collingwood) is that it is only once one begins to examine structures of knowledge and systems of constraint historically that one can come to see that what are taken (and *given*) as absolutes are indeed contingent. But then the question becomes: what does one do when faced with that contingency (especially when we equally recognize that merely recognizing constraints does not in itself remove them)?

Let us look a little more closely at what is being suggested when we are urged to recognize that what was taken as "absolute" is in fact contingent. What is usually meant by contingent, in these contexts, is "not necessary". Something is understood as contingently what it is when it could have been other than it is; that is, something is understood as contingent insofar as, dependent as it is on other things, it only is what it is given those other things,

and insofar as—if those other things could
be other than *they* are—then it need not
be what *it* is. So when one is presented or
confronted with a claim that something is
"necessary" (or treated as "absolute"), one
can always question the claim by examining whether that thing is "necessary" insofar as it is not dependent on other things
(that it is self-subsistent, as it were) or, failing that (given that any particular thing,
as particular, will not be self-subsistent but
dependent on other things), whether that
thing is what it is because the things on
which it depends could *not* be other than
they are. This would give some traction to
the idea that that thing is indeed "necessarily" as it is and not contingently so. But,
of course, there are no guarantees here
because one can then turn one's attention to the claim that those other things
could not be other than they are. The
same process applies. If one isolates any
one thing, one can ask whether or not it
is dependent on other things or whether
it is self-subsistent or self-sustaining and so
on. One might get the sense, from such an
abstract consideration of this process, that
everything is indeed contingent, this then
being a kind of "realization" and a spur to
genealogical projects of debunking claims
to "necessity" through a close examination
of how things depend on other things that

themselves depend on things that could have been otherwise.

However, we shouldn't be too quick to affirm the contingency of everything, because it is, after all, a contrastive concept and if one gets rid of all necessity, then it becomes less clear what reasons one might have for claiming the contingency of something.

Besides, are not some things necessarily the things they are? According to what has been said above, something is necessarily what it is because it does not depend on anything else or else it is because the things on which it depends themselves could not be other than they are. Can we think of any particular things that are what they are because that which they depend on could not be other than they are? What about the facts of the past? For example, my cat is dead. I had her put to sleep about a year ago because she was old and in failing health and that is generally what people do with old cats in failing health. So it is a fact that my cat died on such-and-such a day. This fact is a particular thing. Is it a contingent or a necessary thing? Obviously, we want to say that it is a contingent fact that I chose to have her put to sleep on that particular day. I could have chosen another day. Thus, it seems to make sense to say that the fact that my cat died on

such-and-such a day is a contingent thing.
But the fact that my cat died on such-and-
such a day implies that my cat is dead. And
the fact that my cat is dead is not a contingent fact; it is necessarily the case that
my cat is dead, given that I contingently
had her put to sleep on such-and-such a
date. It is interesting to note what happens
to the contingency of my decision and my
action when looked at in retrospect. That
is, when considered *prospectively*, my decision and my action to end my cat's life on
such-and-such a day was clearly contingent, dependent on things that could have
been other than they were (not today,
maybe tomorrow or next week—maybe
she isn't that sick, maybe she will get better—maybe I won't have this done and let
her die on her own, etc.). However, considered retrospectively, my decision and
my action can no longer be other than
what they are, thus turning certain contingent facts surrounding my cat's death into
necessary ones. We might generalize this
example and say that the facts of the past
are indeed necessarily the things that they
are. This of course does not imply that the
facts of the past are easily determined or
that one cannot get those facts wrong. On
the contrary, it is precisely *because* the facts
of the past are necessarily what they are
that we can be said to get them wrong. But

it remains the case, when it comes to the past, that the facts of the past are necessarily what they are because, as past, *they can no longer change or be changed*; they can be covered over, manipulated, ignored, twisted, misunderstood, forgotten, but they remain what they *have been* as the now actualized possibilities of the past.

But the facts as they are and the facts as we know them need to be put into the temporal context described above (given that this is the way that we relate to them). That is, as "known", the facts of the past (and the present, for that matter) are taken up in particular ways that include constructing a "usable" past given the "presentable" present. What Foucault's work does is not merely recognize the "contingency" of what we are made to think, say and do, but rather gives a genealogical account of the particular ways certain features of the past and present are "taken up" or "grasped", to show that they *continue to be actualized* within our temporal relation to them and that they are thus not immune to the possibility of change, of becoming other than what they are. This is his challenge to "necessity", to the view that present systems of constraint, as structured by a *particular* usable past and *predictable* future, are actually what they are because they are composed of unchangeable features, because they take themselves to be in some sense fully actualized; rather, what works like Foucault's show us is the ways in which they are in effect *actualizing* systems and not yet actualized ones (they are present, not past). This seems to me to be the true sense of his claim to be engaged in a "history of the present".

One might want to ask, though, how effective is this challenge? After all, re-situating systems of constraints within their contingent unfolding frameworks does not in itself remove the constraining effects that the systems have, though it can open up spaces for thinking differently.[7] Foucault can only take us so far here. Indeed, those who follow him probably do so more out of shared sensibility than anything else. I think this is what should be expected of philosophy, given that what we follow in a philosopher is her working out of those obscurities and difficulties that exercise her thought (and our own inas-

---

7. While one should not underestimate the sense of possibility generated by recognizing the contingency of those things that structure our world, one should not overestimate it either; the grip the present may have on us might be theoretically loosened, but transforming the practical engagements we are involved in is an altogether more complex matter.

much as we follow her). But I also think
that we should not, in our present structured as it is, only theoretically point to its
basic contingency and evoke the notion
of possibility that such contingency opens
up. I think we should make use of the principles of immanence and rarity in order to
engage in a concerted effort to re-situate
ourselves, not only in our present, but in
the broader context of an unfolding history considered as a whole in its full sex-
tuple dimensionality. If that temporal
dimensionality is taken into consideration,
we will be responding to the concerns
often raised about the speculative philosophy of history, namely that it encloses
us in a *totality* that would somehow give
over our *future* to something other than
our own efforts. We need to distinguish
between conceiving of the *whole* of history
and thinking of history as a *totality*. The
whole of history involves recognizing the
six dimensions of its unfolding, and in that
sense, history will always escape any totalizing effort, because, as McCumber points
out, "To totalize something is to *claim* to
know it in its *totality*, to know all that it
can be."[8] This is impossible for us, given
that we are placed *temporally within* an
unfolding whole and not before an object

---

8. *RR* 51.

independent of us; we will never be in a position "to know all that it can be".

However, as McCumber goes on to point out, this does not mean that we should not engage in "totalization". Our relation to the *past*, insofar as we distinguish it from the present and the future, can be one of just such totalization, as he shows in the following:

> Suppose a love affair has ended badly, as all love affairs end. I have broken up with my lover, or my lover has died. In order to get on with my life, I must come to see the love affair as no longer existing for me in the presentable present, as no longer offering me future possibilities. I must accept (or, more accurately, decide) that what it has already been is all it can ever be. Only when I see it in this way can it become something which, though I will not forget it, has no ongoing claims on me. In order to free myself of my love affair, I have to be able to tell myself that what it has already been constitutes the totality of what it can be; I deny it new potential. I place it into my past, I "totalize" it.[9]

He then generalizes from this example:

> . . . when we realize that to totalize something is to place it in our past, totalization

becomes the way we recognize our embed-
dedness in a historical tradition without
making ourselves into the prisoners of
that tradition. For if what I have just said
is right, totalizing is the means by which
history becomes ours; *a* past can only be
our past if we somehow, to some degree,
see ourselves as completing it, bringing it
to fruition—and, of course, also of discard-
ing it so we can move on to other things.
To totalize something then means at once
to complete and discard it, and thereby to
acquire it as part of our past. Intellectually
speaking, totalization as the acquisition of
a past is what enables us to escape the past,
even as we construct it.[10]

Thus, for example, we seek to construct
for ourselves a past which "totalizes" slavery,
that turns it, resolutely, into a thing of the
past: something we need to remember and
learn from, but also something we discard
as a now "completed" feature of human
relations, one that can no longer inform
the manner in which we relate ourselves to
our present and future. Similarly, we seek
to construct a usable past that treats other
inequalities built into the relations between
men and women, for example, as "having
been all that it ever could be" and should
no longer be a feature of the presentable

10. *RR* 51.

present.[11] Of course, the construction of such a past is challenged by continuing systematically deployed practices of discrimination in the present that make it much more difficult to "totalize" in McCumber's sense.

But here is where consideration of the future becomes vital. The construction of a usable past is not solely driven by such totalizing efforts; indeed, it cannot be, given that their basic purpose is to *free* us from the particular constraints that structure it as a particular past (that is, a present as it was), even as we learn from the fact that we once related to ourselves in those ways. We might say that the totalized past serves the present only *indirectly*, because it is treated as separate (because "completed") from the concerns of the presentable present. However, that present as presentable also makes use of a usable past in its own self-conception through the various systems of constraint that it imposes on itself. The "rule of law", for example, is a present configuration built out of constant references to a usable past (this is especially evident in the common law traditions). These kinds of relations that the present establishes with the past, those that "justify" and "make sense" of

---

11. The same idea animates those who are fighting "to make poverty history".

its own continuing particularities, are the ones that Foucault teaches us we should be most wary of, if only because such efforts at self-consolidation through an appeal to the past tends to efface the contingency of that relation as it gets constructed. In the terms I have been using, when the present takes up the past in order to justify itself, there is always the danger that it treats what *is currently being* actualized as *having been* actualized in a way that implies a kind of self-evidence or necessity. For example, stating that without the "rule of law" societies would collapse into anarchy is to give the contingent self-consolidation of such a mode of rule an appearance of necessity that its ongoing temporal actualization does not warrant. It seems to preclude the possibility of a future where human relations are not so ordered.[12] Such a

---

12. For example, Ernst Bloch, in his discussion—and Marxist critique—of anarchism, suggests that "we can say that the dream of a society without rule is, when interpreted tactically, the surest means of not realizing this dream; when fundamentally understood, after the economic foundations of the state have been removed, this dream becomes a matter of course." *The Principle of Hope*, trans. Nevelle Plaice, Stephen Plaice and Paul Knight (Cambridge: MIT Press, 1986) 574.

statement, to be honest, needs to recognize itself as in effect a prediction, that is, it is a statement about a predictable future, seen from the vantage point of a presentable present, making use of a usable past. And as such, it can be challenged from a differently configured presentable present making use of different features of the past as it predicts a different future, given that both the original statement and the challenge trade off on the unknowability of the past, present and future in themselves.

This may appear on the surface a recipe for sterile debate, but only, I would argue, on the assumption that the objective is "to get it right". A full appreciation of our temporal engagement in the knowability of the world recognizes that "getting it right" is actually a kind of fantasy,[13] given that we will never be in a position to have this confirmed; any account we devise is subject to our unfolding experience of the world, to an ineliminable temporality. This should not be seen as a loss or a lack, an incapacity or a limitation; all of these merely serve to nourish the fantasy

---

13. A very old fantasy of course, one which sees philosophy's task as articulating the "universal, unchangeable realm of timeless truth". Philosophers still committed to this view are, in McCumber's phrase, committed to a Fantasy Island (*RR* 7).

of omniscience. Rather, we should recognize our temporal engagement with the world as testament to our free relation to it, as the space within which we are called to realize ourselves.

Foucault's work, I have argued, accepts the primordiality of this free relation but places it within the scope of a *critical* engagement that shows how that basically free relation gets taken up in the space of something we traditionally call "reason", where human relations are consolidated and ordered, not so much out of some kind of movement internal to reason itself, but as a response to that which appears to threaten that space, thus configuring a presentable present. Through his genealogical investigations, he challenges the way that present makes use of the past (the way it constructs a usable past) by insisting on the contingency of its self-consolidation. The effect is not only to destabilize any claim to self-evident order and necessity, but to open up that present to something other than its normally constituted predictable future.

But which future? Here is where a speculative philosophy of history becomes relevant, not because it seeks to predict the future on the basis of some general pattern, but because—given its preoccupation with the whole of history—it

tries to include it in our situating efforts
to make sense of the world. It reminds us
that our temporal engagements with the
world include an orientation that takes us
beyond the configurations of the present,
just as it reminds us that those configurations were once other than they are now.
What a speculative approach adds to the
critical work on the present that work like
Foucault's permits is a fuller appreciation
of the function of the future in orienting
our thought in the present.

Foucault himself had little to say about
the role of the future in his work, no doubt
because of his commitment to think outside of the categories of a certain kind of
self-enclosing "dialectical" thought that, in
its appeal to "contradiction", ran counter
to his own modal sensibility keyed more
to possibility than to necessity. However,
it is precisely this sensibility to possibility
that should have us reconsider how we
think and relate to the future. This relation is not exhausted by forms of "predict-
ability" that otherwise govern our practical
and theoretical engagements. The future
is also a realm of *expectation* and *anticipation*, notions that are less tied to the (relatively) "knowable" implied by prediction.
How might the speculative philosophy of
history help us relate to an unknowable
future, the future-in-itself (as McCumber

puts it)? This I think is the principal task set before it, which means engaging the complex structuring role of *possibility* in our efforts to situate ourselves in an unfolding world. There are philosophical resources for doing this. Let me briefly suggest a few in conclusion.

I have made use, in another work,[14] of Michel Serres' idea of framing our unfolding lives within a *modal square* where the necessities of the past structure a contingent present faced with the possibilities of an open future limited only by what is impossible. In his recent works, Serres is exploring further the implications of framing our lives in this way, but he is also engaged in a broader, explicitly *hopeful* reading of our future even as he recognizes the grave dangers we face in the present, given our past.[15] He does so by unabashedly engaging in the articulation of a "Grand or Great Narrative" (*le Grand*

---

14. Réal Fillion, *Multicultural Dynamics and the Ends of History: Exploring Kant, Hegel, and Marx* (Ottawa: U of Ottawa P, 2008).

15. The series of books, recently designated under the general rubric "*Le Grand Récit*", are all published by Le Pommier and include *Hominescence* (2001), where one can find the idea of the modal square (191), *L'incandescent* (2003), *Rameaux* (2004) and *Récits d'humanisme* (2006).

Récit) which essentially explores—through an appreciation of what our developed sciences, works of literature and the writer's personal accounts of his own origins tell us about the world—the story of "hominization", of our *becoming human,* not in order to mark our difference from nature but to reconnect that story to a developing natural world, that is, a world *equally* wrought by transformations. Such a "Grand or Great Narrative" does not pretend to be a *meta-narrative,* that is, one that would pretend to encapsulate and give meaning to all other narratives, but rather, it is literally a work-in-progress (indeed, a work-in-process) that appeals to our various knowledges and common experiences of our natural world and of the historical world that emerged from it. It is a brilliantly executed effort to *situate* us within an evolving and transformable world in a way that is respectful of the principle of immanence as has been discussed throughout this book.

And also respectful, in an interesting way, of the principle of rarity also emphasized, which reminds us that whatever we have constituted and encounter as our world, including the accounts of our experience of it, that world is a rare one, one that does not in its actuality exhaust the very possibilities that render it actual. Our world does not describe a plenitude, not even a hypothetical one. If it is whole, it is an evolving, changing whole that unfolds temporally, as we do. In a recent work,[16] Serres speaks of that world as that with which we are only now coming to realize we have been *at war*, that the "world war" that has in so many ways defined and framed our engagements in the world has been a war *against* the world, waged to ensure our own survival, a war where, in the last few hundred years we have gained the upper hand: until very recently, that is. But this situation, according to Serres, does not indicate merely a reversal in what is too often abstractly considered as a perennial one (our struggle for survival). Rather, we can rather see in our current situation the possibility of calling for a *truce* with the world. A cessation of hostilities. This is *possible* now because we can actually see our struggling relation to what has for so long been deemed a "hostile environment" as, in fact, a battle, a war; we can now see that the world is not the indifferent space out of which we try to carve out a place for ourselves, but an evolving one which responds as much to us as we respond to it, and that such responses can now be viewed more clearly as attacks or aggressions. Hence

16. Michel Serres, *La guerre mondiale* (Paris : Le Pommier, 2008).

the idea of calling a truce, of proposing
a plan for peace, the very idea of which
introduces speculatively a third party, a
third element mediating the claims of
the belligerents (human ingenuity on the
one hand; natural processes—chemical,
organic, viral—on the other). For Serres,
this third element is the Great or Grand
Narrative itself, which oversees the development, the transformations of the other
two. We might also call this third element
more simply: "the future". Attentive to its
terms as far as we can understand them,
we can lay down our arms and attempt to
devise ways to live together.

Or we might also make use of Ernst
Bloch's distinction between the "cold"
and "warm" streams in Marxism which
relate directly to the possibilities of the
future. He takes up a distinction already in
Hegel's logical insistence on the difference
between the notions of *mere* possibility and
real possibility, the former abstract and
many-formed, the latter tied to *actuality* or
the realization of those forms. But while
Hegel ties the notion of "real possibility"
to a notion of necessity, Bloch ties it more
concretely and temporally to the notions
of both actual (and limiting) and *anticipatory* conditions in which our lives unfold.
Bloch ties our thinking relation to the
future-as-possible "to critical *consideration*

of the attainable, to founded expectation of attainability itself"[17] which require both "coldness" and "warmth", both "cool analysis" of the actual conditions of possibility in the world and a prospective "warm enthusiasm" for that within "the Possible which is still unexhausted and unrealized".[18] Around this thought, Bloch writes:

> In Marxism, the act of analyzing the situation is entwined with the enthusiastically prospective act. Both acts are united in the dialectical method, in the pathos of the goal, in the totality of the subject-matter treated, yet the difference of view and situation is plain to see. It has been recognized as one between the respective condition-exploration according to the stipulations of the Possible, and the prospect exploration of What-Is-in-possibility. Research which analyses conditions does equally show prospect, but with its horizon as a *limiting* one, that of the limited Possible. Without such a cooling down Jacobinism or even totally extravagant, most abstractly utopian fanaticism would emerge. Thus lead is here poured into the shoes of overhauling, skipping over, flying over, because experience shows that the real itself has a heavy gait and seldom consists of wings.

17. Bloch 208.
18. Bloch 209.

But the prospect-exploration of What-Is-in-possibility goes towards the horizon, in the sense of the *unobstructed, unmeasured expanse*, in the sense of the Possible which is still unexhausted and unrealized. ... Without such a warming up of the historical and especially of the currently practical conditional analysis, the latter is subject to the danger of economism and of goal-forgetting opportunism; the latter avoids the mists of fanaticism only in as far as it gets bogged down in a swamp of philistinism, of compromise, and finally of betrayal. Only coldness and warmth of concrete anticipation together therefore ensure that neither the path in itself nor the goal in itself are held apart from one another undialectically and so become reified and isolated. And the conditional analysis on the whole historical-situational stretch emerges both as an unmasking of ideologies and as a disenchantment of metaphysical illusion; precisely this belongs to the most useful *cold stream* of Marxism. Through it Marxist materialism becomes not only the science of conditions, but at the same time the science of struggle and opposition against all ideological inhibitions and concealments of the ultimately decisive conditions, which are always economic. To the *warm stream* of Marxism, however, belong liberating intention and materialistically humane, humanely materialistic real tendency, towards whose goal all these disenchantments are undertaken. From here the strong appeal to the debased, enslaved, abandoned, belittled human being, from here the appeal to the proletariat as the turntable towards emancipation.[19]

I quote at this length not to open a discussion of Foucault's relation to Marxism, or even of Marxism's relation to the speculative philosophy of history (at least not here, not at this time), but to point in its direction given everything we have said about history as an unfolding temporal process, within which we situate ourselves. Foucault, having decided to keep his distance from the Marxist mode of framing thought about that process, nevertheless can be seen to have contributed a "cool analysis" of the systems of constraint that characterize our present; but, I have argued, it is one animated by a particular sensibility which we might now characterize in terms of its particular *warmth*, its sensitivity and attention to the "debased, enslaved, abandoned, belittled" especially as these are taken up and made to work for the self-consolidation of those systems. And it is the particular combination of

19. Bloch 208–09.

coldness and warmth manifest in his work
that, I believe, marks both its singularity and continued relevance. Perhaps if
we add something like Bloch's "principle
of hope", an *anticipatory* sense of what is
possible, to Foucault's principles of immanence and rarity, we can flesh out a fuller
philosophy of history which will help us
not only make sense of our unfolding lives
but contribute to giving increasing definition to the "indefinite work of freedom"
Foucault has helped us appreciate is at the
core of our historical existence.

Works Cited

Allen, Amy. *The Politics of Our Selves: Power, Autonomy, and Gender in Contemporary Critical Theory.* New York: Columbia UP, 2008. Print.

———. Rev. of *Sartre, Foucault, and Historical Reason: A Poststructuralist Mapping of History,* by Thomas R. Flynn. *Notre Dame Philosophical Reviews* 2006. <ndpr.nd.edu/review.cfm?id=5721>.

Aymard, Maurice and Harbans Mukhia, eds. *French Studies in History.* Vol. II. New Delhi: Orient Longman, 1990. Print.

Bachelard, S., et al., eds. *Hommage à Jean Hyppolite.* Paris: Presses universitaires de France, 1971. Print.

Baugh, Bruce. *French Hegel: From Surrealism to Postmodernism.* New York: Routledge, 2003. Print.

Beaulieu, Alain and Réal Fillion. "Review essay of Michel Foucault, *History of Madness.*" *Foucault Studies* 5 (2008): 74–89. Print.

Bernauer, James. *Michel Foucault's Force of Flight.* Atlantic Highlands: Humanity, 1990. Print.

Bernauer, James and David Rasmussen, eds. *The Final Foucault*. Boston: MIT Press, 1988. Print.

Bloch, Ernst. *The Principle of Hope*. Trans. Nevelle Plaice, Stephen Plaice and Paul Knight. Cambridge: MIT Press, 1986. Print.

Boyne, Roy. *Foucault and Derrida: The Other Side of Reason*. London: Unwin Hyman, 1990. Print.

Burchell, G. et al. *The Foucault Effect: Studies in Governmentality*. Chicago: U of Chicago P, 1991. Print.

Carr, David. "Narrative Explanation and Its Malcontents." *History and Theory* 47 (2008): 19–30. Print.

——. *Time, Narrative, and History*. Bloomington: Indiana UP, 1986. Print.

Châtelet, François. *La naissance de l'histoire*. 2 vols. Paris: Seuil, 1962. Print.

Collingwood, R. G. *An Essay on Philosophical Method*. Oxford: Clarendon, 1933. Print.

——. *The Idea of History: Revised Edition with Introduction and Additional Material*. Ed. Jan van der Dussen. Oxford: Clarendon, 1993. Print.

——. *The New Leviathan*. Oxford: Clarendon, 1942. Print.

——. *The Principles of History: And Other Writings in the Philosophy of History*. Ed. W. H. Dray and W. J. van der Dussen. Oxford: Oxford UP, 1999. Print.

Connolly, William E. "Beyond Good and Evil: The Ethical Sensibility of Michel Foucault." *Political Theory* 21.3 (1993): 365–89. Print.

———. *The Ethos of Pluralization*. Minneapolis: U of Minnesota P, 1995. Print.

Cousins, Mark and Athar Hussein. *Michel Foucault*. London: Macmillan, 1984. Print.

Daraki, Maria. "Le voyage en Grèce de Michel Foucault." *Esprit* 100 (1985): 55–83. Print.

Dean, Michell. *Critical and Effective Histories: Foucault's Methods and Historical Sociology*. London: Routledge, 1994. Print.

Deleuze, G. *Foucault*. Trans. Sean Hand. Minneapolis: U of Minnesota P, 1988. Print.

———. *Nietzsche et la philosophie*. Paris: Presses universitaires de France, 1962. Print.

Deleuze, G. and Claire Parnet. *Dialogues*. Trans. Hugh Tomlinson and Barbara Habberjam. New York: Columbia UP, 1987. Print.

Derrida, Jacques. "Cogito and the History of Madness." *Writing and Difference*. Trans. Alan Bass. Chicago: U of Chicago P, 1978. 36–73. Print.

Dews, Peter. *Logics of Disintegration: Post-Structuralist Thought and the Claims of Critical Theory*. London: Verso, 1987. Print.

D'Hondt, Jacques. *Hegel: Philosophie de l'histoire vivante*. Paris: Presses universitaires de France, 1966. Print.

Dray, W. H. "The Politics of Contemporary Philosophy of History: A Reply to Hayden White." *Clio* 3.1 (1973): 55–76. Print.

———. "Some Varieties of Presentism." *On History and Philosophers of History*. Leiden: Brill, 1989. 165–87. Print.

Dreyfus, Hubert and Paul Rabinow. *Michel Foucault: Beyond Structuralism and*

422 *Foucault and the Indefinite Work of Freedom*

Hermeneutics. Chicago: U of Chicago P, 1983. Print.

Eldon, Stuart. *Mapping the Present: Heidegger, Foucault and the Project of a Spatial History*. London: Continuum, 2001. Print.

Eribon, Didier. *Foucault*. Paris: Flammarion, 1989. Print.

——. *Foucault et ses contemporains*. Paris: Fayard, 1994. Print.

Eribon, Didier, ed. *L'infréquentable Michel Foucault: Renouveau de la Pensée Critique*. Paris: EPEL, 2001. Print.

Farge, Arlette. *Des lieux pour l'histoire*. Paris: Seuil, 1997. Print.

——. "Le parcours d'une historienne: Entretien avec Laurent Vidal." *Genèses* 48 (2002): 115–35. Print.

Ferry, Luc and Alain Renaut. *French Philosophy of the Sixties: An Essay on Antihumanism*. Trans. Mary H. Cattani. Amherst: U of Massachusetts P, 1990. Print.

Fillion, Réal, "Freedom, Responsibility, and the 'American Foucault'." *Philosophy & Social Criticism* 30.1 (2004): 115–26. Print.

——. "Moving Beyond Biopower: Hardt and Negri's Post-Foucauldian Speculative Philosophy of History." *History and Theory* 44.4 (2005): 47–72. Print.

——. *Multicultural Dynamics and the Ends of History: Exploring Kant, Hegel, and Marx*. Ottawa: U of Ottawa P, 2008. Print.

Flay, Joseph C. *Hegel's Quest for Certainty*. Albany: SUNY Press, 1984. Print.

Flynn, Thomas R. *Sartre, Foucault, and Historical Reason: A Poststructuralist Mapping of History.* Chicago: U of Chicago P, 2005. Print.

Foucault, Michel. *Abnormal: Lectures at the Collège de France, 1974–1975.* Trans. Graham Burchell. New York: Picador, 2003. Print.

——. *Aesthetics, Method, and Epistemology. Essential Works of Foucault, 1954–1984.* Vol. 2. New York: The New Press, 1998. Print.

——. *The Archaeology of Knowledge.* Trans. Alan Sheridan. New York: Pantheon, 1972. Print.

——. *The Birth of the Clinic: An Archaeology of Medical Perception.* Trans. Alan Sheridan. London: Routledge, 1973. Print.

——. *Discipline and Punish: The Birth of the Prison.* Trans. Alan Sheridan. New York: Vintage Books, 1977. Print.

——. *Dits et écrits.* 4 vols. Paris: Gallimard, 1994. Print.

——. *Ethics: Subjectivity and Truth. Essential Works of Foucault, 1954–1984.* Vol. 1. New York: The New Press, 1997. Print.

——. *Herculine Barbin: Being the Recently Discovered Memoirs of a Nineteenth-Century French Hermaphrodite.* Trans. Richard McDougall. Brighton: Harvester, 1980. Print.

——. *The Hermeneutics of the Subject: Lectures at the Collège de France, 1981–1982.* Trans. Graham Burchell. New York: Palgrave Macmillan, 2005. Print.

——. *Histoire de la sexualité, t. 2, L'usage des plaisirs.* Paris, Gallimard, 1984; *The Use of Pleasure,* Trans. R. Hurley. New York: Pantheon, 1985. Print.

——. *Histoire de la sexualité, t. 3, Le souci de soi.* Paris: Gallimard, 1984; *The Care of the Self.* Trans. R. Hurley. New York: Pantheon, 1990. Print.

——. *History of Madness.* Trans. Jonathan Murphy and Jean Khalfa. Ed. Jean Khalfa. London: Routledge, 2006. Print.

——. *The History of Sexuality: An Introduction.* Trans. Alan Sheridan. New York: Vintage Books, 1977. Print.

——. "Jean Hyppolite, 1907–1968." *Dits et écrits.* Vol. 1. Paris: Gallimard, 1994. Print.

——. "Lives of Infamous Men." *Power: Essential Works of Foucault, 1954–1984.* Vol. 3. Ed. James Faubion. New York: The New Press, 2000. Print.

——. *Madness and Civilization: A History of Insanity in the Age of Reason.* Trans. Richard Howard. New York: Vintage, 1988. Print.

——. *The Order of Things: An Archaeology of the Human Sciences.* London: Routledge, 1989. Print.

——. *Politics, Philosophy, Culture: Interviews and Other Writings, 1977–1984.* Ed. Lawrence D. Kritzman. London: Routledge, 1990. Print.

——. *Le pouvoir psychiatrique.* Paris: Seuil/ Gallimard, 2003; English translation: *Psychiatric Power, Lectures at the Collège de France, 1973–1974.* Trans. Graham Burchell. New York: Palgrave Macmillan, 2006. Print.

——. "*Society Must Be Defended*": Lectures at the Collège de France 1975–1976.* Trans. David Macey. New York: Picador, 2003. Print.

——. *Surveiller et punir: La naissance de la prison.* Paris: Gallimard, 1975. Print.

Furet, François. *L'atelier de l'histoire*. Paris: Flammarion, 1982. English translation: *In the Workshop of History*. Trans. Jonathan Mandelbaum. Chicago: U of Chicago P, 1984. Print.

Foucault, Michel and Arlette Farge. *Le désordre des familles: Lettres de cachet des archives de la Bastille*. Paris: Gallimard/Julliard, 1982. Print.

Gros, Frédéric. *Foucault et la Folie*. Paris: Presses universitaires de France, 1997. Print.

Gutting, Gary. *Michel Foucault's Archaeology of Scientific Reason*. Cambridge: Cambridge UP, 1989. Print.

Grumley, John E. *History and Totality: Radical Historicism from Hegel to Foucault*. London: Routledge, 1989. Print.

Habermas, J. *The Philosophical Discourse of Modernity*. Trans. F. G. Lawrence. Cambridge: MIT Press, 1987. Print.

——. *The Structural Transformation of the Public Sphere: An Inquiry into a Category of Bourgeois Society*. Trans. Thomas Burger. Cambridge: MIT Press, 1991. Print.

Han-Pile, Béatrice. "Is Early Foucault a Historian? History, History and the Analytic of Finitude." *Philosophy and Social Criticism* 31.5–6 (2005): 585–608. Print.

Han, Béatrice. *Foucault's Critical Project: Between the Transcendental and the Historical*. Trans. Edward Pile. Stanford: Stanford UP, 2002. Print.

Hegel, G. W. F. *Lectures on the Philosophy of World History: Introduction*. Trans. H. B. Nisbet. Cambridge: Cambridge UP, 1975. Print.

———. *The Philosophy of History.* Trans. J. Sibree. New York: Dover Publications, 1956. Print.

———. *Science of Logic.* Trans. A. V. Miller. Atlantic Highlands: Humanities, 1969. Print.

Heidegger, Martin. *Basic Writings.* Ed. David Farrell Krell. New York: HarperCollins, 1993. Print.

Hyppolite, Jean. "The Concept of Life and Consciousness of Life in Hegel's Jena Philosophy." *Studies in Marx and Hegel.* Trans. John O'Neill. New York: Basic Books, 1969. Print.

———. *Figures de la pensée philosophique.* Paris: Presses universitaires de France, 1971. Print.

———. *Introduction to Hegel's Philosophy of History.* Trans. B. Harris and J. B. Spurlock. Gainesville: UP of Florida, 1996. Print.

———. *Logic and Existence.* Trans. L. Lawlor and A. Sen. New York: State U of New York P, 1997. Print.

Jenkins, Keith. *Re-Thinking History.* London: Routledge, 1991. Print.

Joly, Henri. "Retour aux Grecs: Réflexions sur les 'pratiques de soi' dans *L'usage des plaisirs.*" *Le Débat* 41 (1986): 100–20. Print.

Kant, Immanuel. *On History.* Ed. Lewis White Beck. Indianapolis: Bobbs-Merrill, 1963. Print.

Lawlor, Leonard. *Thinking through French Philosophy: The Being of the Question.* Bloomington: Indiana UP, 2003. Print.

Le Goff, Jacques and Pierre Nora. *Faire de l'histoire.* Paris: Gallimard, 1974. Print.

Lemon, M. C. *Philosophy of History: A Guide for Students.* London: Routledge, 2003. Print.

Lyotard, Jean-François. *The Postmodern Condition: A Report on Knowledge.* Trans. Geoff Bennington and Brian Massumi. Minneapolis: U of Minnesota P, 1984. Print.

MacIntyre, Alasdair. *Three Rival Versions of Moral Inquiry.* Notre Dame, IN: U of Notre Dame P, 1990. Print.

Martin, L. H. et al. *Technologies of the Self.* Amherst: The U of Massachusetts P, 1988. Print.

Marx, Karl. *Selected Writings.* Ed. Lawrence H. Simon. Indianapolis: Hackett, 1994. Print.

May, Todd. *Between Genealogy and Epistemology: Psychology, Politics, and Knowledge in the Thought of Michel Foucault.* University Park, PA: Pennsylvania State UP, 1993. Print.

——. "Philosophy as a Spiritual Exercise in Foucault and Deleuze." *Angelaki: Journal of the Theoretical Humanities* 5.2 (2000): 223–29. Print.

——. *The Philosophy of Foucault.* Montreal: McGill–Queen's UP, 2006. Print.

——. *Our Practices, Our Selves: Or, What It Means to Be Human.* University Park, PA: The U of Pennsylvania P, 2001. Print.

McCarney, Joseph. *Hegel on History.* London: Routledge, 2000. Print.

McCumber, John. *Metaphysics and Oppression: Heidegger's Challenge to Western Philosophy.* Bloomington: Indiana UP, 1999. Print.

——. *Philosophy and Freedom: Derrida, Rorty, Habermas, Foucault.* Bloomington: Indiana UP, 2000. Print.

——. *Poetic Interaction: Language, Freedom, Reason.* Chicago: U of Chicago P, 1989. Print.

——. *Reshaping Reason: Toward a New Philosophy.*
Bloomington: Indiana UP, 2007. Print.

——. "The Temporal Turn in German Idealism:
Hegel and After." *Research in Phenomenology*
32 (2002): 44–59. Print.

McGushin, Edward F. *Foucault's Askesis:
An Introduction to the Philosophical Life.*
Evanston: Northwestern UP, 2007. Print.

Merquior, J. G. *Foucault.* London: Fontana,
1985. Print.

Moses, A. Dirk. "Hayden White, Traumatic
Nationalism, and the Public Role of History."
History and Theory 44 (2005): 311–32. Print.

O'Farrell, Clare. *Foucault: Historian or
Philosopher?* New York: St. Martin's, 1989.
Print.

Oksala, Johanna. *Foucault on Freedom.* New York:
Cambridge UP, 2005. Print.

Perrot, Michelle, ed. *L'impossible prison.* Paris:
Seuil, 1980. Print.

Pinkard, Terry. *Hegel: A Biography.* Cambridge:
Cambridge UP, 2000. Print.

——. *Hegel's Phenomenology: The Sociality of
Reason.* Cambridge: Cambridge UP, 1996.
Print.

Pippin, Robert B. *Hegel's Idealism: The Satisfactions
of Self-Consciousness.* Cambridge: Cambridge
UP, 1989. Print.

Potte-Bonneville, Mathieu. *Michel Foucault,
l'inquiétude de l'histoire.* Paris: Presses
universitaires de France, 2004. Print.

Racevskis, Karlis. *Michel Foucault and the
Subversion of the Intellect.* Ithaca: Cornell UP,
1983. Print.

Rajchman, John. *Truth and Eros: Foucault, Lacan, and the Question of Ethics.* New York: Routledge, 1991. Print.

——. *Michel Foucault: The Freedom of Philosophy.* New York: Columbia UP, 1985. Print.

Ricoeur, Paul. *Time and Narrative.* 3 vols. Trans. Kathleen Blamey and David Pellauer. Chicago: U of Chicago P, 1984–1988. Print.

Russon, John. *Reading Hegel's Phenomenology.* Bloomington: Indiana UP, 2004. Print.

——. "Temporality and the Future of Philosophy in Hegel." *International Philosophical Quarterly* 48(2008): 59–68. Print.

Schatzki, Theodore R. *Social Practices: A Wittgensteinian Approach to Human Activity and the Social.* Cambridge: Cambridge UP, 1996. Print.

Serres, Michel. *La guerre mondiale.* Paris: Le Pommier, 2008. Print.

——. *Hominescence.* Paris: Le Pommier, 2001. Print.

——. *L'incandescent.* Paris: Le Pommier, 2003. Print.

——. *Rameaux.* Paris: Le Pommier, 2004. Print.

——. *Récits d'humanisme.* Paris: Le Pommier, 2006. Print.

Szakolczai, Arpad. *Max Weber and Michel Foucault; Parallel Life-Works.* London: Routledge, 1998. Print.

Taylor, Charles. "Foucault on Freedom and Truth." *Philosophy and the Human Sciences: Philosophical Papers 2.* Cambridge: Cambridge UP, 1985. Print.

Touraine, Alain. *Critique de la modernité.* Paris : Fayard, 1992. Print.

Vegetti, Mario. "Foucault et les Anciens."
    Critique 471–472 (1986): 925–32. Print.

Veyne, Paul. *Foucault. Sa pensée, sa personne.*
    Paris: Albin Michel, 2008. Print.

——. "Foucault révolutionne l'histoire."
    Comment on écrit l'histoire. Paris: Seuil, 1978.
    English translation: "Foucault Revolutionizes
    History." Trans. Catherine Porter. *Foucault
    and His Interlocutors.* Ed. Arnold I. Davidson.
    Chicago: U of Chicago P, 1997. Print.

Visker, R. *Truth and Singularity: Taking Foucault
    into Phenomenology.* Dordrecht: Kluwer, 1999.
    Print.

Wahl, Jean. *Le malheur de la conscience dans la
    philosophie de Hegel.* Paris: Reider, 1929. Print.

White, Hayden. *The Content of the Form: Narrative
    Discourse and Historical Representation.*
    Baltimore: The Johns Hopkins UP, 1987.
    Print.

——. *Metahistory: The Historical Imagination in
    Nineteenth-Century Europe.* Baltimore: Johns
    Hopkins UP, 1973. Print.

——. "The Public Relevance of Historical
    Studies: A Reply to Dirk Moses." *History
    and Theory* 44 (2005): 333–38. Print.

——. *Tropics of Discourse: Essays in Cultural
    Criticism.* Baltimore: Johns Hopkins UP,
    1985. Print.

Index

Apr

Marquis Book Printing Inc.

Québec, Canada
2012